PATRICE MOTSEPE

PATRICE MOTSEPE

An Appetite for Disruption

JANET SMITH

An unauthorised biography

Jonathan Ball Publishers

JOHANNESBURG • CAPE TOWN • LONDON

Published in South Africa in 2022 by
JONATHAN BALL PUBLISHERS
A division of Media24 (Pty) Ltd
PO Box 33977
Jeppestown
2043

ISBN 978-1-77619-182-6
ebook ISBN 978-1-77619-183-3

www.jonathanball.co.za
Twitter: www.twitter.com/JonathanBallPub
Facebook: www.facebook.com/JonathanBallPublishers

Cover image: Gallo Images/AFP via Getty Images

Cover by Sean Robertson
Design and typesetting by Melanie Kriel
Set in 11/16pt Meridien

Dedicated to the ongoing fight against the
terrorism of white supremacy

'Being a disruptor isn't simply about doing something better than the competition; it is about creating something ... that turns the market on its head and puts you at the forefront.'

— Joanna Swash, *Forbes*, 15 October 2021

'You can want success all you want, but to get it, you can't falter. You can't slip, you can't sleep. One eye open, for real, and forever.'

— Jay-Z, *Decoded* (Random House, 2010)

Contents

PART IV: COMING TO THE PARTY

Abbreviations

AFI	African Fashion International
ANC	African National Congress
ARC	African Rainbow Capital
ARCI	African Rainbow Capital Investments
AREP	African Rainbow Energy and Power
ARM	African Rainbow Minerals
ARMferrous	African Rainbow Minerals Ferrous Ltd
ARMgold	African Rainbow Minerals Gold Ltd
ARM MC	ARM Mining Consortium Limited
Avmin	Anglovaal Minerals
BBBEE	Broad-Based Black Economic Empowerment
Busa	Business Unity South Africa
CAF	Confederation of African Football
CEO	chief executive officer
CONCACAF	Confederation of North, Central America and Caribbean Association Football
CONMEBOL	South American Football Confederation
COSAFA	Council of Southern Africa Football Associations
Cosatu	Congress of South African Trade Unions
EFF	Economic Freedom Fighters
F4D	Fashion for Development
FIFA	International Federation of Association Football
JSE	Johannesburg Stock Exchange; Johannesburg Securities Exchange
NAFCOC	National African Federated Chamber of Commerce and Industry

Nedlac	National Economic Development and Labour Council
PSL	Premier Soccer League
REIPPP	Renewable Energy Independent Power Producer Procurement
SAFA	South African Football Association
SANEF	South African National Editors' Forum
SARS	South African Revenue Service
UBI	Ubuntu-Botho Investments
UCT	University of Cape Town
UEFA	Union of European Football Associations
UK	United Kingdom
US/USA	United States of America
VAR	video assistant referee
Wits	University of the Witwatersrand

Author's note

This biography happened because I was looking for a book about Patrice Motsepe to buy when he was named president of CAF in March 2021. I'd long wanted to know his story, and there wasn't a biography out there.

Disappointed and on a mission, I called Jeremy Boraine, then publisher at Jonathan Ball and a brilliant South African. He'd published *Hani: A Life Too Short*, the 2009 biography of the great revolutionary that my friend Beauregard Tromp and I wrote, and is the person behind many of the most outstanding books about South Africa to date. I'm most grateful to Jeremy for calmly and thoughtfully giving me the chance to write about Motsepe, and believing I could do it.

It was tough, though, to decide *how* to do it. The method I knew and trusted was doing interviews myself. I was a journalist and then an editor for 26 years. But Motsepe occupies an uneven, and somehow unsettling, space. Not many people wanted to talk about him as a private person on the record, and it would've been unacceptable to have a series of 'anonymous' viewpoints, even though everyone seems to have an opinion on him. On-the-record interviews may have been possible on the subjects of Motsepe and football, business and philanthropy, but that would have left the book lopsided, with only some areas of his life covered in that way, and others not.

On balance, it seemed research and an agglomeration of studies, reports, press conferences and existing interviews with Motsepe and others would allow me to develop my own analysis and write a biography, which we believed other people might appreciate.

The most important question remained: would Motsepe agree to be interviewed himself? He did so towards the end of the book process, when we were already well into production and we had a date to get the book to the printers. Because of the time constraints and to underline that he did not authorise this book – which was an express wish of his – it is contained in an Epilogue in the final pages. I'm sincerely grateful for his time and input: thank you, Dr Motsepe. I believe it makes the book more insightful in every way and therefore more valuable.

Prologue

Patrice Motsepe isn't a cult personality like Elon Musk, a contradictory visionary who shrugs off antagonists in tweets, or Jeff Bezos, posing in Hawaiian shirts with sunglasses and a girlfriend in a bikini. He's not Ma Huateng, aka Pony Ma, founder, chairman and CEO of Chinese internet giant Tencent Holdings, who's known for being a 'shy geek' who keeps a very low profile.

Often gregarious, Motsepe has an independent style and spontaneity that can disarm a hostile audience. But his tendency to shoot from the hip can also lead to blunders, such as in Davos in January 2020 when he told Donald Trump, then president of the United States of America, that Africans 'love him'. 'Africa loves America. Africa loves you ... We want America to do well. We want you to do well.'[1]

To be fair to Motsepe, a poll at that time revealed that 'Trump was popular in Nigeria and Kenya', and in South Africa a significant 42 percent of respondents reported 'confidence in Mr Trump'.[2] Still, it wasn't a shining moment for the African billionaire.

It hadn't even been necessary for Motsepe to seize it. Trump 'lacked ... aura and respect' and had evoked a 'blasé reaction'[3] at Davos, a place of 'censorious self-criticism' for capitalists. Two years previously, the American president had infamously described African countries as 'shitholes' and tweeted that four American congresswomen, who were not white, should 'go back [and fix] the ... crime-infested places' they 'originally came from'.[4] (Three of the women were born in the USA; the fourth was born in Somalia and moved to the US as a child.)

Motsepe reacted quickly to critics saying that he'd erroneously given himself the role of Africa's spokesman. 'I'm aware of the lively, diverse and at times emotional debate in the global media and on social media relating to my remarks to President Donald Trump at the dinner ... during the World Economic Forum,' he noted on the Motsepe Foundation's website. 'The debate also exposed me to the views of Africans who disagreed with my remarks. I have a duty to listen to these differing views and would like to apologise. I do not have the right to speak on behalf of anybody except myself.'[5]

Motsepe doesn't grovel; he positions himself. A familiar aspect of that is giving credit where it's due; another is hiring people who will stand up to him when he's wrong.

An astute businessman with decades of experience, his view on how to run a boardroom was revealed in August 2020 when he was overruled by the directors of his company, African Rainbow Minerals (ARM), who elected not to follow its rights in subscribing to certain shares.[6] At ARM's annual results presentation, Motsepe was asked why the company had made that decision. He answered, 'I wanted personally to follow the ... rights issue as a good thing for ARM, [but] if management's view is different to mine, then 90% of the time I go with management because it is right. We have smart, bright people ... 99.97% of the time they are right and I'm wrong.'[7]

Motsepe doesn't accept himself being unexceptional, according to his own quote: 'You have to set high standards. I can never be satisfied with a mediocre performance.'[8] A close relative of the great Bakgatla kings, his earliest recognition as a businessman came in 1999, when the World Economic Forum named him a Global Leader of Tomorrow. His many additional acknowledgements and awards include being chosen as Absa's 2002 Entrepreneur of the Year, with Robert Emslie, managing executive of Absa Business Banking Services, saying that Motsepe had 'created a world class company – one that competes on a global stage and that truly

reflects the spirit of our country: energy, determination, persever-
ance, ingenuity and ubuntu'.[9] He was also voted South Africa's
Business Leader of the Year by the chief executive officers of the
top 100 companies in South Africa and by Ernst & Young as its
Best Entrepreneur of the Year in 2002; and the Afrikaanse Handelsinstituut gave Motsepe its prized MS Louw Award for Exceptional
Business Achievement in 2003.

In 2014, he received the BRICS Business Council Outstanding Leadership Award and the Harvard University Veritas Award
for Excellence in Global Business and Philanthropy, and in 2017,
Forbes magazine honoured Motsepe as one of its 100 Greatest
Living Business Minds, while the *Sunday Times* gave him its Lifetime Achiever Award.

A member of the International Business Council of the World
Economic Forum, which is made up of 100 of the most influential
chief executives from all industries, the billionaire isn't a quiet
figure in his favoured field.

* * * *

Patrice Motsepe is a son of the soil, as they say. Passionate about
both the country of his birth and his fellow South Africans, he
noted in 2020 that although he knew friends and colleagues who
planned to leave the country, he wanted to stay and 'work it out'.
'I grew up in a country that was divided, (had) lots of problems
and tensions and was segregated by law, [but] even at that time of
legalised division, I had the privilege of seeing some of the most
incredible people in this country – black people, white people and
everybody else,' he said. 'So my view of the future of this country
is based on this huge amount of support, love, encouragement, as
a young, young boy, over many years, that I've been given by all
South Africans.'[10]

That 'gift', as he describes it, put him ahead of the curve on black economic empowerment, designed to be a feature of all companies' ownership structures, by the time he listed ARMgold, the gold division of his company, on the Johannesburg Stock Exchange in 2002. The national integrated black economic empowerment strategy would be made an Act of Parliament the following year, in 2003.

Known almost as much for his philanthropy as for his business nous, Motsepe credits his compatriots for inspiring this in him. In 2016, he 'noted that there were a lot of people who had "very little in this world ... These are people who sacrifice even when knowing that they may not have a decent meal the next time. Yet they still give. These are the people who encourage us to do what we do."'[11]

It was a heartfelt tribute based on his aspirational equation, money plus 'the confidence of black and white South Africans in the future' equals 'every single one of us [feeling] that this is the best place in the world to live.'[12]

PART I

The beloved game

1

A night in Rabat:
The arrival of the contender

Patrice Motsepe arrived at the Sofitel Rabat Jardin des Roses in Morocco's capital in the early evening. It was 12 March 2021, and the world was firmly in the grip of the covid-19 pandemic.

The luxury hotel, set in a nine-hectare urban oasis of aromatic flowers and orange trees, had a history of hosting royal guests and dignitaries, of whom Motsepe – South Africa's first black dollar billionaire – was certainly one. Still, there would be no deferential greetings and conversations in the lobby on this occasion. The visitor strode quickly down empty marble passages lit by elegant chandeliers, to meet football executives waiting to officially announce the new president for the Confederation of African Football (CAF).

Like many other countries reacting to the rapid and deadly spread of the virus, Morocco had declared a nationwide state of emergency in March 2020, and it remained in place. Mask-wearing in public was mandatory, there were overnight curfews, and local movement was permitted only in exceptional circumstances. Passenger air travel had been suspended – but Motsepe had access to a private jet, so he wouldn't necessarily have had to wait for the easing of restrictions on commercial flights to enter Rabat.

A flurry of diplomatic manoeuvres had finally enabled him and his delegation to get visas during the hard lockdown, as the embassy of Morocco in Pretoria had had to first give them the nod, as it did with all South Africans wishing to visit the kingdom.

Conflict over the African National Congress (ANC) government's recognition of the Sahrawi Arab Democratic Republic, which Morocco had annexed in 1975, and the party's apartheid-era links to the Sahrawi liberation organisation, the Polisario Front, meant there were strained relations between the countries. This had deepened when the South African Football Association (SAFA) had voted in 2018 for the USA, Canada and Mexico to host the 2026 International Federation of Association Football (FIFA) World Cup, instead of Morocco.

Rabat had denied entry to some members of South Africa's Kaizer Chiefs football team – a tussle that delayed their CAF Champions League match in February, a month before the CAF elective congress at which Motsepe would take up his new role.

Securing an endorsement on his passport was but one of the intense behind-the-scenes wrangles to secure him the highest position ever held in football by a South African. Motsepe's election would elevate Anglophone Africa for the first time since CAF's founding in 1957. It had been a Francophone office from the get-go, preferring to promote members from north, east and central Africa. So Morocco, which had used the sport as a less aggressive way than military or political might to build its dominance in north Africa, would have also had to concede control of CAF to a country in the south. Most importantly, Mauritania, Senegal and Ivory Coast, whose countries were represented by Motsepe's rivals – Ahmed Yahya, Augustine Senghor and Jacques Anouma – would have had to agree.

* * * *

A week before his visit to Rabat, Motsepe had been in the Islamic Republic of Mauritania, building hype. He was photographed there with Mauritania's football chief Yahya, president of Senegal's football federation Senghor, and FIFA boss Gianni Infantino. Motsepe had been wearing his 40-year-old Adidas Copa Mundial[1] boots. This model, designed for the 1982 FIFA World Cup held in Spain, had become a bestseller, but Motsepe's specific pair had special meaning: they were the ones he'd laced on back when he was a student.

Putting on a jovial face for the press photographers and smartphone-toting fans, he'd linked arms with the other three men. Such a public display was a disruption to the established order of the CAF and FIFA, but it was of a kind Motsepe had developed over a quarter-century in business and two decades in philanthropy. Confidently representing himself, rather than having a spokesperson do his talking, was a familiar aspect of his persona; so, too, attempts at some *esprit de corps*.

It was also a good-humoured shield for the drama going on behind the scenes. Having 'lurched from disaster to disaster' since 2018, when it was 'on the verge of a total meltdown', CAF had effectively been under the management of FIFA since June 2019.[2]

That was unprecedented. FIFA had always had a hands-off approach to football's six regional confederations,[3] even if it could 'take control' if one of the 211 member associations – which it supports financially and logistically around the world – should 'run into trouble'. But CAF's Madagascan president Ahmad Ahmad was facing 'a torrent of allegations of wrongdoing, ranging from financial mismanagement to sexual harassment',[4] and that gave FIFA a way in.

The Swiss attorney-general was investigating several cases of corruption at the global federation at the time, and some experts felt that FIFA's task at CAF may thus have been to deliver 'a massive slap in the face of African football' because CAF's own structures should have had 'the power to solve the problems of African football'.[5] It appeared that FIFA didn't trust CAF to do its own job.

Angry Afrophile media said clean and committed football administrators on the continent were now also being patronised, with CAF 'treated like … [an] errant child by FIFA, allowed to soil itself and run around with the stench all day while what it really needs is a diaper change and the sacking of the nanny'. Painful pasts came back to the fore, with critics saying 'the white people in FIFA … tell each other, "That's just how Africans are!"'[6]

The picture of African football failing was, however, out there, perhaps cut to fit an unpleasant picture which could only be reframed by FIFA under Infantino. By the end of 2020, when applications opened for a new CAF president, it was obvious that the old way of doing things at its headquarters in Cairo was over.

SAFA announced Motsepe's surprise candidacy in November 2020, at the same time as Yahya and Côte d'Ivoire football federation honorary president Jacques Anouma were endorsed. Senghor was the last to throw his hat into the ring, soon after.

Senghor looked like a favourite to win. Then Yahya. It vacillated, while all the drama was taking place around Ahmad in the background.

Motsepe jumped straight in, setting out on an exhausting itinerary to gather support which culminated in the launch of his ten-point plan for CAF at a press conference in Sandton, Johannesburg, on 25 February 2021. 'African football must become the best in the world,' Motsepe said there. 'It won't happen overnight, but that is the test of what we are going to do over the next few years. For me, the test is what the results are going to be.'[7]

Motsepe had worked hard at bedding down his Africa-first agenda. He'd been to Egypt twice to meet the federation's executive and toured extensively to introduce himself to Africa's football bosses individually over six weeks. In January 2021, he'd met the game's top administrators in Benin, Ghana, Guinea, Côte d'Ivoire, Nigeria and Togo, before travelling to Cameroon, where he spent a few days in the company of most of the 54 African football association presidents who were gathered there for discussions about the continent's most prestigious prize, the Africa Cup of Nations.

The presidents of the member associations of the Council of Southern Africa Football Associations (COSAFA)[8] were the first to get behind him publicly, at COSAFA's annual general meeting in January 2021, in Johannesburg, at which Infantino was present. 'Dr Motsepe is our candidate and we endorse him fully,' said president Phillip Chiyangwa, a Zimbabwean property mogul and former boxing promoter. 'We believe he has the right mix of business acumen and connections in the corporate world to lead CAF through what will be a difficult period in the coming years. The name of Dr Motsepe is synonymous with good governance and integrity, and he is the perfect candidate.'[9]

Motsepe also had the backing of Congolese businessman and politician Moïse Katumbi, who owned big Kinshasa club TP Mazembe, and of Nigerian football association president Amaju Pinnick, who was a member of the CAF executive committee and a FIFA council member. Both had substantial influence in African football. Katumbi had noted that back in 2015 he and Motsepe had discussed 'how people can become interested to sponsor soccer in Africa … [We] were saying let's find a way for people to bring money to African football',[10] while Pinnick – who had, together with Infantino, also propelled the previous president, Ahmad, into power in 2017 – described Motsepe as 'a totally new person, a breath of fresh air'.[11]

In February 2021, Motsepe moved on to Qatar for the FIFA Club World Cup (which is unrelated to the World Cup; they're different competitions, one involving clubs, the other nations), to which all the global organisation's member associations' presidents had been invited. Egyptian champions Al Ahly were in contention, but Motsepe was there less to watch the games than to create ties for Africa with international administrators.

* * * *

It wasn't only the presidential candidates who were campaigning around Africa. Gianni Infantino – whom *Forbes* called 'the most powerful man in sport'[12] in its 'newcomers' list in 2018 – was also travelling around the continent, assessing which country, which national football association and which individuals would deliver his FIFA-friendly agenda.

It seems that by the time Motsepe's España '82 boots had their moment on that field, Infantino had convinced Motsepe's rivals to withdraw their bids. Although it has never been made public exactly why Motsepe ultimately pipped the others at the post, what is known is that CAF had a deficit of nearly R175 million in cash flow and a R640-million-plus loss in cash reserves, while Motsepe was worth an estimated R40 billion, his Pretoria-based football club, Mamelodi Sundowns, was valued at around R300 million and his family's Motsepe Foundation – and the companies in which he had a stake – could afford to donate R1 billion to help save lives during the covid-19 epidemic in South Africa.[13]

Motsepe certainly hadn't volunteered for the CAF job. By the account of SAFA president Danny Jordaan, he'd approached Motsepe to stand only a few days before the closing date for applications, and he hadn't exactly received an enthusiastic reception. 'He asked me if [I] would ask a professor of a university to become the principal of a primary school,' Jordaan told the media,[14] indicating the poor reputation of CAF in terms of governance, debt and in-fighting.

Motsepe corroborated Jordaan's anecdote at the launch of his manifesto, saying that he'd been asked several times to run for the CAF presidency and had turned down the request flat, as he was at the stage of his life where he was enjoying 'the work of my philanthropy', and that the problem was that 'when I focus on doing something, it requires a lot of hard work, sacrifice, and more importantly, tangible progress'. Describing his love for African football as 'stupid', he added, 'There is no one in Africa who has lost more money in football than I have.'[15]

Jordaan had evidently had to get tough on Motsepe in order to persuade him to run, telling the billionaire, 'The principal of this primary school is recognised throughout the world – if you land in any country, the head of the country will want to see the principal of this primary school. It is a job with significant importance on the African continent.'[16]

It was a good gambit. While Motsepe's businesses had made him an ultra-high-net-worth individual in Africa, that wasn't so much the case globally, as his 'world's richest' ranking had fallen 75 places between January 2020 and January 2021 to number 1 050, although his fortune had changed very little. With increasing interests on the African continent and a growing profile at the World Economic Forum,[17] Motsepe would vastly expand his reach if he had success in turning around CAF and making inroads at FIFA.

Jordaan's presentation of Motsepe as SAFA's choice took perfect advantage of CAF's perilous financial position and poor image. At that juncture, what it desperately needed was a presidential contender with their own money who didn't need access to its coffers, and for that, it required an unentitled individual – an outsider, essentially – who was also excited to bring ideas.

2

The dazzle and the dark side: Taking the reins at CAF

Gianni Infantino was in Rabat when Patrice Motsepe arrived for the formal CAF presidential handover on 12 March 2021. The FIFA chief couldn't do much of the razzmatazz, however, as the crackle of concern about the election process had had to be stifled before it turned into a fire. Infantino needed to tread carefully around CAF's member associations to ensure himself a third term at the world governing body in 2023.

For the ten days before CAF's elective conference, things had been tense. Reports said the FIFA president had invited Yahya, Senghor and Anouma to meet with him and some advisors in Morocco on the last weekend of February 2021 in a first such gathering ahead of a presidential election.[1] It was unprecedented to decide on a winner beforehand in that way.

Nonetheless, it was quickly understood that an agreement was reached there with Yahya and Senghor that Motsepe would take centre-stage. Anouma was, however, not on board – he described the process as 'not too democratic'.[2]

As the clock started to wind down, the candidates returned to their countries for consultations, expected to meet on the upcoming weekend in Nouakchott, Mauritania, to finalise the outcome. If Anouma continued to fight against it, it would be a two-horse race. But Anouma appeared to lack the unequivocal backing of enough football administrators, and politicians in his home country, and in the end he decided or was persuaded to stand down.

Visibly delighted, Infantino then announced the deal under which Motsepe would become president for a five-year term, at a conference on 7 March at the Palais des Congrès in Nouakchott, where the African under-20 football championships were being hosted by Yahya. Senghor would be Motsepe's first vice-president, Yahya the second vice-president, and Anouma a 'special advisor'.

Infantino said that 'the agreement obtained by the candidates [was] a strong signal for Africa', and that Motsepe would lead CAF with a 'common program' built from the campaign manifestos of all four.[3] But the plan 'for uniting the disparate interests within the continent's football administration' was rapidly met with derision as 'a uniquely African one: section out more pie slices' – CAF would now have five vice-presidents, as opposed to the former allotment of three, which was rightly flagged as a minus for Motsepe.[4]

* * * *

When the formal CAF handover was done in Morocco, Motsepe instantly became one of the most powerful figures in the world's most popular sport. Importantly, the president of CAF automatically becomes a vice-president of FIFA, football's global governing body, and this role would immediately redefine the man who'd been a disruptor in South African football, business and philanthropy, and even looked to become one in South African politics.

The advent of television and marketing rights and the unprecedented global obsession with football had spurred FIFA's evolution from a tiny amateur operation in 1904 into a multibillion-dollar industry and the guardian of the game. Motsepe could potentially take the opportunity to run for office as its president in the future if he could navigate multiple political hurdles, and traps set by rivals who would need him to fail so that they could rise.

But first, using his network and his influence, Motsepe would be expected to at least double the revenue of CAF and begin to fix its reputation.

When Fouzi Lekjaa, the chairman of the CAF finance committee, had presented CAF's financial situation in January 2021, he'd noted that the reserves were healthier, although it was mooted that these could have been bulked up by a large sum from the FIFA Forward account.[5]

It was easier for Lekjaa to explain why there was more than R350 million missing in commercial income compared to the previous year. That was a result of the cancellation of a broadcasting and marketing agreement CAF had had with French media company Lagardère under Ahmad, who had made a 'deal to sell CAF's TV rights ... for $1 billion [more than R15 billion] over 12 years, a 10-fold increase on the previous deal'.[6]

The federation had been forced to cancel the contract, which had been set to run until 2028, after separate court judgments ruled there hadn't been a tender process. The cancellation happened around the same time as Ahmad was handed a five-year ban (reduced to two years on appeal) by FIFA after being found guilty of misusing finances for his own benefit.

A result of the cancellation of the Lagardère broadcasting agreement was a broadcasting blackout on Africa's biggest pay-TV channel, SuperSport. This was a huge problem. Africans hadn't been able to watch African football since November 2019, and ending that disaster was one of the most notable promises on Motsepe's CAF manifesto. It was something on which he'd have to move quickly. Without the big African football tournaments being broadcast continentally, African fans were turning more and more to European and English football, and millions upon millions of dollars in potential revenue for CAF were being lost to the Union of European Football Associations (UEFA) – and FIFA.[7]

Motsepe addressed the financial crunch at CAF as soon as he could, asking, 'Do we have to cut or must we invest? The way to get yourself out of trouble is not necessarily cutting until you can cut no more and get to the bone. The recognised strategy around the world is to grow. Look at the budget we have at CAF. You can't keep cutting and cutting. We will reorganise and reposition.' But, he warned, the significant benefits would 'take some time – they don't happen overnight.'[8]

* * * *

The so-called Moroccan protocol that saw Motsepe become president was quickly and warmly welcomed by, among others, Paul Kagame, president of Rwanda, when Kagame hosted the CAF executive committee meeting in May 2021 in Kigali. Infantino was also present.

Kagame heralded 'the new mindset that is supporting African football to achieve its aims' and said the new CAF leadership was 'a badge of honour for us'. 'The two brothers [Motsepe and Infantino] I am sitting with here, I have known for a long time, and our minds are synchronised on what to do for sport, for football. I have enjoyed working with them, and we are a family.'[9]

Controversial Zambian icon Kalusha Bwalya,[10] president of his country's football association from 2008 to 2016 and the most successful player in its history, was another Motsepe supporter, pointing out that CAF needed 'visionary leadership with an emphasis on strong teamwork, and at this moment if anyone can do that, with the right people around him, it is Motsepe'.[11]

South African football legend Jomo Sono publicly applauded Motsepe, too, saying that 'you can see that he loves the game'. 'I think he will [perform] better than all former presidents. We just hope by the time his term ends [in 2026], he would have restructured African football. Look at what he's turned [his championship-winning South Africa football team] Mamelodi Sundowns into today. It's difficult to compete with Sundowns in South Africa, and even in Africa.'[12]

Accomplished international sports administrator South African lawyer Norman Arendse said there was 'much to admire' about the new CAF chief. 'He commands great respect and ticks all the boxes. His appointment is a masterstroke by SAFA and FIFA.'[13]

Those who were drawn to the dazzle of Motsepe taking the seat in Cairo described him as 'oozing class from every pore', 'a self-made man ... close to power', 'a leader with impeccable credentials and ... endless influence across the spectrum' and 'synonymous with success and wealth'.

The darker opinion, that there could be some sort of dual leadership between Motsepe and Infantino at CAF if Motsepe was 'indebted' and perhaps expected to 'repay [Infantino] at some point',[14] wasn't held by most of those who'd dealt with Motsepe in business and football, and knew what CAF was getting: an unflinching straight-shooter. If Motsepe saw no point in pursuing something – a project, a conversation – he wouldn't give it his time. If he was angry, he showed it; and if he felt the need to celebrate, he had no qualms about doing that in public.

Motsepe had repeatedly shown he wasn't insecure about the expertise of people he chose for key positions, and that was part of a self-belief that some took for conceit. Yet no one would have been as hyper-aware of the steep learning curve represented by CAF than Motsepe himself. He was only going to have one chance to get it right.

There were two key perceptions at play about his new job. The first was that he could 'expect to have more freedom to implement whatever changes he [saw] fit' at CAF, as he was 'taking charge of the confederation at a difficult time in its history'.[15] The other was that he would be a lackey of Infantino. That would likely be proved wrong, even if only in the longer term: Motsepe tends to wait to make what he believes will be his best impact.

When he was in the spotlight for his first address as the incoming president at that conference in March in Nouakchott, Motsepe had strongly pushed a pan-African agenda. 'African football needs collective wisdom, but also the exceptional talent and wisdom of every president of every country and every member association. That's what gives me confidence ... The commitment to improve and continue to invest is there, and the governance transparency is an excellent foundation.'[16]

* * * *

It was more than a month after his election in Rabat, in April 2021, that Motsepe officially arrived at the CAF headquarters in Cairo with his Congo-born general-secretary, Véron Mosengo-Omba, who'd been the subject of contention due to his Swiss citizenship. The pair were accompanied on their first day there by FIFA council member Hany Abo Rida, a former Egyptian Football Association president, and they met the rest of the staff before a boardroom sit-down with CAF's senior managers.

Motsepe encouraged the federation's executives 'to come with pride and without any uncertainty'. 'Real success takes time to happen, and you are real leaders. Success is built on trust. We are going to be successful, and we will be judged on our results.' He told the staff it was 'essential [that they] all shared the ambition to make African football more competitive at the global level'.[17]

Motsepe addressed disputatious comments around Mosengo-Omba, saying his general-secretary was the 'right person' with the expertise 'to give the administration the necessary impetus'.[18] But Mosengo-Omba's Swiss passport wasn't the only cause of controversy. His previous designation was as chief officer of FIFA's member associations based in FIFA's headquarters in Geneva with Infantino; he and Infantino had known each other since they were law students together in Germany in the 1980s. That closeness between the two men was highlighted against concerns about FIFA getting too enmeshed in the business of CAF.

Yet Mosengo-Omba had the relevant experience: he'd interacted with not just most African football association heads, but most in the world. And for Motsepe, his general-secretary's nationality wasn't an issue. Referring to Africans 'who are what I call part of the diaspora,' Motsepe said 'that many of those I've met, even those whose parents left and they grew up in Europe or America, have a deep emotional bond with Africa. We need them. For me, it [is] important to send a message ... that in Véron we have got world-class material. Véron loves Africa deeply.'[19]

Motsepe pledged that he would 'keep looking for some of the best, smartest Africans, whether they are in China or Japan,'[20] but insisted he needed 'results'. This echoed how he'd staffed the executive of his mining companies and then his equity investment vehicles: his priority was appointing people who could 'hit the ground running'.[21]

He told the CAF staff in Cairo, 'We must keep the promises we made to the football community, and I know we will leave a great legacy for this continent. Today I am delighted to be here, and I need people who will do a good job. There is a lot to do, and we need you to give 100%'.[22]

Indeed, Motsepe himself hadn't been idle over the preceding months. By the time he and Mosengo-Omba were welcomed at the building in 6 October City, Cairo, they'd already started work. That continued.

Motsepe joined dignitaries on 28 April for the draw of the FIFA Arab Cup Qatar at the Katara Opera House in Doha, where he had talks with Asian Football Confederation president Salman bin Ibrahim Al Khalifa. Another major mission was a visit to Kinshasa which involved a beloved project, a football competition for children; and once that was signed off by the Democratic Republic of Congo's minister of sports and recreation, Marcel Amos Mbayo Kitenge, Motsepe paid a courtesy visit to the country's president, Felix Tshisekedi, who was also the African Union president for 2021. Motsepe would go on to meet President George Weah of Liberia, President Julius Maada Bio of Sierra Leone, President Macky Sall of Senegal and President Alassane Ouattara of Côte d'Ivoire over just a few weeks.

It was on this last stop, in Abidjan in May 2021, that Motsepe announced that the Motsepe Foundation was donating R145 million to the FIFA-CAF Pan-African School Football Championship. Children aged 12 to 15 would be eligible to join the continental event, taking place in 2022/23. This was Motsepe's first personal gift made publicly to the confederation as CAF president. 'The best investment we can make to ensure that African football is amongst the best in the world and self-sustaining is to invest in schools' football and youth football development infrastructure for boys and girls at club and national level,' he said.[23]

The Motsepe Foundation had long been running such a venture in South Africa by way of the Kay Motsepe Schools Football Cup, inaugurated in 2004, which was named after Motsepe's mother. It was the biggest tournament of its kind in South Africa, with more than 5 000 public, private and independent high schools taking part every year. There was a grand prize of R1 million for the winners, and R600 000, R500 000 and R400 000 for the second, third and fourth placed, and the payouts were designed especially for development of schools' infrastructure.[24]

Motsepe and Mosengo-Omba then attended the 45th UEFA congress in Montreux, Switzerland, where Motsepe discussed

collaborations between CAF and UEFA with his European counterpart, Aleksander Čeferin, a Slovenian lawyer who'd been a
football administrator in his home country. This marked a heightened presence for Africa at football's European 'parliament'.

* * * *

The CAF staff in Cairo would also soon feel the presence of its new
executive. During the night of 24 May, claimed one report, some
15 employees were informed by email that they had been let go,
the recipients all having received the same cryptic message: 'Your
mission at CAF is over. Don't come to headquarters anymore. You
will receive your salary for the month of June.'[25]

Among those who lost their jobs were 'strategic' role-players,
such as the human resources head, a long-time finance department head, the director of information and technology, and the
legal director. Ahmad's former advisor and his assistant were also
axed, while the commercial director 'chose to resign'. 'An internal
source' alleged it wasn't about cruelty from management 'occur-
ring on a daily basis', but that there was 'little communication
between [Mosengo-Omba] and the various departments, [and]
many unanswered emails and blocked projects, with a very peculiar atmosphere which generated a lot of stress'.[26]

FIFA's influence at CAF was again alluded to, although it wasn't
specifically stated that Motsepe was even aware of what some staff
felt was that 'peculiar atmosphere' at the offices.

While this relative upheaval was going on in Cairo, Motsepe's
diary was filling up to extend CAF's reach internationally and 'even
during a global pandemic, [he] maintained a penchant for globe-
trotting', attending the congress of the Confederation of North,
Central America and Caribbean Association Football (CONCACAF)
in Miami, the Copa América final in Rio de Janeiro, and the Euro

2020 final in London in July, and the CONCACAF Gold Cup final in Las Vegas and the Olympic football tournament in Tokyo in August. But the focus remained on Africa, and tensions that had been simmering for some time.

In October, Ghana Football Association president Kurt Okraku welcomed Motsepe at a press conference in Accra, where Motsepe was enthusiastic about prospects for the continent. 'Ghana has produced some of the best footballers in the world. This country has the talent and resources to produce a national team that can win the [Africa Cup of Nations], but also win a World Cup,' he said. 'We must stop being excessively pessimistic and negative [about the World Cup]; there is no continent that has succeeded by dwelling on its failures. An African team must win ... in the near future.'[27]

But the mood wasn't as jovial a month later when Okraku was sending a message to the CAF president about neutrality. This came after SAFA made allegations about dirty tricks and laid a formal complaint with FIFA over a qualifier for Qatar 2022 in Ghana, during which Bafana Bafana were ousted by their hosts. The ignominious 1-0 loss had left South Africans broken-hearted, and SAFA had initially refused to accept that the national team was out, claiming there might have been match-fixing related to decisions by Senegalese referee Maguette N'Diaye.

The Ghana Football Association was every bit as fiery, insisting nothing of the sort had happened, and sending its own eight-page letter to FIFA, decrying SAFA's complaint as 'a hoax'.[28] Okraku was said to not be expecting the CAF president to take sides in the ongoing matter, 'despite his nationality'. 'Motsepe is the president of CAF and not the president of SAFA. He doesn't call the shots as SAFA. We voted for Motsepe to represent a truly democratic African Confederation Football and not to take sides.'[29]

It was a crucial moment for Motsepe, whose CAF presidency of course went hand-in-hand with his senior role at FIFA. He had to strike a balance, which could be a bit of a tightrope-walk for a man who didn't carry a script. Perhaps it was no surprise then that, when FIFA was in the process of deliberating SAFA's complaint, Motsepe 'sensationally waded in on the standard of referees' after four Ghanaian referees were suspended with multiple complaints lodged against them.

Speaking at a CAF general assembly in Cairo in November 2021, Motsepe noted that 'Africa has got good referees, we've got world-class referees. We've also got referees who are not so good. Then we've also got referees who are even further from not so good, but they all try. We want to train them, and also pay them good money and look after them so that they can make a career out of being referees.'[30]

Ten days after it laid its complaint, SAFA was told its protest was inadmissible. Bafana Bafana wouldn't be at the World Cup.

SAFA had other problems, too, with the DStv Premiership plagued by high-profile errors by match officials.

It was a pivotal moment for Motsepe, who would surely not want to get caught up between his home country's football advancement and the global governance organisation's rules.

He would have to hone his diplomatic skills.

3

The birth of the Brazilians: How Sundowns was made

Motsepe had grown up in the stands and out on the fields as a boy, squeezing into buses for road trips to matches. He'd wanted to own Sundowns football club for a long time, perhaps from when, as a 'little boy, he would pester his ... dad, ABC Motsepe, to part with money for the lot of them to travel by suburban train to Marabastad to watch Pretoria Sundowns'.[1]

Motsepe recalled that when he was at the University of the Witwatersrand (Wits) in the late 1980s, 'I used to say ... that one day I will own a soccer club. You must remember, at that time I didn't even have five cents in my pocket. I had no money'.[2]

In 2003, he bought a 51 percent share in Sundowns, but Motsepe really got his wish when he took total control of the club the following year by buying the remaining shares.

As soon as he'd bought the club, there were rumours that he would serve on the board of SAFA. Irritated, Motsepe dismissed them. Tussles over how to fund football in South Africa threatened to become an immediate distraction and he still had significant business goals unrelated to the sport. He refused to get involved publicly in the association's messy politics – a conviction extended even towards the media. Motsepe would talk about Sundowns-related matters at press conferences he called, but he controlled the space.

Motsepe's ambitions for his club were greater even than those of its previous owners: pioneering Mamelodi doctors Motsiri Itsweng and Bonnie Sebotshane; the crooked tycoon Zola Mahobe; casino and skin-whitening cream magnates Solly and Abe Krok; and formidable husband-and-wife duo Angelo and Anastasia Tsichlas.

* * * *

Pretoria Sundowns had been created with fervour as an amateur outfit in the 1940s, and revived with even more enthusiasm by young football fans Frank Motsepe, a relative of Patrice, Ingle Singh, Roy Fischer and Bernard 'Dancing Shoes' Hartze in 1964.

The club had made its debut as a professional team under the South African Soccer Federation, sharing a dusty base at the Muslim Grounds in Marabastad, central Pretoria, with a cricket oval, and its dressing room – a rare thing – with cricketers. Encouraged by Sundowns pioneer and early director Joseph 'Fish' Kekana, Itsweng and Sebotshane moved the club to the township of Mamelodi, their neighbourhood, after securing it in 1970.

As a backdrop to this, world football had by that time mobilised against the apartheid regime, although it had been an erratic process. CAF had acted first, expelling South Africa in 1960.[3]

In 1976, an agonising year in South African history, there was still beauty in a boot that could shave a mud spatter off a ball – and Motsepe, who was 14 years old in a football-mad family, would have cheered that level of skill.

In a most memorable game of the time, the people got five razor-sharp goals – 5-0 for a South African 'International XI' against a morally bust South American side. Kaizer Chiefs star Pule 'Ace' Ntsoelengoe's attack on the Argentine Stars opened the scoring. Then came another four goals pounded in by Orlando Pirates hero Jomo Sono in front of 30 000 spectators segregated in the stands at Rand Stadium – whites occupied the western and northern seats; black fans got the sun-facing southern and eastern blocks.

Many gathered outside to hear the roars in the Johannesburg suburb of Rosettenville, which was packed with Portuguese 'retornados' from Mozambique who'd fled after Lisbon's Carnation Revolution of the previous year. They loved Sono the way they loved Eusébio, their compatriot from Lourenço Marques. Both were Africans to rival Brazil's Pelé, the Netherlands' Johan Cruyff and Germany's Franz Beckenbauer.

That match between South Africa and Argentina, wangled to try to satisfy FIFA, featured the first-ever team of black and white footballers after the apartheid regime had slightly pushed the boundaries of its sports policy from 1971. The international governing body had wanted South Africa excluded completely from international pitches, and so the chummy face of Pretoria, sports minister Piet Koornhof, coined the term 'multi-nationalism' to hedge the bets of the government. Black, white, Indian and coloured soccer sides could compete, but not in integrated teams. White sides mostly won such encounters.

FIFA wasn't fooled and kept up the pressure until eventually Koornhof relented momentarily and roped in General Motors as sponsors for that big 'international' game in March 1976. But all the show was on the field. Black supporters could attend, of course, but they couldn't sit with or have a drink with white supporters after the South African victory. The players weren't officially able to celebrate together either. The Sabotage Act, the 180-Day Detention Law, the Group Areas Act and the Suppression of Communism Act covered a range of illegal contact that even FIFA couldn't strike down.

Jubilance went on into the night anyway, lovers of the game rejoicing from city to village, one such being Mmakau outside the capital, Pretoria, where the Motsepe family closely followed the careers of the football superstars – Orlando Pirates' Malawian goalkeeper Patson 'Kamuzu' Banda and his opposite number, Motsau

Joseph 'Banks' Setlhodi at Kaizer Chiefs, Amos 'Shuffle' Mkhari, Abednigo 'Shaka' Ngcobo, Lucky Stylianou and many more.

Motsepe's father ABC always had a special interest in Sono, a fondness probably with its roots in time gone by when ABC was a teacher at Orlando High School and Sono a student. (The school produced other illustrious soccer alumni, including Kaizer Motaung, Irvin Khoza and Ephraim 'Shakes' Mashaba.) A young Patrice must have also heard impassioned discussions about Pretoria Callies, Arcadia Shepherds and Pretoria Sundowns.

A teenager when the Soweto Uprising happened, Patrice would have internalised the brutality enacted on black people, including black footballers. One of those was Kaizer Chiefs captain Ariel 'Pro' Kgongoane, who was killed on 16 June 1976. 'Though agile in the field of play, the midfielder could not duck a police bullet which hit him on the head.' He was in the wrong place at the wrong time. 'He died on the spot.'[4] The skipper's black granite tombstone was engraved with the team's logo.

A few months later, football's most admired hype man, Ewert 'The Lip' Nene, known for his fast-talking style and habit of driving around with a loudhailer to publicise matches, was murdered by thugs during a transfer deal for Chiefs with the parents of the young talent, Nelson 'Teenage' Dladla, in a township outside Johannesburg. It was Nene's flourish and daring that had given rise to the club being known as the 'glamour boys'.

There were also incalculable losses to international football competition as the regime was intensifying its white supremacy, and therefore still refused to field a united South African team that could have taken on the world's best.

The FIFA Congress in Montreal in 1976 finally decided on the total expulsion of the Football Association of South Africa, six years after the Olympic movement had thrown the country out.

Continued racism at home and FIFA's decision meant the greats like Ntsoelengoe and Sono had to play abroad. Ntsoelengoe would tally 87 goals in 244 games in the North American Soccer League where he played during the local off-season for the Miami Toros, the Denver Dynamos, the Minnesota Kicks and the Toronto Blizzard over 11 seasons. That put him in the North American all-time top 10, while he scored around 250 goals over 17 years with Kaizer Chiefs.

Sono, 'the Black Prince', scored more than 200 goals in a playing career that would include Pirates, the New York Cosmos, the Colorado Caribous, the Atlanta Chiefs, and the Blizzard alongside Ntsoelengoe.

* * * *

South African football was increasingly isolated, becoming an internal affair in which the commercial value of clubs was based only on domestic leagues. And Sundowns was one of the most demoralised. In 1980, it was relegated to the second division of the National Professional Soccer League, which was where it stayed until 1985 when 'Mr Cool', Zola Mahobe, entered the frame.

The young Sowetan business owner put down enough money to become a Sundowns director, shelling out about R100 000 for an 80 percent stake in the franchise. His purchase of the club 'coincided with vast improvements in the match experience: Saturday afternoons in South Africa became more accessible, cleaned-up, family-friendly spectacles. Soweto's elite, bolstered by people moving from other parts of the country into areas like Hillbrow, Yeoville, Berea, Mayfair, went to these matches. They were places to be seen, unlike in the past when violence was a strong likelihood and no-one in their right minds would take their girlfriends, let alone their children, to a stadium.'[5]

In 1986, Sundowns won the Mainstay Cup, a major tournament,

beating Jomo Cosmos 1-0. The following year, it snared the BP Top Eight, the JPS Cup and the Castle League Championships.

But while Mahobe had a blueprint for success in mind, he lacked the mega-funds big clubs around the continent could tap into to bring that to life. It was superstar players Mahobe needed to turn himself into a talisman, and when his lover, bank teller 'Snowy' Moshoeshoe, started moving money around in his favour, Mahobe was able to buy them.

The tale of Mahobe and Moshoeshoe, who stole from her employer to benefit Mahobe to the tune of some R10 million over three years, is part of football legend. Mahobe 'arrived on the ... scene as a brazen unknown, flashing a fat chequebook and ushering in the era of soccer sugar daddies',[6] and used his dirty loot to fashion Sundowns into a club finally capable of taking on the best in the league. For some fans, that prosperity wiped out his lawlessness; they even nicknamed him the 'Robin Hood' of the game.

At the same time, Mahobe understood branding, and together with coach Stanley 'Screamer' Tshabalala, brought in the yellow and blue Brazil colours that have powered Sundowns for more than 30 years. (Brazil had won three FIFA World Cups by then.) The club was soon dubbed 'the Brazilians', and was also affection-ately known as 'Bafana ba Style' and 'Masandawana', slang for 'Sundowns'.

Screamer, a Pirates coaching legend and one of the few black coaches in what was the top flight in South Africa at the time, perfected what's known as 'shoeshine and piano', a heavily skills-oriented footballing style that focused as much on performing tricks and embarrassing an opponent as it did on creating chances or scoring goals. Sundowns would pick up and drop this showman-ship over the years, depending on the intensity of the competition.

In 1989 Mahobe was convicted of fraud and sentenced to

16 years behind bars. The twin Krok brothers then acquired the club from Standard Bank after it was repossessed, and went into partnership with the Tsichlases. Angelo was a former goalkeeper for Athens-based club Atromitos, and then for Corinthians (a Greek Football Club) in Johannesburg, where he met Anastasia, who'd started her working life in football as a secretary at Moroka Swallows. Her father was a former chairperson of Atromitos. She would become Sundowns' managing director and serve on sub-committees at FIFA and CAF.

There was silverware aplenty while the Kroks and the Tsichlases were partners, and they brought a total obsession for soccer to the club. In 1986, there was the BobSave Superbowl; in 1988, the Top 8, the Telkom Charity Cup and the Ohlsson's Challenge Cup; in 1990, the Top 8 again; and in 1991, the Telkom Charity Cup for a second time. The BobSave Superbowl came back in 1998, and the Telkom Charity Cup in 2000. And Sundowns won seven league titles while the Tsichlases were at the helm, including three in a row under the newly formed Premier Soccer League (PSL) from 1998 to 2000.

But there were even greater goals. Sundowns reached the CAF Champions League final in 2001, losing to Al Ahly (the 'Red Devils') when the Egyptian giants won 4-1 on aggregate.[7] It was then, with all that potential on display, that Motsepe bought 51 percent of the club, quickly making an offer to take 100 percent control.

It was 'impossible' to keep up with the money Motsepe could invest, Anastasia said later. 'We were partners with Patrice for a year, and of course Patrice Motsepe … can afford to spend a lot of money … he wanted to go further. He had his dream. Everybody has his own dream … So we took the team to that top level, became a recognised force in South Africa … and then Patrice came, he took the club … a step further. That's why I say Sundowns is a very lucky team.'[8]

When he first bought the club, Motsepe wasn't impressed with its style of play and lack of flair: he felt his team were missing the entertaining flash that had made Sundowns 'a spectacular side' in the past.

In 2003, Sundowns offered Wits University 'an amount of money they have never seen before' for midfielder Manqoba 'Shakes' Ngwenya: R1 million, which was a record signing. A sure talent, Ngwenya had been playing for Wits University when he scored a late equaliser at Orkney Stadium in North West in a 2003 match against Kaizer Chiefs. Motsepe was present, said Ngwenya, adding that he'd 'come there ... to watch me',[9] having taken a private jet.

That would have been typical of Motsepe's no-nonsense approach. And it showed the weight of his wallet.

4

A crisis of coaches: Sundowns' battle for control

Motsepe started as an owner the way he meant to finish, patient enough in the beginning, and issuing a light warning: 'Just like in my job, I am expected to deliver, or else I will get fired. I have a duty to perform and everybody knows his responsibility. It is the same with our coach, he has to deliver.'[1]

His first major appointment at the club was Argentinian Ángel Cappa, who'd coached in Mexico, been an assistant coach at Real Madrid and was popular with Diego Maradona.

Cappa did well by winning the 2005 Charity Cup with Sundowns, but then suddenly stepped down, citing 'personal and domestic problems'. Some newspapers speculated he 'jumped before he was pushed'.

Motsepe said he'd 'decided to let him go because these [problems] could have a profound effect on his ability to focus on the team'. But the boss also referred to a run of underwhelming results, saying, 'We need to win games and trophies and make sure that the club is one of the best in South Africa and on the continent.'[2]

In December 2005, Motsepe brought in another Argentinian, Miguel Gamondi, as caretaker co-coach with former Bafana Bafana captain Neil Tovey, who was the head of Sundowns' youth academy. Motsepe said that he expected 'good results' from the pair. 'I can't tell a coach who to field and what to do. I need results and I don't compromise.'[3]

The caretakers shone, winning the PSL, but Motsepe's tolerance for in-fighting was short. In October 2006, after spats between Tovey and Gamondi as to who was the more in control, and three draws and one loss, they were out.

Motsepe had indicated when Cappa left that he wanted a head coach who was a 'local' – 'someone that understands township soccer and furthermore understands the mentality of South African and township players'[4] – and so next came Gordon Igesund, a highly successful South African coach who delivered a 'skop, skiet en donner' (slang for 'cowboy tactics') style of football.

Igesund had won three League titles with Manning Rangers, Pirates and Cape Town team Santos by the time he joined Sundowns in 2006. Sundowns was triumphant under him, too, and snatched the SAA Supa 8 again.

But Motsepe had his eye on a greater prize: the CAF Champions League. When Igesund tried twice, and failed both times, he was fired in February 2008. It wasn't as if Motsepe hadn't warned him. 'When he let Tovey and Gamondi go, [he] said he was always three months late in firing his coaches, and he looked to be on the warpath, [saying], "If you're a coach, you've got to win, and if you don't win, I say there is trouble ... very, very serious trouble."'[5]

Igesund and the players 'got an earful' from an 'irate' Motsepe when they were handed an 'abject defeat' by Platinum Stars just before the coach was dismissed. Reports said Motsepe and Igesund left the Loftus Versfeld stadium – Sundowns' home ground – in the same car that night after two hours of 'crisis talks' which included separate meetings with the players and the technical staff.[6]

There were no hard feelings on Igesund's part when he was let go. When Sundowns won the Absa Premiership title in 2014 under coach Pitso Mosimane, Igesund said, 'I'm really happy for Patrice ... I know how much this title will mean to him. He has a real passion for the game, and I'm glad that passion has been rewarded'.[7]

South African coach Trott Moloto took over from Igesund on an interim basis for nine months in 2008, until Frenchman Henri Michel signed his contract in October of that year. But that also appeared to be doomed. Motsepe wasn't amiable about how Michel handled a miserable match against Ajax Cape Town not long after he arrived. Sundowns lost the game 1-0, and Michel didn't attend the post-match interview with South Africa's national broadcaster, the SABC, and pay-TV channel SuperSport. Although it's believed he ultimately did go back, it was too late.

There was no way around this but an appearance at a PSL disciplinary committee, as there were agreements in place about live-broadcast comments from managers after the games. Motsepe said he was 'very disappointed and embarrassed' and offered his 'unreserved apology on behalf of Mamelodi Sundowns'.[8]

It may have been that Michel was under pressure, and, with Sundowns' fans, this could get very personal. In March 2009, Michel had to be whisked away by police from Lucas 'Masterpieces' Moripe Stadium in Pretoria after Sundowns lost 1-0 in extra time to Platinum Stars in the second round of the Nedbank Cup. The crowd was angry enough to pose a threat to his life.

That was hard on Motsepe, but he could be gracious when coaches failed to complete their campaigns, blaming neither fans nor managers. In Michel's case, he said the former head coach had 'made a huge contribution to the standard and quality of football at Sundowns and in South Africa', and paid tribute to his 'commitment and loyalty'.[9]

Motsepe would be honoured for his commitment, too, in 2009 at a special event before the 2010 World Cup in South Africa. He was named among South Africa's 'big brothers' in football at the launch of a campaign by the Coalition of Supporters Unions of Africa, founded in 2006, to build solidarity for Africa's qualifying nations Algeria, Cameroon, Ghana, Côte d'Ivoire, Nigeria and

South Africa. The Coalition paid tribute to Motsepe, Sono, Chiefs' owner Kaizer Motaung, former Robben Island political prisoner and politician Tokyo Sexwale and SAFA executives Jordaan and Molefi Oliphant, at a ceremony that also marked the anniversary of the Sharpeville massacre.[10]

* * * *

Motsepe appointed Romanian Ted Dumitru on an interim basis in 2009 to replace Michel until the end of the season in June, when Bulgarian Hristo Stoichkov joined Sundowns as manager.

Stoichkov arrived off a low base of poor performances he'd had as Bulgaria's national coach and coach of Celta Vigo in Spain. Known as 'El Pistolero' or 'The Dagger', he was a riddle of a man: he'd been named by Pelé on the 2004 'FIFA 100' list of the greatest players of all time, but was also notorious for his aggressive temper.

Stoichkov signed a one-year contract with Sundowns, and when it was approaching completion, with Sundowns second in the League, he resigned. His assistant, Antonio López Habas, stepped in and saw a good start to the season in 2010, with Sundowns in contention for the title as they topped the log with seven points.

The high wasn't destined to last, however, and after a slump in form over six matches, Habas resigned in February 2011. This wasn't through Motsepe wanting him to leave before the end of the season; rather, dangerous antagonism from some Sundowns' supporters was a feature, as they created 'turmoil and scenes of anarchy at matches and at the club headquarters in Chloorkop', and issued death threats against the coach.[11]

Motsepe told the media that Habas's wife had 'been hospitalised' through the trauma, but he insisted that Habas's resignation was 'not a case of the club bowing to the violence'. 'Indeed, it is something we abhor and intend holding investigations and disciplinary hearings in order to determine if there are ring-leaders involved in this matter.'[12]

After the regrettable period with Habas, Motsepe decided to take a chance on one of his heroes, Dutch legend and former Barcelona assistant coach Johan Neeskens, and it was rough going. Sundowns finished fourth and was only a runner-up in the Nedbank Cup in Neeskens' first season.

Motsepe decided to give the coach time to develop in his role, but the faction of fans who wanted a say in how the club was run saw no point in that. Like Michel and Habas, Neeskens would need police intervention when fans threatened him after Sundowns lost a game in September 2012.

The PSL appointed an internal security task team to look into the matter and come up with ways to deal with the hooliganism, yet things quickly got much worse. After a loss to Moroka Swallows in October, Sundowns fans staged a frightening pitch invasion in which 'missiles were thrown and the dugouts knocked over [as] supporters breached security to reach Neeskens in the tunnel'. It wasn't a healthy picture for Motsepe or Sundowns at all. Photographs 'emerged showing the coach, twice a World Cup runner-up as a player with the Netherlands, covering his head with his hands in an attempt to shield himself from blows'. The attack had happened 'despite policemen flanking him on both sides'.[13]

Motsepe stood up for Neeskens, and said he believed the coach could still turn the club's fortunes around, but now Sundowns was making international headlines for all the wrong reasons.

The PSL said it would pursue criminal charges against the attackers, and Motsepe came out firmly, noting that the club would back a plan for police to act against fan violence. 'It is important for us to create an environment where supporters are educated to accept the outcome of a match. You win, draw or lose some of the games, teams do go through ups and downs. Those who threaten violence must not be allowed to enter stadiums. Stadiums are a place of entertainment and not violence.'[14]

The problem was that there was another side to the chaos for Motsepe which was, perhaps, not as easily solved as acting against the thugs. Sundowns hadn't won the league since the 2006/07 season, and Motsepe had had to buy out the contracts of four coaches in six years. So once the club reached the unbelievable point of being in the relegation zone at Christmas 2012, it was all over for Neeskens. Motsepe knew he had to let him go, with the payout on the Dutchman believed to be in the region of nearly R20 million.

Sundowns wasn't yet a money-spinner for Motsepe, although he continued to shrug off difficulties. It was only later that he admitted 'we never thought we would lose so much money', and put the actual cost at 'millions of rand a year'. He remained resolute, however, that 'we went mainly into soccer not to make money, but as a means of giving back'.[15]

A decade of 'giving back' surely had to eventually have returns.

5

The big time:
The Pitso Mosimane years

If fate had dictated that 2012 would again be a disappointing year for Sundowns, it was even more terrible for Pitso Mosimane, who was the national team coach until the qualifiers for the prestigious Africa Cup of Nations and South Africa's last match against Sierra Leone. That ushered in a nightmare for him.

There had been a sense of imminent glory in the Bafana Bafana camp when goalkeeper Itumeleng Khune delivered a magical punch in the 71st minute to keep them at 0-0 by the closing whistle. Then Egypt ended its simultaneous game against Niger with a 3-0 score, setting Niger back on goal difference.

The Bafana players and Mosimane were overjoyed, jumping into the air and embracing each other. But SAFA's technical staff had made a shocking error: CAF's rules stated that if there was a tie for points at the end, the result would be decided on a head-to-head of wins, not goal difference. Niger had six victories, and South Africa three, meaning Niger won the group.

Mosimane wasn't officially blamed. The technical team was blasted, but they decided to put it behind them and continue, together with Mosimane, to try and secure a place for South Africa at the 2014 World Cup. But that also wasn't meant to be, and when South Africa drew 1-1 with Ethiopia in the qualifier, it felt like the right time for Mosimane to head for the exit. Despondent, he decided to take a break from football for a few months.

Motsepe was, meanwhile, also weighing up his mistakes.

Sundowns had been 10th on the table in the 2011/12 season, and by the start of 2013, the media was beginning to lose faith in the club under his ownership. It was calculated that 'the last five years of the Tsichlas reign [had] yielded more success than Motsepe's entire tenure'.[1]

It hadn't helped that Sundowns' popular captain at the time, its gifted centre-back Method Mwanjali, and one of its top strikers, Nyasha Mushekwi, who were both Zimbabwean internationals, were among nearly 100 Zimbabwean players, personnel and football writers implicated in 'Asiagate', one of the biggest football scandals of the early 2000s. It concerned friendlies between the Warriors (the Zimbabwean national team) and Asian teams being fixed between 2007 and 2009, and ultimately put the Zimbabwe Football Association into serious financial jeopardy as its internal investigation dragged on for three years.

FIFA, which was taking the biggest beating in its history, wasn't impressed. African football fans were shattered. When an official list of banned and exonerated players and officials was finally released by the Zimbabwe Football Association in October 2012, Mushekwi had at least escaped a life ban after volunteering information. So had Khama Billiat, who was playing for Ajax Cape Town and would sign a five-year contract with Sundowns the following year, becoming one of its greatest players before moving on to Kaizer Chiefs.[2] But Mwanjali – who wasn't only Sundowns' captain but also the captain of the Warriors – was in the 'banned' group.[3]

Those were bleak times.

After five years without a trophy, beset by the pressures of competition and not wanting to give up on a dream that was about not only financial success but also deep emotional ties, the chairman wanted to give his investment one last, massive push, to see if it could finally rise domestically and in Africa as a whole.

Motsepe at last made a decision that would fundamentally change his own and Sundowns' future. He hired Pitso Mosimane.

* * * *

Mosimane knew Sundowns very well, having played for the team under Itsweng and Sebotshane, and under Mahobe in the 1980s, then having played and also coached under the Kroks and the Tsichlases. He was ready to make the comeback of his life, and that would start with him repairing the cracks caused through a series of doomed coaches at a club whose fans weren't going to give up on their intense reactions to its failures and achievements.

Joining in February 2013, Mosimane decided to play the first team as a unit of attackers and defenders, and his run started exceptionally well. They were unbeaten with four wins and two draws in his first half-season.

Hearing Mosimane's argument that Sundowns needed three top-class players in each position if it was to continue to compete at the highest level, Motsepe was increasingly prepared to spend. The coach marked his first full season in 2013/14 by bringing in serious talent like Zimbabweans Billiat and Cuthbert Malajila, and South African midfielders Bongani Zungu and Katlego 'Mahoota' Mashego.

In 2014, a 3-0 win against SuperSport United in the Tshwane derby secured the league. South African midfielder Teko Modise 'scored a gorgeous chip 35 yards from goal to make it two on the night'. '[That] added to the party atmosphere' inside the packed Loftus Versfeld.[4]

The seven-year drought had ended, and Mosimane had elevated the club from the danger of relegation it had faced to being the best in South Africa – in just over a season and a half.

Meanwhile, '32-year-old Modise, a man who had never won a

league title despite a fantastic career up to that point', saw his own 'curse ... finally broken'. 'To be honest I have won a lot of awards and crossed a lot of milestones, but lifting the PSL trophy was an overwhelming experience. I could not believe it and it was very emotional,' he said.[5]

Motsepe, now intent on building 'the club into the equal of any major outfit in Europe',[6] hired top trainers, medical personnel and analysts so that Sundowns couldn't help but keep winning. It was relentless effort on the parts of coach, players and chairman, but it would take them to the heights of African football. As Sundowns midfielder Hlompho Kekana said, '[This] tests you as a person, it tests your character ... There's a lot of sacrifices ... to ensure that the team plays [in the top tournaments] regularly.' But, he emphasised, 'It's more mental than anything. When you are mentally strong, you stand a good chance of winning those matches.[7]

And, indeed, finally, in 2016, Sundowns triumphed in the CAF Champions League by beating Egyptian club Zamalek 3-1 on aggregate in the final in Alexandria. Motsepe's club was only the second PSL team to win that prize, after Orlando Pirates had done so back in 1995.

The previous time Sundowns had tried to win the Champions League, in 2015, they'd been knocked out by TP Mazembe, the club that Motsepe's mentor, Congolese businessman and politician Moïse Katumbi, had owned for 33 years. Katumbi explained afterwards that Sundowns would soon outdo the opposition, and that wasn't only because the PSL was in a strong financial position, but because Motsepe had the money to keep improving his club.

Motsepe wouldn't take any personal credit after the dazzling 2016 win in Egypt, saying, 'This is more about South Africa than about me individually. We've won the league. That was for the supporters. But the Champions League is for South Africa. It's for all our people. We have the most loving and caring and generous people, and it's an honour for us. This is a humble contribution from Mamelodi Sundowns. We have a duty to always make humble contributions to make South Africa a better place for all.'[8]

Motsepe applauded Mosimane: 'The irony is that I had coaches from all over the world, but I had to wait for a young man from South Africa to show us something we already knew – that we've got so much talent in South Africa.' He added to that patriotic fervour, saying, 'We must just give our coaches a chance, and also invest in our youth – the future of South African football.'[9]

He compared Mosimane to legendary Manchester United manager Sir Alex Ferguson, saying, 'I … want to see him grow because can you imagine, for example, if he were to coach one of the European clubs? Pitso is black, he is African, he is South African, and he is one of us. You have to feel a sense of unique pride.'[10]

* * * *

There were also controversies that tested Motsepe while he was chairman of the club. One of the most public was the Keagan Dolly saga, which was a messy way for Sundowns and Motsepe to start 2017, and revealed a darker side to relationships between clubs, players, agents and the league. The Dolly story also put Motsepe in the headlights of European clubs making offers for South African players.

Dolly was a gifted young midfielder from Westbury, Johannesburg, who'd been a member of the iconic 'CBD' attacking trinity with Billiat and Colombian forward Leonardo Castro in Sundowns' shining 2016 season. Together with Mosimane, the trio had made it 'their business to dictate the side's tempo, rhythm, positional play and movements in each encounter'.[11] With 30 goals between them, they were fundamental to Sundowns winning the domestic treble that season.

Dolly, who'd been scouted for the Sundowns youth structures from the Football School of Excellence based outside Johannesburg, had won the PSL Young Player Award in 2013/14. An outstanding prospect, he then signed for Ajax Cape Town, but Sundowns wanted him too and put up a better contract in 2014. This was followed briefly by a loan back to Ajax before Sundowns re-registered Dolly with the league in 2015 and offered him a four-year contract with a one-year additional option.

Dolly's supreme performance in 2015/16 earned him the attention of European football scouts, and that year, Olympiakos of the Greek professional league put in a bid for R14 million to buy the young winger. But then came an explosive argument between Dolly's side and Sundowns over his contract. It was ostensibly about money, but essentially it was about control.

The battle was traced to when Dolly had signed for Sundowns, with his agent Paul Mitchell and father Ramon putting forward a contract with a buyout clause.[12] Ramon Dolly said the clause 'was the only way we would let Keagan go back [after leaving Ajax]'. 'They [Sundowns] didn't want to put that in, [but] eventually they came around.'[13]

But when Olympiakos did its paperwork, the fight began. Dolly's side said the buyout clause was R12.5 million, which is what Mitchell had put to the Greeks. Motsepe and Sundowns insisted it had instead asked for R25 million, and that is what it would be expecting from Athens.

Each camp was equally adamant that its number was correct, and soon the debacle threated to undermine the jubilation of the player and the club's success. Sundowns had won the PSL title in 2016, and Dolly had been nominated for midfielder of the season, players' player of the season and footballer of the season at the PSL awards, but the heat in the background was stifling as Sundowns took the Dolly stalemate to the PSL's dispute resolution chamber.

Christmas 2016 came and went as the PSL's chamber considered the facts. Then, as the clocked ticked into the new year, the pace to pass a verdict quickened: French club Montpellier also wanted the player, upping the ante by offering Motsepe R14.3 million.

It wasn't enough.

On 4 January 2017, the league announced it had found in favour of Sundowns, although the chamber acknowledged there had been some 'negligence' on the club's part in the 'handling' of the contract. The buyout clause was restored to R25 million.

Dolly's team was furious. Motsepe wasn't happy with the miserable trajectory of events, either. In an interview after the findings went public, Motsepe would only venture that Sundowns had made one change in the contract when it had had to re-register Dolly with the PSL in 2015. But he also quipped that he 'would sell Dolly for "R5" [if he did not have] a board of directors to answer to'.[14]

That annoyed Ramon Dolly and Mitchell, who claimed it wasn't a simple error, as suggested by Motsepe. Rather, said Mitchell, 'the president's been misadvised by his people there'.[15] Dolly's agent warned they could take the PSL's findings to the SAFA appeals board, and that if Dolly won, Sundowns could ultimately be referred to FIFA. It was a shaky moment, but in the end, it didn't go that far.

Sundowns' management met to try to establish how it had got itself into a dispute over a contract it had drafted for its own player, but Motsepe decided not to sanction anybody at Chloorkop since the PSL had found that 'negligence is not grounds to reject a rectification, and the rectification was granted'.[16]

'It's a very simple issue,' Motsepe explained. 'There was an agreement. Done. [Then, when the contract was re-signed], a mistake was made. An official in Sundowns made a mistake.' There were suspicions, Motsepe said, 'that there's bribery or corruption

… but my starting point was, no guys, come on, I think it's a genuine error and we only became aware of it – we didn't know about it – when an offer arrived from Olympiakos … Clearly,' Motsepe concluded, 'there was a mistake [made] in good faith.'[17]

He said he'd promised Dolly he could still leave Sundowns during the transfer window of January 2017 if his buyout clause was met in full. And it was.

Dolly – who'd won everything he could possibly win with Sundowns when he was there – ended up going to Montpellier in a deal believed to be worth about R28 million, a modern record for a South African player and a South African team.[18]

Nonetheless, there were critics of how the PSL had intervened in the dispute, with one analyst saying that 'the [dispute resolution chamber is] not a fair, objective body fit to judge on player contracts'. 'With the same people representing Kaizer Chiefs and Sundowns as well as the PSL against players, justice is currently unavailable.'[19]

* * * *

Sundowns would have to keep an increasingly sharp eye on its administration. 'In 2007, [Venezuelan striker] Jose Torrealba [had] challenged the club, and won, with regards to a contract extension that he claimed he didn't sign … In 2014, the club accepted [Dutch defender] Alje Schut's card from the PSL despite it showing the wrong year. [In the 2018/19] season, Sundowns were found guilty for fielding an ineligible player.'[20]

But the highs – such as the Montpellier windfall over Dolly – were very high. And in January 2017, when the annual CAF awards took place, Sundowns was named African club of the year, Mosimane was voted African coach of the year (the first South African to take this honour), and Sundowns goalkeeper, Ugandan international Denis Onyango, was named African player of the year. It was a spotlight moment for Dolly, too, as he, Onyango and Billiat were chosen for the honorary CAF team of the year, also known as Africa's Finest XI.

Kaizer Motaung announced collegially on the glamour boys' website 'on behalf of Kaizer Chiefs' that he wished 'to congratulate Mamelodi Sundowns for their achievements' at the awards. 'Well done to club president Patrice Motsepe for his leadership and for making the country proud.' Motaung had a history with those same prizes, as Chiefs were the first South African club to win the African Club of the Year prize, in 2001. 'I wish to also congratulate coach Mosimane and his players for their individual achievements … they augur well for the quality and the standard of the PSL.'[21]

Another highlight was the 2018 Barcelona friendly against Sundowns in Pretoria. Announcing it, Motsepe said, 'I know how big this is for the youth. I remember when I was a young follower of football and I went to Orlando Stadium and watched all the great players. They inspired me. Some of them are alive today and they don't know it was such an honour for me to just touch them.'[22]

The match, which formed part of the Nelson Mandela Foundation's 100-year Mandela celebrations, was played in front of 90 000 fans and broadcast widely around the world. Legends Lionel Messi and Andrés Iniesta headlined the visiting team.

As the Sundowns chair so aptly put it, 'There are many young footballers who we know that watching Messi and Iniesta will inspire them to realise their dreams, whatever dreams those might be.'[23]

6

The broadsides and the bucks: A new era begins

The year 2017 would be momentous for CAF as it marked its 50th anniversary with its showcase, the Champions League, expanded to include 16 teams instead of eight. Motsepe wanted in.

The money was meanwhile starting to come in too, in a serious manner, for Sundowns. In terms of the Champions League, whoever won in 2017 would take home a previously unheard-of R49 million, with clubs that made it into the quarter-finals and the semi-finals each receiving a certain amount for getting that far in the competition, too.

Motsepe was certainly seeing a harvest. In 2016 alone, Sundowns had taken home around R50 million in prize money through its successes in national and African competitions. And by July 2017, 'the Brazilians' had already banked about R8.5 million for reaching the last eight of CAF's golden jubilee Champions League.[1] (To put this into perspective, PSL sponsors Absa presented R10 million to its winners.)

Motsepe responded to Sundowns reaching CAF's quarter-finals with bonuses for Mosimane and the players. He had a tendency for incentives – Sundowns players were believed to have guarantees that they would receive performance bonuses for winning PSL matches, for instance, of reportedly 'between R5 000 and R8 000 per PSL match won ... payable after every four PSL matches won by the club'.[2] (It was thought by 2021, when Sundowns had won eight in nine league games, that the players would be 'already closing in on R100 000 [each] before the campaign had even reached the halfway mark'.[3])

Motsepe had pledged the entire CAF Champions League prize money of R20.9 million to the players who lifted the trophy in October 2016, saying 'All of [it] – it's all theirs. They must now sit down and start thinking about how they are going to divide that money amongst themselves.' And he had 'some sage words for the players regarding their windfall'. 'I just said to them, "Guys, don't waste the money now. Take some of that money and invest it. It will benefit you when your football days are over."'[4]

Motsepe's incentives were presented as a positive form of intergenerational wealth-building. Sundowns wanted 'the boys to become millionaires and build houses for their parents and for themselves'.[5]

More money would follow as Sundowns were paid around R15 million for finishing sixth in 2016 at the FIFA Club World Cup – the most important tournament of its kind hosted on Asian and developing nations' soil.[6] The loot from that outing in Japan was significant, but that didn't seem to matter as much as having got there in the first place, as Sundowns was the first football club from southern Africa to represent CAF at the event.

The sensational team under Motsepe and Mosimane were crowned PSL champions for the fourth time in 2018, meaning they would qualify for the CAF Champions League again, and '[inflict] Egyptian powerhouse Al Ahly's heaviest continental defeat with a 5-0 home win against [the] record eight-time Champions League winners in April 2019'. 'The accomplished tactician [Mosimane] then masterminded an 11-1 win over Côte d'Or of Seychelles in September 2019, and Sundowns broke the previous record for the highest number of goals scored in a single match in the competition.'[7]

Mosimane was more noticeably motivated after those successes by the notion that South Africa was becoming too small a market for Sundowns. He said in an interview in 2019 that '[the club] would continue to attract players because of [its] insistence on participating in the Champions League every single year'. 'It is important to sell the right story to these players and not the myth that we are a big club and we have many supporters because that story doesn't work anymore.'[8] It was, rather, the drive for that more immense stage, and the refusal to be mediocre.

Mosimane didn't see money as the only route for the club to push to win any more. 'Everybody likes to say Sundowns is supposed to win the league because they have a big chequebook,' he said. 'Sundowns has always had a chequebook before I came here and there were seven years of drought. Probably the cheque at that time was bigger than the one I have.'[9]

* * * *

Then, in September 2020, Mosimane turned his back on Sundowns and signed with the Cairo-based African super-club Al Ahly. This came as a shock to most South African football fans, who knew there was drama in the Sundowns camp, but never quite expected Mosimane to leave.

It was likely the cause of significant friction at Chloorkop, and no one has described exactly what transpired behind the scenes between Mosimane and Motsepe when Mosimane told the chairman he was resigning. After all, when Mosimane made his announcement, he was only four months into a new contract at Sundowns, and had recently said that being the club's coach was 'no longer a job; it's a home, it's a family'.[10]

Motsepe would, however, have known by the middle of 2020 that he was facing a challenge to keep Mosimane. It was inevitable. South Africa's most successful coach wouldn't be without offers, and Al Ahly could put more cash on the table than Motsepe was prepared to do. Mosimane admitted later than he'd also had 'an offer from Qatar [with] more money than Sundowns', although he'd decided to rather stay in South Africa, 'to be part of [Sundowns'] 50th anniversary'. He'd called the relationship he had with Motsepe 'special'.

'If you ask me if I want to go, I will say I want to stay,' Mosimane noted. 'When two people want each other, they will end up in the same place and same kraal.'[11] He expressed his gratitude for a 'special love' from the Sundowns supporters: 'We have so much history. We've got people singing, making a song about me.' Mosimane was referring to the new 'matorokisi' dance at Loftus invented by musicians Makhadzi and DJ Call Me which had gone viral, almost eclipsing the dance Sundowns supporters conventionally did to the sound of drums, usually led by midfielder Tiyani Mabunda.

'There is a flag going around with my face [on it],' enthused Mosimane. 'You don't take that for granted.'[12]

But Motsepe wasn't game to again hike Mosimane's salary, which was said to be between R800 000 and R1 million per month. Al Ahly was reported to have offered Mosimane R2.5 million monthly, excluding bonuses. In any event, it would be an historic event for Mosimane to move there as he would be the first black sub-Saharan African to coach the club in its 113-year history.

That switch in plans by Mosimane to leave Pretoria and move to Cairo didn't go smoothly. It quickly led to a breach-of-contract claim from Sundowns being delivered to Mosimane's manager (and wife) Moira Tlhagale, who had kept 'her 10 percent commission for getting her client to sign a new contract with Sundowns', the amount 'reportedly paid in full instead of divided over the four seasons that Mosimane would have been head coach'.[13]

Motsepe refused to express animosity himself, however, saying,

'I have on several occasions over the past few years expressed my support for Pitso Mosimane leaving Sundowns to coach in North Africa or Europe or Bafana Bafana. I have received a warm and emotional note from Pitso and am very proud of his achievements at Mamelodi Sundowns. Pitso has been the most successful coach in the history of Sundowns and will always be a member of the Mamelodi Sundowns family.'[14]

Mosimane's agency then also noted how grateful they were to Sundowns for the years Mosimane had spent with the club and how they 'would not like this glorious legacy to be soiled by tussles that could easily and rapidly be handled professionally and privately'.[15]

* * * *

Still, the tension between Mosimane and Sundowns didn't ease, and Mosimane even endured abuse from the Brazilians' fans – who were formerly his greatest supporters – when he arrived for a Champions League match between Sundowns and Al Ahly in Pretoria in May 2021.

But Mosimane held a 'secret', which he treasured.

A few months later, in July 2021 when Al Ahly were going for 'a record-stretching 10th title' against Kaizer Chiefs in the Champions League final in Morocco, Mosimane said he expected Al Ahly would win as Motsepe would be present at the game. He called Motsepe his 'lucky charm', saying that every time Motsepe had attended an Al Ahly match when he, Mosimane, was coach, Al Ahly had performed brilliantly. 'When he came to Zamalek [in 2020], we won. When he came to the [Club] World Cup, we won bronze. And when he came to Qatar last month, he handed us the African Super Cup. So he must just keep consistent and keep coming!'[16]

Chiefs lost 3-0, and Mosimane won his third Champions League as a coach.

However, when Sundowns beat Al Ahly 1-0 at a Champions League encounter in Johannesburg in March 2022, Mosimane showed a somewhat uncharacteristic bitterness. Goaded by unforgiving Sundowns fans, he conceded that his old club had 'won the game fair and square', but added that he believed 'they're still after me, these people'. 'They don't want to leave me alone, but ... I've moved on. They have a good team and they have three coaches. What do you want? You've won. Leave me alone. I'm gone. I've done my best and given you a great team.'[17]

Then he 'fired a broadside' and indicated he had 'stories to tell' about Sundowns: 'It's very dirty and I'll reveal it one day. There's a lot and it's too much. Don't play dirty ... There's only one person behind all of this.'[18]

Patrice Motsepe didn't comment.

A few days later, Mosimane lashed out directly at Motsepe in his capacity as CAF president, likening Motsepe's administration to that of 'long-serving former CAF president Issa Hayatou, who hogged the position for close to 30 years'.[19] Hayatou, a Cameroonian former teacher who'd overhauled the federation formed in 1957 by Ethiopia, Sudan, Egypt and South Africa on the brink of the mighty wave of independence for many African nations,[20] had certainly stayed on for far too long. But he had handed [CAF] over to his successor Ahmad with in excess of R1.9 billion in the bank and an ever-increasing array of competitions'.[21]

Apparently fed up that the video assistant referee (VAR) wasn't being used routinely in the federation's fixtures yet, including at the Champions League game which Al Ahly had lost to Sundowns, Mosimane 'put the blame for the slow progress ... squarely on Motsepe's doorstep', believing the system should now be 'standard in CAF competitions'.[22]

The use of VAR was becoming urgent in Africa due to the poor state of refereeing on the continent, and that put Motsepe at the front of the crisis, as he'd promised when he became president of CAF to address both the prevalence of the tech[23] and problems with referees. He saw that VAR was used at the inaugural CAF Women's Champions League in Egypt in November 2021, at the Africa Cup of Nations in Cameroon in January 2022, and for the Qatar 2022 World Cup African qualifiers.

But that wasn't enough for Mosimane. 'Egypt has it for every match,' he'd railed. 'There is always talk that it is going to be better and what-not, but better where?'[24]

The confederation's head of media Luxolo September was quick to defend Motsepe. 'There are costs. Africa is vast, and while some countries have this infrastructure, some don't. These are objective realities. The costs of rolling out VAR ... can run up to millions of dollars in a single month. There is progress but it's not something we should approach in an emotional or sentimental way. We must be practical and give an objective view of our continent. President Motsepe is committed to this mission ... We should also not forget that the pyramids were not built in one weekend.'[25]

7

A millennial in the chair:
Tlhopie Motsepe

There was a touch of tears in February 2021 when Patrice Motsepe told the media in Johannesburg that he would leave the chairman's seat at Sundowns if he became CAF president. But his jersey would simply be 'retired', not replaced, because 'Sundowns will never lose me … My heart and soul will always be with Mamelodi Sundowns'.[1]

He would be passing responsibility to his eldest son, Tlhopane (better known as Tlhopie), which was a cultural rite of passage, he explained, while also referring to the Motsepe family's 'deep, deep emotional commitment' to the club. His wife, Tlhopie's mother, Dr Precious Moloi-Motsepe, would 'assist in running the "family business" alongside [Fulbright fellow and Sundowns director] Dr Rejoice Simelane and [Tlhopie's] brothers Kgosi and Kabelo'.[2]

Coach Manqoba Mngqithi gave Tlhopie the thumbs-up, saying, 'The least I can tell you is that, this is one of the best decisions that a father can take. Tlhopie is a very good boy, he is very intelligent, he is very humble, he is very principled and, for me, there is no chance that he will fail.'[3]

Off the cuff, Motsepe promised he would keep funding Sundowns: 'I'm talking here not just of the love, but also the financial commitment'.[4]

* * * *

At just 32, Tlhopie Motsepe – whose LinkedIn profile records that he has a BA in international relations with psychology from Wits – was young to be taking over a top-flight football club. He saw it as an honour, telling the media that 'you can't play down being in a position like this'.[5]

It was a transitional moment overall, as the new chairman was also taking over without the multi-trophy-winning Mosimane. Yet while many clubs aren't able to keep flourishing after a significant manager or a leading chairman leaves, that wasn't the case with Sundowns, which was testament to the work Mosimane and Patrice Motsepe had put in, together.

Admittedly, it took three men to do what Mosimane had done alone. Former Chiefs coach Steve Komphela, and Mngqithi and Rulani Mokwena, who'd been Mosimane's assistant coaches at Sundowns, made a formidable trio as they prepared to come into their own. It was as if the club's 50th anniversary party in December 2020 was the bridge to a different level.

Sundowns was looking polished. Three months earlier, its marketing team had got German sportswear company Puma to design new home and away shirts in 'a slim-fit cut with a Johnny collar reminiscent of 1970s-style playing jerseys ... intended to link the jersey to the era in which the club was established'.[6]

Its celebratory gala dinner in Sandton had an A-list, including African football legends El Hadji Diouf of Senegal, Samuel Eto'o of Cameroon and Siaka Tiene, a midfielder for Côte d'Ivoire who'd once played for Sundowns. Diouf told the media at the event that he believed Sundowns was 'one of the biggest clubs in the world'.[7]

Tlhopie, who, like his father, had been 'football-crazy' as a child, set out determined to take advantage of being a millennial chairman, noting, 'If we don't make sure young people are inspired by football, there are so many things contesting for their attention now, like Netflix ... your laptop, your phone or TV.'[8]

Echoing his father's willingness to give credit where it was due, he paid tribute to Sundowns' 'icons and role models' Komphela, Mngqiti and Mokwena, saying their appointments had been 'a wonderful opportunity for us as a football club to bring South Africans to the fore again, and actually employ from within our ranks'. Impeccably poised, likely a leaf taken from his mother's playbook, Tlhopie also made mention of 'the incredible … technical staff' who 'do so much work behind the scenes'.[9]

His father must have had faith in him, as Tlhopie took over the club at a particularly demanding time in world football, and he would have to be up to competing at an international level. There was no going back to the outer rings of the CAF tournaments for Sundowns. The club had earned 14 titles in total after clinching the 2020/21 PSL honours. Four-times-in-a-row defending champions in South Africa's DStv-sponsored premier division, Sundowns was yet to be beaten or concede a goal as of October 2021.

This was an exciting position for the fans, whose 300 branches were now spread across South Africa, eSwatini, Botswana, Zambia and Zimbabwe. There was even a branch in Cincinnati in the US.

Many competitions lay ahead. For example, the Club World Cup tournament had been expanded to include 24 teams, as opposed to the original seven, and those clubs would now play in eight groups of three teams each, with group winners qualifying for quarter-finals in a knockout format. Spain's legendary Real Madrid was that event's most frequent historical winner, with four cups. The reigning champions in 2021 were England's popular Chelsea Football Club.

The tournament, which replaced FIFA's long-running Confederations Cup, would next be held in China, although no date had been confirmed by May 2022 due to reshuffles in international football resulting from disruptions caused by covid-19.

In April 2022, Sundowns had won its fifth straight league title with four games to spare, and co-coach Mokwena was spreading Mosimane's gospel of a team that was a phenomenon, noting that the club now needed 'stronger rivals to improve football in the country'.[10]

* * * *

Patrice Motsepe was perhaps a little late in giving Sundowns' future to sports scientists to determine, but the club did finally enter into a five-year agreement with the University of Pretoria in March 2021, just as he was on his way out. Motsepe said he wanted the benefits of 'technology and ... research'[11] – essential to keep Sundowns at the top in Africa, and capable of playing on FIFA's biggest stages.

To an extent, Motsepe may have been inspired by Austria's national coach Ralf Rangnick, who had been using state-of-the-art scientific methods in football clubs for years. But Motsepe was also mirroring his only rival in South Africa's billionaire owner rankings.

Johann Rupert, who'd recently dethroned Motsepe as the country's richest football boss, with a net worth in the region of R100 billion, had got in slightly ahead of Motsepe in how he linked his club to science. His company, Remgro, had bought the Stellenbosch Academy of Sport in the Cape winelands, and then also picked up a lower-leagues football club called Vasco da Gama in 2018, soon transforming it into the Stellenbosch Football Club. The Academy then exposed Stellenbosch's players to 'the best developmental support' under 'sport scientists, doctors, coaches, physiotherapists and biokineticists, with performance-nutrition catering'. Rupert saw it as an 'agent of social change' – an investment in the community living around his multimillion-dollar wine estate.[12] But when it was announced in July 2022 that the Motsepe Foundation would back the SAFA first division, adding to its sponsorship of the third-tier ABC Motsepe League, Motsepe had undoubtedly trounced Rupert.

The major difference was that the Afrikaner billionaire – who would go into a rugby-club partnership with Motsepe not long afterwards – didn't attend his club's games much. This was according to Stellenbosch Football Club and Academy chief executive Rob Benadie, although he noted that 'Rupert gives them the support they need'.[13] Patrice Motsepe was the opposite, tireless about attending Sundowns' big matches.

Tlhopie Motsepe would surely have to similarly devote himself to the club's cause, and he got off to a strong start. In October 2021, Sundowns lifted the MTN8 Championship at last; it hadn't done so since 2007. The victory came after a 3-2 sudden-death penalty shoot-out against Cape Town City FC at the Moses Mabhida Stadium in Durban.

Sundowns' women's team were meanwhile emulating the men's famous continental successes, having qualified as the COSAFA entrants to the eight-team finals of the inaugural CAF Women's Champions League in November 2021. The joy was boundless when they conquered the continent by beating Ghanaian side Hasaacas Ladies 2-0 in Cairo.

Since their male counterparts had lifted the CAF Champions League trophy in 2016, the Sundowns' women's team made it a double to match Spanish giants Barcelona, the only other club in the world to have both their men's and women's sides win an elite competition on their own continent. Patrice Motsepe had long wanted to see that happen, and that it took place in his first year as CAF president was a personal achievement.

* * * *

Inspiring as that was, Tlhopie also had no choice about accepting some of the drama left over from his father's era. That would include Mosimane, and, by extension, Al Ahly. Following on the Sundowns' fans' attack on Mosimane at the Champions League fixture in Pretoria in 2021, came another bout of unpleasantness in March 2022. When Al Ahly and Sundowns met in Johannesburg for their fourth fixture in the group stage of the 2022 Champions League, the Egyptians claimed they were 'forced to arrive late for the game', their allegation being that Sundowns fans had created an obstruction in the road near FNB Stadium.

Tlhopie quickly sent a letter to his Red Devils counterpart, Mahmoud El Khatib, saying the delay had been caused by a traffic jam and that the snarl-up had also affected Sundowns.[14] Tlhopie added that he was 'committed to building and maintaining a good relationship' with Al Ahly, and undertook to investigate the incident. In June 2022, Al Ahly announced that it had parted ways with Mosimane.

Tlhopie may not have to spare too much time himself on handling that kind of encounter in the future, however. In his raft of business objectives was a deal to take Sundowns global with Roc Nation Sports,[15] the talent agency belonging to American hip-hop superstar and billionaire businessman Jay-Z.

Roc Nation, which created communication strategies, among other services, for top brands, had already signed World Cup-winning Springbok rugby captain Siya Kolisi (who played for the Durban-based Sharks rugby team) and fellow South African rugby players Cheslin Kolbe (who played in Toulon, France), Sibusiso Nkosi (the Sharks), Aphelele Fassi (the Sharks) and Zimbabwean-born Tendai 'Beast' Mtawarira (who played for Old Glory DC in Washington DC), in 2019 and 2020.

Tlhopie put his signature on Sundowns' contract with Roc Nation in August 2021, marking the American company's 'grand entry into

African football'. Its director of operations for Africa, Isaac Lugudde-Katwe, described Sundowns as having 'a vision that is aligned with ours ... We want to show the world what [they are] about. We are not about quantity, we are about quality. Our clients are athletes who strive to be great ... We do have a lot of people who would love to be part of Roc Nation, but only a few are chosen.'[16]

Roc Nation would also soon represent South African national team cricketers Temba Bavuma and Lungi Ngidi, while consulting for top Italian football club AC Milan and the United Rugby Championship. The choice of who to sign and who to turn down lay with Roc Nation co-CEOs Brett and Michael Yormark, brothers who were not only interested in representing sports achievers, but also 'the potential to mould [brands] based on ... political and social outlook'.[17]

This was certainly a change in strategy for Motsepe as the owner of Sundowns, his thinking perhaps best explored in how Brett Yormark explained the future of sports marketing in December 2021. The American said that many sports organisations in South Africa, including the 'top three' of rugby, cricket and football, were facing increasing financial challenges, and needed to 'develop a model that ensured their survival'. Decrying the power of centralised control – such as SAFA in the case of football, and the South African Rugby Union and Cricket South Africa – he told the audience that 'the influence of private ownership [was] an area that South Africa [was] going to have to accept'.[18]

'In rugby and football, it's the clubs who are paying the players, enriching the local community, and creating jobs on a consistent basis in each of their local markets. The clubs are super, super important. They can't be treated like the stepchild, and they can't be just a feeder system to the national teams. It's not right, it has to change, and we're going to do everything we can to impact that change.'

Yormark said he believed 'other South African franchises should follow suit' as 'they [needed] capital infusion', and Sundowns was surely a prize in that respect. It was already backed to the hilt by a billionaire with a taste for disruption and a willingness to put his own money into enterprises such as those Yormark was describing.

Michael Yormark was part of an American company that acquired a 51 percent controlling share in the Sharks rugby franchise in 2021, but Patrice Motsepe had beaten them to it in terms of the concept. In December 2019, he'd gone into a deal with Johann Rupert at the Blue Bulls rugby franchise in Pretoria, in which the Bulls would hold 26 percent of the company, Rupert's Remgro 37 percent and Motsepe the remaining 37 percent. Early in 2020, Rugby World Cup-winning coach Jake White joined the Bulls as director of rugby, with Motsepe heralding 'the Jake White-led revolution' as the team looked to again becoming 'a dominant force in southern hemisphere rugby'.[19]

* * * *

Sundowns had made history with its fourth consecutive DStv Premiership title by the time Tlhopie broke the news of a multi-year partnership with the global company Herbalife Nutrition in December 2021. That was Sundowns' first deal brokered by Roc Nation.

Herbalife, which manufactures a range of nutrition, wellness and sports-performance products, would become the football club's official and exclusive nutrition and sports nutrition partner, just as it was for international football superstar Cristiano Ronaldo and the Los Angeles Galaxy soccer club.

Competition for that kind of sponsorship was fierce around the world.

8

Not a moment's silence: The first year at CAF

Sponsorship and investment in African football were Motsepe's parallel quests at CAF. But while back at home Tlhopie was putting together deals for Sundowns relatively unfettered by interference, Motsepe was managing the expectations of FIFA and Gianni Infantino against the criticism of those who insisted the African federation remain steadfastly independent of the global body.

Here was his Catch-22: if Motsepe was to be his own man, he would have to ensure he could increasingly pull away from Infantino, but if he pulled away from Infantino, Motsepe might find himself in the crosshairs of a powerful man.

It appeared that Infantino was intentional in placing Motsepe, FIFA's choice for CAF president, at the centre of lobbying for two legacy projects whenever he could, these being a biennial World Cup and an Africa Super League.

Motsepe had been clear that 'Africa must be put in a fundamental position to benefit financially' from football's ability to attract fans and money. He told Ghana's media during a conference with them in October 2021 that he believed that 'could happen if the World Cup happened more frequently ... I am very clear in my mind that one of the biggest beneficiaries of football every two years is the developing world.'[1]

Fifty-four, or a little more than a quarter, of FIFA's 211 affiliated member associations are in CAF, which is why it was critical for Infantino to up his stakes for and with the African federation from the time he became FIFA president in 2016. His first success in this regard came in 2017 when FIFA agreed that it would increase the number of African nations competing at the World Cup in the USA, Mexico and Canada in 2026 from five to a guaranteed nine.

And there was a chance that a tenth African nation could take part as FIFA, under Infantino, had further agreed to a six-team play-off before that event, involving one country from each of its six continental federations, to decide the final two qualifiers. If an African country was successful during that play-off, it would also feature at the World Cup. That news had been warmly welcomed by African football lovers who had long bemoaned poor representation at the spectacular showcase.

* * * *

Infantino perhaps wanted to build on that momentum by generating a feasibility study for a biennial tournament, mooting that this would also be 'good' for Africa. He said he wanted to give 'more playing and hosting opportunities to countries that rarely or never qualify', and cited 'speeding up the development of talent worldwide to close the gap on the soccer powers of Europe and South America who have dominated the World Cup from its launch in 1930'.[2]

A biennial men's World Cup had first been proposed 20 years earlier, and then, due to pushback, fell off the radar, although the theory remained that the more visibility Africa's football associations had at the global level, the closer an African country would get to winning the trophy.

Infantino had been accompanied by FIFA's head of global development, French football administrator Arsène Wenger – a long-term former manager of Arsenal Football Club in England – when he'd attended a CAF extraordinary general assembly in

Cairo in December 2021. 'During their presentations, the two FIFA officials went to great lengths to present a strong case for a biennial World Cup ... They argued that this project would extend its focus far beyond the game's elite.'[3]

While the anti-elitist argument about the Cup has value, it should also be noted that each World Cup earns FIFA up to about R100 billion in broadcasting and commercial deals.

Motsepe had had to drive support for such an event among CAF members ahead of that extraordinary congress, amid an outburst of anger towards the suggestion in Europe and the Americas, with UEFA and the South American Football Confederation (CONMEBOL) threatening a boycott if a biennial World Cup went ahead, and the global football players' union FIFPRO[4] warning 'of players facing burnout and injuries from bigger workloads'.[5]

This had put Motsepe in a somewhat precarious position. He has a deeply ambitious nature, which suggests he might chase the FIFA presidency at some point, and that meant he would have to make sure he didn't lose support for himself among FIFA's other federations.

Under Motsepe, CAF voted and gave Infantino and Wenger its wholehearted support, with no objections. Critics said FIFA had found 'a willing ally' in CAF, through Motsepe, as it tried to 'muscle its way down world football's corridors of power with confrontational agendas'.[6]

The biennial cup concept faced criticism from federations other than CAF, and Infantino had sought to emphasise that 'those who were against the move "were afraid of change"'. But in March 2022, he put it forward in Doha, Qatar, before the World Cup draw, that FIFA had in fact 'not proposed a biennial World Cup', adding, 'Let's get the process clear here [that] the last FIFA congress asked the FIFA administration ... to start a feasibility study into holding the World Cup every two years'.[7]

The FIFA administration under the leadership of Wenger did exactly that, Infantino continued, and 'came to the conclusion that it is feasible, that it would have some repercussions and impact. [FIFA] found it would be ... even positive for a big part of the world, but there is of course also big opposition to it and that is where the discussion has to start.'[8]

* * * *

Then came the announcement of an African Super League, a new competition that could happen 'side by side' with the World Cup. Although the plan hadn't been raised with any prominence at the time of Motsepe's election in Morocco, it would come up over the following months with Motsepe in charge, especially as he now had a focal role as one of FIFA's six vice-presidents.

An African Super League would fall under CAF. Twenty-four teams would contest three groups of eight teams ahead of a knock-out stage. Teams would be taken from the best-ranked African clubs, with groups to be played on a regional basis. The Champions League and the CAF Confederation Cup would likely continue, as an African Super League would not be 'a breakaway, but integrated in the institutional structures of African and global football'.[9]

Motsepe offered the lure of sharing an African Super League kitty to the 54 national governments whose football associations fell under CAF, but made it clear that their buy-in would have to come through the chairs of the football clubs. 'You can't, in Africa, have initiatives of this magnitude that do not involve everybody, so every nation in Africa is part of this process,' he said. 'What I like is that it will allow CAF to get some money to develop African football and make it world-class, but also to use some of the money to share amongst all of the 54 nations in Africa – from the smallest one to the largest one.'[10]

'There has to be fundamental changes in how we do things in football so that African football can be noticed across the world,' Motsepe told the Ghanaian media in October 2021. He emphasised that 'we do not want aid from anybody'. 'We can work on our own and that's what I am here to do. My job is to make sure that African football grows and succeeds.'[11]

Similar plans for a private seasonal European Super League involving 20 permanent teams had failed in 2021. Among the richest of those – Arsenal, Chelsea, Liverpool, Manchester City, Manchester United, Tottenham Hotspur, Barcelona, Atletico Madrid, Real Madrid, AC Milan, Inter Milan and Juventus – had ventured the idea, before fans, who are of course the power behind the football throne, threatened to boycott them if they went ahead. Since so few teams would be involved, the rest – which were not as wealthy or powerful – would effectively be sidelined, leaving fans questioning the meaning of true competition.

Unlike in Europe, fans in Africa were thought to be in favour of an African Super League as this would put more money into their continental football. Conditions are such that African clubs are nowhere near as commercialised as European clubs, which would be likely to oppose an African Super League because Europe might lose financial support for their national teams and their clubs if the African iteration became popular. Broadcasters and sponsors might ultimately prefer the African version over the European version.

A significant threat also lay in African players – who boosted European club sides – finding a more attractive option at last in African clubs, and leaving to play on their home continent instead.

In July 2022, Motsepe jubilantly announced that the African Super League had been ratified by CAF's 54 Member Associations and would go ahead. He explained that Infantino had participated in the process to reach that point because 'FIFA [brought] a wealth of experience in terms of running the best competition in the world, [the World Cup]'. 'We want the African Super League to be world-class and to compete against the best in the world in terms of quality of football, resources, infrastructure, pitches, referees, stadiums and ticketing.'[12]

August 2023 was announced as the start date for the first event, with each Member Association to be given $1 million every year from the proceeds.

For Motsepe, an African Super League meant much more cash directly into the coffers of a still-stuttering CAF, with Infantino claiming in 2020 that it would generate more than R3 billion in revenue. Motsepe said CAF had been inundated with investors and sponsors for the event by mid-2022, he and Infantino having already had 'really exciting discussions with some of the biggest TV companies in the world' in 2021.[13]

Motsepe had made a promise to sort out African football broadcasting so that fans could watch the big games on pay TV anywhere around the continent, and almost as soon as he started work in Cairo, an invitation to tender had gone out. By December 2021, CAF could announce that a deal had been concluded – with the Swiss-based Infront Sports & Media headed by Philippe Blatter, the nephew of the disgraced former FIFA president Sepp Blatter.[14]

Infront – which also represents the Olympic winter sports federations – is owned by Chinese conglomerate Dalian Wanda. It had supported the FIFA World Cup since 2002, distributing its Asian media rights and managing broadcast production.

Knowing its choice could send a shiver through some media, CAF quickly noted that Infront France had a strong record, 'having covered the ... Chinese Basketball Association and national team, the German Football Association and Italy's Serie A'.[15] It's been reported that '[Philippe] Blatter has often had to confront scepticism over his relationship with FIFA, but he has always claimed accusations of nepotism are unfounded'.[16]

Perhaps the desperation to have African games back on the continent's screens meant that not much attention was paid to the CAF deal. Meanwhile, Motsepe continued to present a picture of clean, renewed governance.

* * * *

It was a coup for the new chief of African football when TikTok partnered with the confederation for the Africa Cup of Nations in January 2022 for what was the social media platform's first major brand partnership in Africa. And Motsepe could boast that CAF had come second only to UEFA in attracting TikTok as a digital entertainment platform sponsor – it had only worked on Euro 2020, UEFA's top tournament, before.

It would be a year-long sponsorship that would cover the Champions League 2022 and the Women's Africa Cup of Nations 2022, set to be held in Morocco. TikTok promised innovation, which Motsepe always chased, to expand fan communities around Africa's unique football culture. These were areas into which CAF had not previously ventured, even though TikTok's research showed that the hashtags #football and #soccer raked up an incredible 273 billion and 108 billion views, respectively, in 2022. #African-Football had more than 48.3 million views.[17] Drawing millennial, Gen Z and younger fans around the world to African football was becoming easier.

But Motsepe was not going to have a smooth run in his first year at the helm of CAF. At his first major tournament, the 2022 Africa Cup of Nations in Cameroon, an entirely unexpected picture emerged of him.

The event would mark the first time in 50 years that Cameroon had hosted the tournament, and Motsepe had fought hard for it to happen. Many in world football had tried to have the Cup postponed or moved, as the country – situated on the Gulf of Guinea in the west-central region of the continent – was in the midst of a violent battle between those who wanted to preserve its Francophone identity and its equally nationalist Anglophone citizens, who demanded separation.

Cameroon had lost a previous hosting opportunity in 2019 due to infrastructure problems, and as late as December 2020, detractors were still lobbying Motsepe to change the venue, but he gave it the go-ahead.

European football administrators who had urged him to postpone as they didn't want to lose some of their top players who were Africans for the weeks required in preparation and matches, were sorely disappointed. Their protestations had essentially been dismissive of Africa's basic rights to equal footballing time on the calendar, and had sounded more racist as they grew louder.

It was a key moment for Motsepe: if he'd blinked, and allowed European clubs to have a say, it would have been game over for him. In any event, it was a fist in the air for Africa when he didn't budge – but he couldn't have known that it was neither civil war nor infrastructure, nor even Afrophobia, that would leave a tragic legacy for the event.

The Cameroon national team, the Indomitable Lions, were playing Comoros at the Olembé Stadium in the capital, Yaoundé. A gate had been briefly locked at an exit to an area where covid-19 vaccination certificates and test results were being checked, and as soon as it was opened, a crowd of people pushed security guards aside and forced their way in. The stampede resulted in the deaths of eight people – one of them a child – and injuries rose to nearly forty.

Motsepe would have clearly remembered how 43 people had died when there was a crush at Ellis Park Stadium in Johannesburg in 2001 after spectators without tickets bribed gatekeepers to gain access to see Kaizer Chiefs and Orlando Pirates play in a packed derby. And Ghana, Zimbabwe and Egypt had had their own horror stadium stampedes over the years.

CAF called an urgent press conference at Ahmadou Ahidjo Stadium in Yaoundé the following day. 'Looking wary and devastated ... Motsepe expressed "deep condolences to the families" of the victims on behalf of CAF and the local organising committee. He added that CAF, the committee and the government should all shoulder the blame even though security is the responsibility of the local organising committee'.[18] 'If that gate was open as it was supposed to, we wouldn't have had this problem we have now, this loss of life. Who closed that gate? Who is responsible for that gate?'[19]

All remaining matches started with a moment's silence. Players of all teams wore black armbands.

The tragedy immediately seemed to quieten Motsepe's more sociable profile, but as the months tracked on after that, little information emanated out of Cairo about the disaster.

It could be that for Motsepe, that moment would be one of his most significantly disruptive. He'd told *Forbes* magazine in 2011 that 'people must see you as someone who is fallible, who also makes mistakes. I'm a sinner. I fumble. People must see me as one of them.'[20]

A test now lay ahead to prove that to be real.

In April 2022, Motsepe gave a steely response to questions about Côte d'Ivoire's ability to host the 2023 Africa Cup of Nations when he visited Abidjan to assess readiness. Having met Côte d'Ivoire president Alassane Ouattara during his mission, he said CAF had 'identified areas where we can improve and will improve'.

'We are going to [Côte d'Ivoire] next year, but we are not going to make the same mistakes again. There are certain preconditions, and in the public domain, I have to be nice and polite, and of course respectful. But I think behind closed doors, we will be significantly more assertive and more uncompromising in terms of safety, the police, the security, the army where appropriate, football pitches – and hopefully covid-19 will be less of a challenge.'[21]

PART II

Ties that bind

9

Crushing the devil:
How a family was made

Patrice Motsepe was first named a billionaire in 2008, exceeding his brother-in-law Cyril Ramaphosa's fortune by a considerable sum. Ramaphosa had become a member of the so-called 'three comma club'[1] a few years earlier, having left politics for business in 1996, returning in 2012 when he was elected the country's deputy president.

But the Motsepes are not, by South African standards, nouveau riche. Patrice's father, Augustine Butana Chaane (better known as ABC) Motsepe, was a self-made man during apartheid, and Patrice's three adult sons represent the third generation of building wealth, so the Motsepes are comfortable with it, and growing the family name into a dynasty.

Uncovering their history is, however, a challenge, as so little has been written directly regarding Motsepe and his family.

* * * *

Patrice Motsepe's paternal grandparents, Joseph Tlhopane Motsepe and Stephina Motsepe, embraced the ideas of the free market but battled catastrophic land theft and the economic crises of two world wars which further impoverished black people. Both born towards the end of the 19th century, they became shopkeepers and businesspeople determined to see their children educated.

Joseph had left home to work in the Cape and was a devoted

member of the Anglican church; he'd lived in the eastern city of Grahamstown (now Makhanda) and enjoyed attending the cathedral services there. When he returned home to Mmakau, the family's village outside Pretoria, he intended to introduce Anglican beliefs to his clan, but the traditional leadership were initially opposed to it. 'He was told that everybody who embraced Christianity would have to leave the village and live outside [it]. However, because his father was a member of the royal family, he was allowed to remain ... and given a chance to start a branch of the Anglican Church there.'[2]

Joseph and Stephina's son, ABC, born in Mmakau in June 1915, vigorously pursued an economically viable life after his parents ensured he attended Fort Hare, one of Africa's finest universities, with his brother, Cuthbert. That was in the mid-1940s, when the Second World War had ended and the working class was in dire straits.

The connections ABC and Cuthbert made at Fort Hare were to play out later in life, not only for them, but also for ABC's children. A notable classmate of theirs was Nelson Mandela, who met ABC decades afterwards at the funeral service of struggle veteran Peter Magano,[3] who was from Ga-Rankuwa, the area into which Mmakau falls. Reports say Mandela, a keynote speaker at the burial, 'broke away from his security detail and threw his arms around [ABC] in a warm embrace'.[4]

Another distinguished peer was Seretse Khama, who would become the first president of Botswana. Khama had completed his primary and secondary years at the London Missionary Society school, the Tiger Kloof Educational Institute, in Vryburg in South Africa, not far from the border. He and the Motsepes came from chiefly lineages whose bloodlines crossed in Botswana, and he and ABC's children would be linked in dramatic ways decades later.

In the 1950s, ABC worked as a teacher in Hammanskraal

outside Pretoria, and Cuthbert was based not far away at a school in Mamelodi, a township in Pretoria. In 1960, South Africa's crimes against humanity finally became an international disgrace after the Sharpeville massacre, but that only had the effect on the National Party of prompting it to legislate more oppression. It banned the ANC and arrested the Communist underground at Liliesleaf Farm in Johannesburg. Mandela was already behind bars.

Cuthbert soon left the country, heading for Lobatse in Botswana in 1963 on the same route taken by many who wanted to join the liberation movements and fight for their freedom. He settled in the capital, Gaborone, and is remembered for 'contributing tremendously towards the formation of the Botswana Christian Council'.[5] He was later awarded a Presidential Order of Meritorious Service.

A third brother of ABC's – there were six siblings – was the most revolutionary. Godfrey Motsepe was a leading member of the ANC who was living in exile in Belgium when Patrice was a promising young undergraduate studying towards a Bachelor of Arts, and on track to become a lawyer.

Four assassination attempts were made on Godfrey's life, and he was South Africa's High Commissioner to Ghana when he gave his submission about this to the Truth and Reconciliation Commission in Pretoria in August 1996. Accompanied by his daughters (Patrice Motsepe's cousins), Jacqueline Masebilanga and Tamaria Motsepe, Godfrey told the Commission that he'd arrived in Brussels in 1980 to set up an ANC office there. 'As soon as I was ensconced [there] I noticed that I was being constantly tailed by what subsequently turned out to be South African agents. Firstly, they used ... psychological warfare against me. I would ... find that they had opened the office overnight and searched through documents, but nothing would be stolen ... I would go perhaps to Amsterdam to a meeting and when I [came] back, I would find that they had opened my apartment. They [left] the windows open, had rifled through the desks in the house, rifled through everything, but nothing would be stolen.'[6]

His wife was also subjected to threatening phone calls, and his family 'were terrified of living with' him, Godfrey testified.

On a night in February 1988, Godfrey was standing at a window when a man outside fired two shots at him. 'I was very, very fortunate in that I dove out of the way, and I lay flat on the ground, but a splinter from the bullet had hit me ... and I was bleeding a little bit.'

About a month after that, he was woken up by the authorities in the early hours of a Monday morning. A 17-kilogram bomb had been placed on the doorstep at the entrance to the building where the ANC offices were housed, timed for 9 am. The bomb squad had to supervise an evacuation.

Two days later, his colleague, Dulcie September, the ANC's chief representative in Paris, was shot dead at their workplace. While that tragedy was followed by public mourning in the French capital, and got the attention of international media, it has yet to be resolved.

That experience held a lot of pain for Jacqueline and Tamaria; Tamaria said the assassination attempts on her father 'changed my perspective on many things while growing up'.[7]

Godfrey returned to South Africa after the ANC was unbanned in 1990.

* * * *

ABC had long left the little university town of Alice in the Eastern Cape, and moved from Pretoria to Johannesburg, where he was teaching at Orlando High School in Soweto, when he fell in love with and married nurse Margaret Keneilwe 'Kay' Lekoma. Kay, who was from Noordgesig in Johannesburg, was believed to have been 'designated coloured' under apartheid. It's understood that one of her grandfathers was from Scotland and 'designated white'.

ABC openly discussed politics with his pupils, and since the government had no appetite for dissent, this was risky. Orlando High School, nicknamed 'The Rock', would be at the centre of the Soweto Uprising in June 1976.

Although it's not known exactly when ABC and Kay acquired the 'matchbox house' that would be the long-time family home in Adams Street, Orlando East, it's believed four of their children – Tshepo, Bridgette, Rozette and Patrice – were born in Johannesburg. Tshepo, who married Cyril Ramaphosa in 1996, was born in 1953, so it could be surmised that ABC and Kay moved into their home in the early 1950s. At that time, Orlando East – neighbourhood of Archbishop Desmond Tutu and Mandela, at different times – was about 20 years old, having been the first township developed by the Johannesburg municipality.

Patrice and his wife, Precious – who's also from Soweto – would later extend their philanthropy to the community in Orlando East through their Motsepe Foundation. Patrice said it was 'a humble way to give back to the place where I was born. It's part of the broader obligation that I have'.[8]

ABC and Kay raised their children to be ambitious and enterprising. Tshepo, the first-born, got degrees in medicine and surgery at the then University of Natal's medical school for 'non-white' students in Durban, before leaving for the USA, where she gained a Master's in Public Health at Harvard in the 1980s. She was a high-achieving medical doctor and figure in public health when she married aspirant businessman Cyril Ramaphosa.

Bridgette, who was born in 1960, was 16 years old when the Mmakau community was deprived of royalty payments for mineral rights leased to a Canadian company. Its people marched to the mine seeking justice, and were met with teargas, dogs, police and guns. A fiery teenager, Bridgette swore then that she would become a mining lawyer, although she ultimately graduated with a BA in political science from the University of Botswana in the early 1980s.

That didn't mean she left behind her aspirations in mining. Bridgette went on to be the first black South African woman to become a deep-level hard-rock mining entrepreneur, later launching her own company, Mmakau Mining, which steadily gained interests in platinum, gold, uranium, coal and ferrochrome, and a range of other resources including anthracite, kaolin and silica.

A contrarian, Bridgette got under some politicians' skin when she started getting involved in the government's policy determinations, to the extent that by the early 1990s, she was drafting submissions to ensure that not only black junior miners gained access to changing legislation, but also black women miners and black women mine owners. Bridgette was the president of the junior mining chamber of South African Mining Development Association by 2001 and then, six years later, vice chair of the minerals and mining development board that advised the minister of minerals and energy on matters relating to the pivotal Mineral and Petroleum Resources Development Act.

When Jacob Zuma became president in 2009, he and Bridgette battled over the nationalisation of South Africa's mines, which was a thorny issue for the ANC as it scuttled to appease its South African Communist Party and Congress of South African Trade Unions (Cosatu) alliance partners, who had been promised so much after previous president Thabo Mbeki had been recalled. It was contentious that one of the richest women in South Africa seemed to be 'an advocate of nationalisation'.[9]

Explaining that, to her mind, the problem was 'the capitalist mining model', Bridgette pointed out that 'when we created a new South Africa, 83% of the resources were owned by the (racial) minority. Now 91% is owned by monopolies ... We are sliding backwards.'[10]

In terms of how she advanced it, nationalism was about giving black South Africans access to capital through broad-based black economic empowerment (BBBEE), which insisted even foreign companies comply with rules around black management, black ownership and black shareholding. Bridgette wasn't necessarily picturing the masses directly benefiting from the extractive industries; she was arguing about adherence to principles of empowerment that had been government policy for more than a decade.

For South Africans who didn't like the sound of Bridgette's politics, her marriage to top ANC member Jeff Radebe didn't make them any more partial to her. Radebe served in every national administration from 1994 to 2019.[11]

ABC and Kay's third-born, Veronica Rozette Kuki Motsepe, was a beautiful young woman who won 'Miss Africa South', the country's 'black' beauty pageant, in 1976, and went on to compete in the Miss World contest in November that year at the Royal Albert Hall in London. That was when the world was still reeling from images of dozens of black children and teenagers injured and murdered by the apartheid security forces during the Soweto Uprising.

South Africa's segregationist pageants and 'the state of the Miss World contest [was] a lot like the state of the world: a mess,' *People* magazine reported at the time. 'Seventy-one countries sent representatives; nine of them walked out [in protest against South Africa's racial policies], two of them were locked out, and almost up to the moment that the new Miss World was announced, her own government was trying to yank her out of the competition.'[12]

A few years later, in 1979, Rozette was targeted by South Africa's hate laws. She and a white British immigrant, 28-year-old

Richard Watson, pleaded guilty to having sexual relations, a violation of the Immorality Act. Their sentence was suspended for three years but it was a shock for the family.

After the court ruling, Rozette moved to the USA, where in 1983 she married Kelly Miller Alexander Jr, the son of Kelly Miller Alexander Sr, chairman of the board of the National Association for the Advancement of Colored People and a veteran of the civil-rights movement in his home state of North Carolina. ABC and Kay hosted the wedding at the Friendship Baptist Church in Charlotte, with the nuptials making the society pages and Rozette's wedding gown winning delighted attention.

* * * *

Patrice was named after Patrice Lumumba, first prime minister of the independent Republic of the Congo and a revolutionary hero for many Africans, likely including ABC. His and Kay's first son was born on 28 January 1962, just more than a year after Lumumba was killed by political opponents.

Motsepe seemed at one stage as if he might become a professional soccer player. A neighbour of the family in Mmakau, Reggy Morale, remembered him playing for boyhood teams Magnificent FC and Dynamos FC, while another Mmakau resident, Matsuwa Taukobong, said he would himself take Motsepe to watch Pretoria Sundowns playing in the apartheid leagues. Taukobong, who'd worked at 'the landmark Kay Motsepe Bottle Store' when Motsepe was a child, said 'the boy would jump for joy' when their team scored. Had ABC not insisted on his children devoting themselves to school work, said Taukobong, Motsepe, 'a good laaitie (youngster)', could have been a football star.[13]

But even at a tender age, so the narrative goes, Motsepe was good at business. He would wake up early in the morning during the school holidays in Mmakau to help ABC at the counter of the family shop, which catered mainly to mine workers, who had a liking for the enthusiastic little boy. His fond memories of those days included counting the chickens in the family's yard, and Decembers, when his parents' shop was full of customers spending their Christmas pay packets.[14]

Perhaps ABC would have wanted his son to take over the business when he grew older, but Motsepe was nursing a different aspiration: to be a lawyer.[15]

ABC and Kay were fiercely opposed to the National Party's 1953 Bantu Education Act, which specified that black children be trained for the manual labour and menial jobs that the government deemed suitable for those of their race, while explicitly inculcating the idea that black people had to accept being subservient to whites. For this reason, they sent Patrice for part of his schooling to St Joseph's, a Catholic, 'coloured-designated' Afrikaans-language boarding school in the farming community of Aliwal North (today, Maletswai) on the border of the central province of Free State and the Eastern Cape.

Motsepe recalled that his father 'wanted to give me a good education and, just as important, he wanted me to speak proper Afrikaans'. 'At boarding school, I spoke better Afrikaans than any other language.'[16]

He was a highly motivated student. 'Even at school I had to be first ... for me it was always about hard work, blood and sweat and coming out top.'[17] And it was at St Joseph's that Motsepe discovered a liking for rugby, as it was the hinge for a happy life at the school. (Although rugby teams were racially divided during apartheid, the sport has had black and white players and fans in South Africa since the late 1800s.) Those kinds of race, culture and language intersections in Motsepe's early years played out to his advantage throughout his life.

Motsepe was at St Joseph's until he was 15, and then moved to St Mark's in Mbabane, the capital of Swaziland (now eSwatini).

* * * *

In 1970, all black people within South Africa had their national citizenships revoked by the Bantu Homelands Citizenship Act, which instead enforced citizenship of the 'bantustan' designated to their respective ethnic group.

Although it's difficult to confirm a timeline, it seems the Motsepes went back to their family home in Mmakau at around the time it fell under Bophuthatswana, which was nominally declared 'independent', in 1977.[18] Tshepo would have been at the University of Natal at the time, while Rozette was in Johannesburg, and Bridgette and Patrice were teenagers.

The new homeland had considerable economic potential, accounting for two-thirds of the total platinum production in the western world and also being rich in asbestos, granite, vanadium, chromium and manganese.

In Bophuthatswana, ABC and Kay opened a general dealer, a funeral parlour and a hostel in Mmakau to complement their liquor services. And it's clear where Patrice got his business savvy: ABC was an exceptionally good businessman who was driving a Jaguar in 1973.[19] In 1979, when Patrice was 17 years old, ABC was honoured by the National African Federated Chamber of Commerce and Industry (NAFCOC), which named him one of the top three entrepreneurs in South Africa.

Founded in 1964, NAFCOC's objective was to promote black business and black entrepreneurship, and his recognition there was redolent of everything ABC had worked towards over his life, from Mmakau to Fort Hare, back to Mmakau, to Soweto, and finally back to his village again – building, building, building when a chance to compete on an equal footing with whites wasn't yet imaginable.

But ABC didn't abandon the world of education once he was living more permanently in the village expanding his enterprises. He founded a school, Sekitla High, which was still operating by the 2020s. But there were many stresses throughout.

Patrice Motsepe was born when community power was at a crossroads as the regime set about shutting down opposition forces. In the cities, there was solidarity in trade unions, the Communist underground and townships, where there were boycotts and acts of insurgency. In the rural areas like Mmakau, however, sufficient local economies and traditional leaders, the closest equivalent to a black political elite, were essential to how black people operated. Black shopkeepers had to be 'highly sensitive to ... local concerns because they relied very directly on community support to remain profitable'. At the same time, however, 'legitimate African traders needed a satisfactory working relationship with white local and central government because of the high degree of state control'.[20]

Living in Soweto had come with all the violence and exclusion inflicted by the apartheid regime. In Mmakau, there were additional harms. The Motsepe children would know the impact of corporate raids on the mineral resources in their village and surrounds, and the strong-arming from the bantustan police and soldiers there to keep ordinary people and black businesses in line.

* * * *

The family had a right to benefit from their ancestral land. Ga-Rankuwa, northwest of Pretoria, was where their lineal tribe, the Bakgatla ba Mmakau, had lived for over a century, and for several centuries in terms of historical links.

When the Great Trek – the movement from the Cape to the South African interior by Afrikaners, the descendants of white Dutch colonialists – arrived there in 1839, the boers found the tribe locked in combat with the armies of Mzilikazi, a former lieutenant of Shaka, founder of the Zulu kingdom. The boers joined the Bakgatla to drive Mzilikazi away, following which an uneasy alliance developed between boer and Bakgatla. In 1886 officials of the independent boer republic, the Zuid-Afrikaanse Republiek, registered the Bakgatla land in the government's name – in trust for the tribe. As ABC told a reporter in 2000, 'The land is ours [but] if there is one mistake that God made, he forgot to give my grandfather a title deed.'[21]

But that wasn't the only complication the family had to cope with. In 1870, over half the Bakgatla population had moved northwards into the Bechuanaland Protectorate (today's Botswana) to escape the increasingly violent demands for labour from boer leader Paul Kruger's authorities. 'Some stayed, however, and the Bakgatla kgosi [a hereditary leader, paramount chief or king] has remained the recognised traditional authority of those resident in either country.'[22]

But in the 1970s and 1980s, before the platinum boom of the 1990s, the bantustan government was negotiating mining rights directly with Anglo American subsidiary Anglo Platinum, and Canadian prospectors, among others, as if this was on behalf of the communities who had that nominal tenure over the land. So the Bakgatla had to fight not only white capital but work within patronage networks institutionalised under chief Lucas Mangope, president of Bophuthatswana.[23]

Royalties had to be deposited into the government's account, and getting money back to the community was a struggle. ABC was one of the leaders of demonstrations for restitution, but those had bitterly mixed results. There didn't seem to be agreement around how royalties could be shared, and who should rightfully receive those.

This manifold strife undoubtedly had an impact on Patrice when he decided to specialise in mining law, and its traces remained on him as the battle for who would lead the Bakgatla ba Mmakau intensified in the 2020s.

* * * *

ABC Motsepe was 92 when he died at his home in Sandton in 2007. His coffin was draped in the regalia of his beloved Orlando Pirates football club for burial at Ga-Mmakau Cemetery in the village where he was born. As the club's slogan goes, 'Once a pirate, always a pirate!'

The Buccaneers' choir sang at the funeral, as did the Mamelodi Sundowns choristers and Pretoria gospel star Solly Moholo, who performed the mokhuku dance of the Zion Christian Church, leaping in the air to crush the devil under his feet as he landed.

Motsepe's family's burial sites bonded him ever more deeply to the land.

10

The careful curation:
Precious Moloi-Motsepe

When Precious Moloi-Motsepe was 7 years old, she experienced the loss of her beloved grandmother from complications of hypertension. It was that, she later said, that fuelled her ambition to be a doctor, so that she could prevent these kinds of needless deaths.

She registered for a degree at Wits in 1982 and qualified with an MBBCh in 1987; and it was between those years that she met the man who would be her husband, Patrice, who was also studying at the university.

Denied most of the social distractions of student life under apartheid, young Patrice and Precious quickly became very close. Recalling the 'social injustice' of the time, Moloi-Motsepe recalls, 'Patrice and I laugh when we tell [our] children that we were not even participating in sports at university because we were only accommodated as far as the academics were concerned. On the social side, interacting with students, getting that holistic type of exposure to an institution of higher learning, was not possible because of the apartheid system. But I was very lucky in life that I met a partner who was very committed, very hard working, and our values were very much aligned.'[1]

By 1989 the pair were married and had their first child, Tlhopie. The little family moved temporarily to the USA when Patrice – a star graduate in mining and business law who'd been selected for a prized position at the prestigious South African firm Bowman Gilfillan – was chosen by the American Bar Association for a two-year lawyers' fellowship at the elite McGuireWoods in Richmond, Virginia. Moloi-Motsepe furthered her studies in women's health at the Medical College of Virginia while she was there.

But this certainly wasn't a path without its bumps. Deliberating about choosing between studying medicine and having a family, Moloi-Motsepe said, 'Professionally, my goal was to specialise in women and children's healthcare, and personally I wanted to have a family. I wasn't willing to compromise one dream for another. Many women … who were my role models either opted not to have families of their own in order to advance their careers, or if they [had] children, they [would] make the difficult and really painful trade-offs in a never-ending [balancing] act.

'I found this troublesome because it seemed to me that in order to flourish … in any career, it … required some form of personal, deep sacrifice. Although some men contend with this same dilemma, this opportunity cost, as economists would call it, is a loss unique mostly to women.'[2]

She must have made her peace with it, or come up with a workable plan, because when the Motsepes got back to Johannesburg in 1993, Moloi-Motsepe opened one of the inner city's first women's health clinics, and went on to specialise further in paediatrics. But a change in direction a few years later, which at first seemed to make no sense, gave her a more distinctive identity: 'I realised that just working in health would not help me achieve what I wanted to do, which was really helping communities be self-sustaining. I have a passion for fashion, and I realised early on that we [needed that] platform.'[3]

'I … admired other women's style, including Jackie Kennedy Onassis, Miriam Makeba, Coco Chanel and Adelaide Tambo. Their grace in their professions inspired me.'[4]

Fashion and design were already highly traded spaces in South Africa, and exclusive to a few, mainly white, prominent names.

But instead of entering as a designer herself, Moloi-Motsepe went in with the aim of backing black creatives using the supporting structure of her international humanitarian work.

She'd established that categorical identity in 2000 when she spoke on women and health in the workplace at the United Nations Global Summit of Women in New York. That was in her role as the head of the Motsepe Foundation, but it built links for her personally as much as it expanded the family's philanthropy.

In 2003, Moloi-Motsepe launched an international fashion week in Cape Town, but not all reactions to her initiative were positive. There was already an established event of that nature on the calendar in Johannesburg, and one media outlet said the Cape Town event was 'forcing local designers into a schizophrenic split', with the designs presented lacking 'refinement' and the standards set 'not seeming to reach the international level'.[5]

The existing showcase in Johannesburg was, however, hardly diverse, with black designers as scarce as black models.

Nonetheless, as an entrepreneur, Moloi-Motsepe accepted the criticism. She had a different vision, anyway – not only to sell, but to mobilise fashion through specific projects, such as the Design for Life Breast Cancer Campaign that emanated out of her work as president of the Cancer Association of South Africa from 2002 to 2007. (She received the Elizabeth Tshabalala Award for Raising Breast Cancer Awareness in 2012.)

Moloi-Motsepe's plans in fashion were long term. She bought a South African events company called Leisureworx in 2006 and transformed it into her own vehicle, African Fashion International (AFI), 'a platform of [fashion entities] that enables social and economic development in the continent through one of the world's favourite passions'.[6] AFI became a subsidiary of Patrice Motsepe's company, Ubuntu-Botho Investments (UBI).

Before Moloi-Motsepe bought Leisureworx, she and Motsepe

'had, in fact, wanted to buy Edcon [which was on sale at the time] and turn one of the country's biggest retail chains into a South Africa-first department store. Motsepe had wanted to diversify his investments ... But as fate would have it, Bain Capital beat the duo to the deal and Moloi-Motsepe found herself exploring other options.'[7]

The AFI packaging became more authentic as Moloi-Motsepe gathered African brands to go global.

And there was another angle to this for South African designers, as the government was doing little to promote the advancement of clothing and textile workers, even though they had a significant history of supporting the liberation movements by way of active trade unionism. Moloi-Motsepe observed that fashion gave 'opportunities to bring back manufacturing to developing countries, which can offer work to large amounts of people since it's so labour intensive'.[8]

AFI went on to own Joburg Fashion Week, which took place in October, and Cape Town Fashion Week, in March, with partner Mercedes-Benz, which already sponsored similar shows in London, New York, Zürich and Berlin.

AFI would eventually be staging up to five events a year, and Moloi-Motsepe was in the front row of almost every one. 'I have really only missed a handful of shows,' she said. 'It [is] important for me to support all the designers ... joining us on this journey.'[9]

* * * *

When she was invited to the Herald Tribune Luxury Conference in Rome in November 2012, Moloi-Motsepe was as fascinating to the media there as regular headliners Donatella Versace, Jean-Paul Gaultier, Manolo Blahnik and Vivienne Westwood. The then *International Herald Tribune*'s fashion editor, Suzy Menkes, had travelled to South Africa as a guest of AFI earlier that year to look at the work being produced in the country, and that close contact paid off. Over time, editorials featuring Moloi-Motsepe became more common in prominent fashion media.

A turning point came when Moloi-Motsepe was selected as an 'agent of change' for Fashion for Development (F4D). This is a private-sector global platform founded in 2011 to support the United Nations' Millennium Development Goals (a group of ambitious goals set in the year 2000, aimed at eradicating extreme poverty) and United Nations secretary-general Ban Ki-moon's initiative Every Woman, Every Child (launched in 2010 to advance the health and wellbeing of women, children and adolescents everywhere). That presented a much wider reach for her in terms of developing a network for fashion, women's issues and philanthropy around the world.

Moloi-Motsepe stayed on board with that new agenda with other F4D agents, including Austrian-American businesswoman Nadja Swarovski, Somali American entrepreneur and model Iman, British fashion designer Victoria Beckham, crown princess of Norway Mette-Marit, American designer and label-owner Donna Karan, British model and businesswoman Naomi Campbell, Chinese entrepreneur Mengqing Fan and Oscar-winning South African-born actress Charlize Theron. Soon, F4D had taken its campaign to more than 20 countries.

Moloi-Motsepe went on to work especially with Mette-Marit, with whom she shared global panels, including as the princess's co-chair of philanthropy group Maverick Collective, founded by Melinda Gates as a women-only assemblage for health solutions in the developing world. That brought Moloi-Motsepe into the tighter ambit of billionaire women of the world.

In 2017, the year her husband won a Sunday Times Lifetime Achiever Award, Moloi-Motsepe was given the inaugural F4D

Franca Sozzani Award[10] at the United Nations in New York for promoting African designers and supporting disadvantaged women. That promoted her cause on a global scale.

In 2018, AFI and F4D partnered to couple designers from Africa with luxury European brands Gucci, Salvatore Ferragamo and Bottega Veneta to create looks to match handbags from the brands.[11] Moloi-Motsepe said that legendary Tunisian couturier Azzedine Alaïa – who'd worked for many of the greatest fashion houses in Europe and had a devoted fan base that included Madonna, Naomi Campbell, Rihanna, Janet Jackson and Grace Jones – had told her he, too, was open to 'taking on one or two designers who showed with AFI to work in his studio'.[12]

* * * *

AFI's Joburg Fashion Week 2018 was the year Moloi-Motsepe was able to take her plans up a level as she forged a bond with Tokyo Fashion Week under the theme #AfroAsia. 'Africa and Asia are both celebrated for promoting local authenticity while achieving covetable global style,' she said. 'This could lead to inspiring fashion and business partnerships.'[13]

Selected designers would get an opportunity to showcase in Japan, with Moloi-Motsepe looking for the 'most adventurous' who could 'collaborate, and exchange ideas and knowledge with their peers, intersecting Africa with Asia'. Among them were MaXhosa by Laduma, Mnolim by Matte Nolim, Haute Baso founded by Candy Basomingera and Linda Mukangoga from Rwanda, Khosi Nkosi, Orapeleng Modutle's Style Avenue and Rich Factory's 100 Colours by Rina Chunga.

Moloi-Motsepe's sister-in-law Bridgette Radebe also turned up, in a dazzling pants suit and Japanese-inspired headpiece, accompanied by her brother, Patrice.

The influential fashion publication *Women's Wear Daily* wrote afterwards about the event, mentioning how 'designers including Thebe Magugu, Rich Mnisi and Tuelo Nguyuza [had] benefited ... by being able to maintain a sustainable business and expand distribution', which had been Moloi-Motsepe's dream with AFI.[14]

When the blockbuster Hollywood movie *Black Panther* was embraced worldwide in 2019, it drove an increased interest in African designers, and, out of the blue, gave Moloi-Motsepe extra leverage to approach government agencies around Africa about improving trade and distribution for fashion businesses.

The searching gaze for style ideas was certainly turning south for Europe and across the Atlantic for the USA. That gave Moloi-Motsepe the confidence to approach iconic Belgian fashion designer Diane von Furstenberg about possible partnerships.[15]

Moloi-Motsepe attracted the attention of Edward Enninful, the Ghana-born British editor-in-chief of British *Vogue*, when he attended the Condé Nast International Luxury Conference, which was co-sponsored by AFI, in Cape Town in 2019. Suzy Menkes, arguably the world's most famous fashion journalist, curated and hosted the event.

Others who attended and spent time with Moloi-Motsepe there were Gucci CEO Marco Bizzarri, Tiffany & Co CEO Alessandrio Bogliolo, Susan Akkad of Estée Lauder Companies and Sylvie Bénard of LVMH and Paris Good Fashion. That level of interaction indicated Moloi-Motsepe was past being a novelty in the USA and Europe, with her company beginning to operate alongside foreign partners who sought out its attention.

* * * *

The daughter of a teacher, Precious Moloi-Motsepe has pointedly credited her 'township education' for her enterprising nature.

Unlike her husband, she didn't always go to a private primary school. Her earliest school years were instead spent in Soweto, where she grew up.

Her parents raised their five children 'on Christian values and held up education as a very important commodity [to acquire] to get out of the poverty cycle, so I went to a school that really tried to give us the best education given the circumstances. I think one of the people that influenced me as a child outside my beloved parents was the [principal] at my primary school in Soweto, Mrs Wacey.'[16]

That was a time when apartheid's security forces routinely patrolled in tanks with guns. It was an extreme atmosphere, and there were not many ways to escape it – but the Moloi parents enabled that for their children, later putting them in a Catholic boarding school in Rustenburg which 'offered, for most of us, some of the best education'.[17]

Moloi-Motsepe was just 10 years old when she was sent to Rustenburg. 'I recall that we had no electricity and the school was in the middle of the forest, so the nuns had to switch the electricity off at about seven o'clock, and we all went to bed to save power. The only place I could find a light was in the bathrooms, so I would go there, sit on the floor and study. I think that was an early development of my hunger for knowledge and just hard work and discipline.'[18]

It came at an emotional cost to the young girl, though. 'It was a difficult, difficult system because you had to be away from home.'[19]

Moloi-Motsepe was able to complete her medical studies at Wits with the assistance of a loan from the Helpmekaar Study Fund, established in 1914 under the Helpmekaar Society of the Cape Province to 'promote the general development, upliftment and welfare of the Dutch-speaking section of the South African population and develop a distinctive Afrikaans culture'.[20] But the study fund didn't isolate itself to white Afrikaners, and by the 1980s, it had extended its assistance to a few black students.

This is a clue as to why the Motsepes found an early affinity with the white Afrikaner business community. Moloi-Motsepe's philanthropic work through the Motsepe Foundation would later extend to funding individual students at the University of Cape Town (UCT), in a sense taking that tradition forward.

In 2017, Moloi-Motsepe's *The Precious Little Black Book* was published. A guide containing advice for women across South Africa – domestic workers, students, job-seeking graduates, professionals, businesswomen – it was also a way for Moloi-Motsepe to answer a need. She had conceptualised the book when she was a medical student, 'after realising that many people fall ill because they [don't] have information they could use to empower themselves and change their livelihoods'. Developed out of 'meetings with women' with a 'common hunger for information', the book was donated to schools and communities.[21]

A founding member of the South African Universities Chancellors Forum and of the Gender Equality, Wellness and Leadership Department within the Motsepe Foundation, Moloi-Motsepe continued to define her image through mentorship and investment in young people. The Martha Rose Scholarship, named after her mother, funded aspiring nurses in South Africa, while Moloi-Motsepe was able to attract attention to such endeavours by serving on the Harvard Kennedy School's Women's Leadership Board and Center for Public Leadership Council, and the World Economic Forum Global Agenda Council.

African youth was also at the heart of her drive to invest 'in preserving Africa's cultural heritage' through the ABC Motsepe Schools Eisteddfod of choral music, a four-day competition that transported children from around the country to Johannesburg to deliver spectacles small and large. Thousands of performers feature, each act specialising in opera, izitibili (church hymns and traditional African songs) or indigenous folklore.

'Something happens to us when we see our children sing and dance to our traditional music,' Moloi-Motsepe said. 'The way they perform songs in our languages gives us hope that who we are as people will not be lost in the changing world.'[22]

* * * *

Given that Precious Moloi-Motsepe and Patrice Motsepe have always shone a light on their own parents as role models, it follows that they'd want to have the same influence over their children. Moloi-Motsepe described her mother as 'very charming, gracious and elegant. Just by observing her, I was moulded into the woman I am today.'[23]

But very little is known about the couple's three sons, Kgosi, Kabelo and Tlhopie, and their relationships with their parents, as these didn't play out in the public's view. The careful curation of the Motsepes' private lives includes complete confidentiality about their family life.

Only those parents whose sons were the same age as Kabelo when he attended St John's College from pre-school in 2009 to matric in 2020 might have caught glimpses of the Motsepes with their children. Even then, they weren't flamboyant about their wealth at the most exclusive private boys' school in Johannesburg.

On rare occasions some news slipped out, such as Moloi-Motsepe making a mention to *Sunday Times* writer Craig Jacobs in April 2019 when they met at a reception at the Zeitz MOCAA art gallery in Cape Town. Jacobs wrote that 'Dr P [glowed] with pride as she [told] me her and Patrice's second-born, Kgosi, [had] graduated with a BCom in business marketing from the University of Pretoria a few days earlier'.[24]

11

Bottomless flutes:
How the billions get bought

Back in 2005, *Time* magazine dubbed Patrice Motsepe, Cyril Rama-phosa, Tokyo Sexwale and former political prisoner and prominent business figure Sakumzi 'Saki' Macozoma 'the Fab Four', telling how 'a new breed of tycoon' was walking the wood-panelled cor-ridors and sipping whiskey in the stuffed leather chairs at 'the imposing Rand Club in downtown Johannesburg, [where] South Africa's mining magnates and millionaires had been meeting for more than a century'.[1] 'The neo-Baroque building boasts the long-est bar in Africa and is filled with paintings of such celebrated past members as British coloniser Cecil Rhodes as well as, of course, the ubiquitous portrait of Queen Elizabeth II. Built on the wealth of the largest goldfield in the world and the sweat of black labour, the club's membership was, until a few years ago, closed to South Africa's blacks. But these days ... a black elite has crossed over from politics.'[2]

The 'quartet of rich, well-connected black businessmen [sym-bolised] South Africa's new corporate elite ... for their growing power and wealth', according to the magazine. 'Between them, they [have] more than a billion dollars' worth of interests in some of South Africa's largest companies.'[3]

Ramaphosa was angered by this, retorting that he'd 'let his membership of the Rand Club lapse'. Regarding a comparison made to Russian oligarchs, he said, 'That's absolute rubbish.' 'None of us have been able to make headway in business riding on the coattails of government. I've been an entrepreneur from the age of 16 ... I started as a hawker buying and selling things.'[4]

Motsepe didn't comment publicly on the article, but since it addressed issues that were directly personal, rather than biographical, that wasn't unusual. Motsepe only gave hints of his private individuality by being a stylish but not flashy dresser. He apparently had a taste for the bespoke Florentine clothing brand Stefano Ricci, having once been photographed wearing a 100-percent crocodile leather belt with the iconic SR eagle-head motif buckle made of galvanised palladium, which retailed for more than R40 000.[5]

Motsepe and his wife were careful to keep their private life private, even though they tended to hold hands and speak intimately in public where they were seen together on multiple, complementary stages. There was an allure to their lifestyle, a fascination with their charisma. Motsepe said once, 'It's important for people to know they can relate to you, that you are not an arrogant, aloof, uninvolved person.'[6] But their personal lives seemed to be untouchable.

The occasional inside glimpse revealed that the Motsepes lived exceptionally well. A family home in Bryanston, Johannesburg, was 'reminiscent of a state house', with a lengthy driveway up to the front and vast gardens 'scented with blooming spring flowers and the lawns spread out like lush green carpets'.[7]

In 2014, the family bought 'a sprawling retreat' in the prestigious residential suburb of Bishopscourt in Cape Town for 'a record price' of R68 million. 'Nestled against the backdrop of Table Mountain' and offering 'spectacular views' of Kirstenbosch Botanical Gardens, the luxury estate reportedly included a main bedroom suite with his and hers dressing rooms and bathrooms, coupled with a separate lounge with a fireplace. There were five additional en suite bedrooms with dressing rooms, and all the rooms in the main house led to a terrace or balcony with spectacular views of the surrounding terrain.[8]

The upscale home, which had a lift between floors, also featured a formal 24-seat dining room with a spacious gourmet kitchen, a cigar lounge, a climate-controlled wine cellar, a state-of-the-art theatre, a music room, a billiard room, a gym and a ten-bay garage. Outside, there was a floodlit tennis court, a pavilion, a swimming pool and a landscaped garden full of indigenous flora.

Neighbours included 'famous author Wilbur Smith' and the Spanish and German embassies, which were apparently situated directly opposite the Motsepe property.[9]

In 2022, Motsepe bought the famous wine farm, Hidden Valley, near Stellenbosch in the Western Cape for something between R100 million and R120 million – in cash.

* * * *

Patrice Motsepe wore a staple striped dress shirt when he was *Forbes Africa*'s first cover star, in October 2011. At the magazine's launch party at Johannesburg's Montecasino hotel complex, he wore a tuxedo. Moloi-Motsepe was in a strapless gold and honey-bodiced dress with a sensational gold rope neckpiece with a beaded fringe.

By coincidence, Motsepe had – for the first time – topped the local *Sunday Times* 'Rich List' two weeks earlier with his R23-billion fortune. This 2011 tally isolated South Africa's 20 wealthiest people on the Johannesburg Stock Exchange (JSE), who were worth a combined R112.2 billion. The newspaper noted that 'the top 20 make up more than 70% of the wealth of South Africa's 100 richest people'.[10]

Most were 'much richer than is recorded, as they have other investments including cash, property, offshore investments and business interests which are not on the JSE', the only apparent downside of the prevailing global economic crisis being that the number of South African billionaires had 'slipped' from 30 to 28.

'Seven of the top 10 are self-made,' the *Sunday Times* noted, 'and those who come from family money have made even more than the wealth created by entrepreneurial parents and grandparents ... Old money has got richer.'[11] This pointed to the Ruperts, who have had control of the world's largest luxury watchmaker, Compagnie Financiere Richemont, brands Jaeger-LeCoultre and Cartier, and investment vehicle Remgro, which has stakes in more than 30 companies; the Oppenheimers, who trace their fortune to the 1917 formation of Anglo American, which later took control of De Beers, and who now operate investment firm Oppenheimer Generations; and the Ackermans, who have governance over retail behemoth Pick n Pay, which operates more than 2 000 stores in eight countries on the African continent.

Yet that was certainly the case with Motsepe too, even if the 'old money' notion derived by the 'Rich List' did not stretch to village-based bottle stores, funeral enterprises and general-dealer consortia. At least not then.

Motsepe had 'JSE-listed investments worth R22.99 billion, up from R19.91 billion the previous year', reflecting 'his stakes in ARM and Sanlam, though it excludes the value of his other investments, including ... Mamelodi Sundowns'.[12]

Poll position on the *Forbes* list of 'The World's Billionaires 2011', meanwhile, was Carlos Slim, the Mexican telecommunications mogul valued at $74 billion. (Slim was ousted from that spot in 2013 and is now positioned around the 16th-richest in the world, although he is still the wealthiest person in Latin America.) Motsepe came in there at number 336, with an estimated fortune of $3.3 billion (about R53 billion), while Nicky Oppenheimer – number three on the *Sunday Times* list[13] – was at number 136.

At that time, Ramaphosa was considering running for the position of deputy president of the ANC. He'd been out of politics and in business from 1997 to 2007, when he was again elected to the ANC's national executive committee. Ramaphosa was some way behind Motsepe in the 'Rich List' ranks, his stakes in MTN, SABMiller, Bidvest, Assore, Mondi and Standard Bank worth R2.22 billion.

The five wealthiest Africans on the *Forbes* list in 2011 were Nigerian businessman Aliko Dangote, South African Nicky Oppenheimer and family, Egyptian construction magnate Nassef Sawiris, Rupert and family, and Nigerian mobile tech investor Mike Adenuga. Motsepe was at number 10 on the list of richest Africans.[14]

* * * *

The Motsepes inevitably made exclusive guest lists, such as for the 2013 'nuptials of minister of police Nathi Mthethwa and his lovely bride, prominent businesswoman Philisiwe Buthelezi'. 'It was one of the most elegant and high-profile celebrations the country has ever seen,' gushed a report, calling it 'an exquisite fusion of Parisian chic and African flair'. 'Half of ... cabinet' was there, including Jacob Zuma and former president Kgalema Motlanthe, and 'mingling with South Africa's top politicians were a number of ... business leaders including Robert Gumede and his wife, Portia, and Vivian Reddy and his wife, Sorisha Naidoo'.[15]

The Motsepes didn't only appear on those lists in South Africa. In May 2013, the American Foundation for Aids Research held its 'Cinema Against Aids' fundraiser at the legendary Hôtel du Cap-Eden-Roc at Antibes on France's chic Côte d'Azur between Cannes and Nice.[16] *Vogue* magazine highlighted the couple in an atmosphere of 'glittery attire [and] bottomless flutes of Moët champagne'. The runway fundraiser, attended by Leonardo DiCaprio and compered by Sharon Stone, revealed a collection of 38 outfits which was bought by the Motsepes for about R16 million.

When brought onstage, Patrice – who, one report noted, was wearing a velvet embossed tuxedo jacket – seemed 'surprised'. 'He looked out into the crowd and shrugged his shoulders sheepishly.'[17] Precious, meanwhile, told *Vogue* that she planned an exhibition 'as inspiration for emerging African fashion designers'.[18]

The Motsepes met Leonardo DiCaprio again in 2014 when their fellow philanthropist held an evening fundraiser and auction in the Riviera resort of Saint-Tropez to support his foundation, which is dedicated to the protection of the environment and endangered species. The event raised about R300 million. A few days later, the headline 'Billionaire buys $1m Picasso sketch at Leonardo DiCaprio gala' attracted attention.[19] That billionaire was Patrice Motsepe.

Among the celebrities who mingled with 'a bevy of art buyers' at the DiCaprio event were actors Jared Leto and Marion Cotillard, model Cara Delevingne, and musicians Bono and Julian Lennon. The 500 or so guests paid upwards of R90 000 each to attend the gala.

'World auctions guru' Simon de Pury presented a prestigious if unusual collection which included rock 'n' roll memorabilia, a Damien Hurst sculpture (for which a Russian billionaire parted with nearly R100 million), two walk-on roles in an upcoming DiCaprio film, and one of DiCaprio's own motorcycles signed by Hollywood legends Robert DeNiro and Martin Scorsese.

But 'one of the most interesting sales of the night was undoubtedly a Pablo Picasso drawing purchased by South African mining billionaire Patrice Motsepe, who paid a cool $1m [about R10.5 million] for the piece.'[20]

It's not known if the Motsepes have an art collection, but in September 2015, two pieces worth nearly R260 000, seemingly first purchased by the Motsepe Foundation, were bought at a South African Revenue Service (SARS) auction for R2 500. The valuable works included 'Good Days' by Rashid Johnson and a piece by Carrie Mae Weems from her 'Roaming' series. Johnson and Weems are among the world's great African American visual artists.

'Durbanite Justin Titus was the lucky buyer, having bought the paintings on a whim without even seeing them. [But] why and how the artworks landed up at a SARS auction remains a mystery, with Motsepe Foundation officials having gone to ground.'[21]

Titus explained that the auction – his first – was 'so large, [and] things are scattered around at the … depots so I didn't actually see the paintings'. But when he examined the provenance documents – which authenticate art pieces with details like the work's creator, history and appraisal value – he saw the previous owner had been the 'Patrice Motsepe Foundation'. The value was listed at around R300 000, and the contact person on behalf of the ultimate consignee was Patrice Motsepe.

'When I saw the value and who had bought them, I was elated. It is hard to describe the feeling. It was like fireworks.'

The 'savvy-minded Titus' realised he could turn 'a massive profit' on the paintings, but still approached the foundation to see whether they would like to be reunited with the auctioned items, to 'buy the art back'. 'They seemed interested,' Titus reported, 'although apparently Patrice is travelling overseas.'[22]

* * * *

Another inlet for art for the Motsepes came through their company African Fashion International (AFI), which bought online art marketplace Wezart in 2020 for an undisclosed amount from Durban-based Sihlesenkosi Majola, a young former law student who'd founded it in 2016.

Majola said he reckoned AFI's acquisition of his start-up was 'part of a strategic plan by Moloi-Motsepe's firm to become a digital hub for Africa's creative industry'.[23] And, indeed, Moloi-Motsepe's intention, she said, was to 'explore diverse narratives and contribute to global creative critiques', with AFI operating as an aggregator platform, not only for designers, but also for writers, photographers and visual artists.[24]

Majola had met Moloi-Motsepe while he was at a panellist at a World Economic Forum event in Cape Town in September 2019. He moved from Durban to Johannesburg after the sale of his website to work more closely with AFI.

Wezart was generating about R200 000 in annual sales at the time of the acquisition and had five permanent employees; its platform was showcasing 200 artworks from 65 artists. AFI would have appreciated that South Africa's 'growing black middle class' was 'fuelling local art purchases', which Majola said had 'grown at 28% over the last decade, compared to just 10% globally'. 'Expensive art works and prohibitive gallery fees act as a barrier for many local artists and these new up-and-coming art buyers, [as] galleries can typically take 40% on each sale an artist concludes.'[25] Wezart, by comparison, took only 15 percent.

AFI introduced Wezart during Cape Town Fashion Week in 2020 through an auction at the Cape Town International Convention Centre.

* * * *

Art, fashion and football weren't the only Motsepe investments that attracted the media's attention more readily than business.

Patrice arrived at the Bull Ring auction site in Mpumalanga in April 2021 by helicopter for South Africa's first sale of regal Ankole cattle – known for their extra-long, widely curving horns.

Organisers were 'thrilled by the astronomical prices achieved' by 'some recognisable faces', including Motsepe. Of the more than R10 million sold, a quarter by value 'came from the herd of [Cyril] Ramaphosa, who is the biggest breeder of the majestic cattle in [the country] at his Ntaba Nyoni Estates in eastern Mpumalanga'.[26] Motsepe spent R1 million.

That amount increased markedly in March 2022 at Ramaphosa's next cattle sale at his Phala Phala Wildlife game reserve in Limpopo. The South African president arrived, all smiles, wearing 'a light pink shirt, black formal pants and clean black shoes', and stopped to chat to Motsepe 'who would be responsible for a record-breaking bid'.[27]

The star of Ramaphosa's show was Fafa, a young pregnant heifer 'with iconic horn shapes that [stretched] up to about 80 centimetres.'[28] Motsepe bought Fafa for R2.1 million – the highest price yet for an Ankole in South Africa and part of a total R5 million he spent on four Ankole cows. Since Ankole are known for their longevity, living for up to 30 years, the Motsepes may have these queens of their herd for the rest of their lives.

Ramaphosa, meanwhile, drew headlines when it was claimed he might have failed to report a burglary in 2020 of about R62 million in cash from sales at Phala Phala.

12

The patriotic bourgeoisie: Inside the club

Established in 1999, the Motsepe Foundation has long donated considerable sums to causes as divergent as the Nelson Mandela Foundation, Motsepe's home village, the Cancer Association of South Africa, and disaster alleviation efforts.

Motsepe has repeatedly acknowledged his advantages of a good education, relative economic stability and family support when he was growing up – he doesn't believe in merit alone. So, theoretically, the more advantages the Motsepe Foundation (and other philanthropic entities) could offer society, the more successful society would become.

Access to quality education is a central mission of the Foundation, and this is upheld through the distribution of university bursaries as well as school infrastructure development. The bursaries, 'guided by Dr Moloi-Motsepe, are focused in skills areas that are acknowledged to be necessary for the growth of South African and African industries ... science, technology, engineering, the arts and mathematics (STEAM), as well as entrepreneurship, medicine, law and agriculture. School infrastructure programmes, which operate in high-density areas, have constructed ablution facilities, communal gathering spaces, and fully equipped computer and science labs.'[1]

The Motsepe Foundation paid out over R41 million to 338 young people to go to university from 2014 to 2021, with Moloi-Motsepe injecting a further R2 million to assist those who'd completed their studies at UCT, where she's the chancellor, but couldn't graduate because of student debt.

In March 2019, the Motsepes and the South African government donated a combined R75 million to victims of Intense Tropical Cyclone Idai, which wrecked parts of Zimbabwe, Mozambique and Malawi. The cyclone claimed close to 800 lives in the three countries, while hundreds went missing.

In KwaZulu-Natal, South Africa, when floods resulted in nearly 500 deaths and multiple injuries in 2022, the Motsepes gave R30 million to recovery assistance there.

In March 2014, Guinea's ministry of health was alerted to an outbreak of ebola in the southeast. Soon, one of the world's most terrifying diseases had taken hold, moving into Liberia and Sierra Leone, with some incidence in Nigeria and Mali, Europe and even the USA. In the October, the Motsepe Foundation committed more than R15 million to African Union efforts to assist.

When covid-19 took hold globally, 'although the rich got spectacularly richer during the pandemic, some did humanitarian good with their wealth. For example, the Oppenheimer, Rupert and Motsepe families each pledged R1 billion to help financially distressed small businesses get through the pandemic.'[2]

* * * *

In 2015, Patrice and Precious Motsepe were honoured at the 12th annual Keep A Child Alive Black Ball, a night of awards at New York's Hammerstein Ballroom. American musicians Alicia Keys and Lenny Kravitz, Nigerian-American rapper Wale (Olubowale Victor Akintimehin) and American comedian Chris Rock were among the superstars at the iconic venue, which had been reimagined as an Afrofuturist space, with a dinner prepared by Ethiopian-born Swedish-American celebrity chef Marcus Samuelsson.

A project of the Alicia Keys Foundation, Keep A Child Alive had seen millions of dollars donated since 2004 for HIV treatment, care and support to children, young people and families affected by the virus. Rock emceed the fundraiser that took in more than R40 million that night. Keys said the next day that the energy had been 'electrifying'.[3]

The Motsepes were 'recognised for their efforts addressing the issues of social and economic inequality of Africa's poorest people, and for their generous support of HIV and Aids initiatives over the years'.[4]

The couple reunited with musical artists who work in philanthropy when the Motsepe Foundation hosted and presented the Global Citizen festival with major partners including House of Mandela and Coca-Cola Africa in 2018. They'd decided to take on a South African date for the festival after meeting its organisers at the United Nations. A unique activist platform that generates 'commitments and policy announcements from leaders around the world', Global Citizen was valued at over R300 billion by July 2018, with the goal of reaching 501 million people by 2030.

The showcase was part of the Mandela 100 campaign, which marked the centenary of the birth of Nelson Mandela and aimed to give people around the world an opportunity to reflect on the statesman's life and promote his legacy. Global Citizen said it would be the largest concert in Africa's history, with 'a live audience of around 200 000 … [and] hundreds of millions more through global broadcasting and streaming'. Mandela 100 featured 'the most heads of state to attend a festival since [it] launched in 2011'.[5] Among them were Ramaphosa, Paul Kagame, who was also the chair of the African Union at the time, Uhuru Kenyatta of Kenya, Nana Akufo-Addo of Ghana and Erna Solberg of Norway. Kagame and Motsepe shared a vision for Africa in general, having been together on many stages around the world discussing it.

Fans were thrown into often-chaotic, sometimes-heroic 11th-hour commitments to charity to qualify for Global Citizen's main attraction: a concert at FNB Stadium hosted by Trevor Noah where Beyoncé, Jay-Z, Ed Sheeran and other international acts would perform on a bill that included South African artists Sho Madjozi and Cassper Nyovest, and hosts Sir Bob Geldof, Naomi Campbell, Gayle King, Bonang Matheba, Tyler Perry and Forest Whitaker. Oprah Winfrey gave a keynote address. Tickets were free but had to be 'earned' by raising societal issues.[6]

Two years after Jay-Z and Beyoncé hypnotised South Africans with their flow of passion for each other and their music on the Johannesburg stage, the Motsepe Foundation had progress to report. Commitments of R104 billion had been made, with the World Bank exceeding its more-than-R15-billion pledge to increase investments in its Human Capital Project, a global effort to accelerate more and better investments in people for greater equity and economic growth.

By 2019, which marked a decade of the campaign, the collective voices of dedicated Global Citizens had mobilised more than R700 billion worth of commitments, which had already affected the lives of 880 million people living in extreme poverty.[7]

* * * *

The year 2020 marked two decades since Patrice Motsepe had first made an impact at Davos, the event at the start of the new century set up as 'a profound reframing of the very definition of success'. 'No longer was ... status a simple function of material wealth. Rather it became a function of the "value" of what you did with your wealth.'[8]

Motsepe had then been a 40-year-old billionaire and South Africa's most sought-after young business mind, projecting himself on the World Economic Forum's 2000 stage as an independent and willing investor in his own country.

A decade later, Davos repositioned itself under the theme 'The Great Transformation', which challenged capitalism 'to adapt to harder times'. 'Philanthrocapitalism' was thereby popularly introduced, and in 2013, Motsepe chose Davos as a platform to announce he'd joined the Giving Pledge, by way of the Motsepe Foundation. The Giving Pledge was founded in 2010 as a project of American billionaires Warren Buffett and Bill Gates (formerly, at different times, the world's wealthiest men) when they both committed large chunks of their sizeable wealth to charitable causes.

Many academic studies would be done into how individuals' great wealth could be deployed 'in the service of humanity, especially to purchase a more sustainable future for the next generation'. Among relevant observations was that wealthy individuals do 'not need to jump bureaucratic hurdles before they commit resources [since they tap into their personal fortunes]'. Also, that 'the reach of their impact can defy artificial national borders'.[9]

His signature to the Giving Pledge was a key element of integrating Motsepe 'into this very exclusive club' and 'placed him in a position of high global visibility'. It also built on the 'historic relationships between Davos (representing international capital) and South Africa'.[10]

The Motsepes were the first Africans to take on the audacious billionaires' challenge to donate half of their fortune, but that wasn't the prompt for them to do so. In his undertaking to the Giving Pledge, Motsepe stated, 'I decided quite some time ago to give at least half of the funds generated by our family assets to uplift poor and other disadvantaged and marginalised South Africans.' He noted that he was 'duty-bound and committed to ensuring that [such donations] would be done in a way that protects the interests and retains the confidence of our shareholders and investors'.[11]

When the Motsepes answered the call to the Giving Pledge, 91 billionaires – mostly Americans – had signed up. By 2022, there were 231 from 28 countries. Among the Motsepes' friends who were 'pledgers' was American billionaire Michael Milken, whose think-tank, the Milken Institute, established deep bonds with the Motsepe Foundation, including the Milken-Motsepe Innovation Prize worth a total amount of more than R30 million. The prize seeks technologies to tackle Africa's agriculture and energy challenges.

By the time the Motsepes got to know Milken, he'd paid about R17 billion in fines and settlements and served 22 months in prison after pleading guilty in 1990 to six criminal charges stemming from securities transactions. A United States federal grand jury had indicted him on 98 counts of racketeering and fraud in 1989, nailing him on insider trading, stock parking, tax evasion and illicit profits when he was a Wall Street trader in high-yield, or 'junk', bonds.[12]

Motsepe had none of those kinds of reputational distractions. He was also able to highlight in his pledge that he 'was a beneficiary of various people, black and white, in South Africa and in the US who educated, trained, mentored and inspired me and whose faith and belief in me contributed to my success in my profession, business and elsewhere. The same can be said about my wife, Precious, and we are deeply indebted to them and many more.

'Most of our donations have been private, but the need and challenges are great, and we hope that our Giving Pledge will encourage others in South Africa, Africa and other emerging economies to give and make the world a better place.'[13]

ANC spokesman Jackson Mthembu drew political attention to Motsepe's signature in 2013, saying Motsepe had given 'expression to our view of the patriotic bourgeoisie' through the Giving Pledge: 'This unprecedented act of goodwill in South Africa ... reflects a deep understanding of [the] development challenges and limitations facing [the country].'[14]

In 2020, SAFA emphasised Motsepe's participation in the 'movement of philanthropists' in its endorsement letter for him as a candidate – indeed, the 'revolutionary choice' – for CAF president, saying this highlighted 'his commitment to contribute to the improvement of the living conditions of the poor, unemployed and marginalised in Africa and globally'.[15] 'Building relationships and partnerships is a fundamental first.'

But it remains moot as to whether philanthropy can ever really offset the harms that people experience when they believe their land and history are under destruction.

13

A royal family:
The Bakgatla ba Mmakau

The Bakgatla occupy several ancestral seats in South Africa, including in Mmakau and Moruleng, and each area has to have a leader. But the Motsepes' relationship with Botswana is intricate, as the Bakgatla capital is in that country, in the town of Mochudi, and Motsepe's cousin is the tribe's paramount chief, king or kgosi, Kgafela Kgafela II.[1] He was crowned in 2007 after the death of his father, Kgosi Linchwe II, who'd ruled between 1963 and 2007.

Linchwe was, however, long isolated from his chiefly duties in Botswana after Seretse Khama's government sent him to Washington as an ambassador in 1963, and while he was away, stripped some of Botswana's chiefs of community control. Linchwe said he was revitalised in the US capital when he witnessed the American civil-rights movement evolving into the black power movement, having 'always thought of [himself], first and foremost, as an African chief'. 'I was very much influenced by the black Americans who were sorry they had lost their culture,' he said when he returned to Botswana in 1973 after his ambassadorial duties ended. 'We here, too, had been brainwashed by the Europeans into being ashamed of ourselves. We were standing on a no-man's land of culture.'[2]

Back home in Mochudi, Linchwe began a crusade to reacquaint the Bakgatla with their traditions. The tribal regiments (mephato) and 'associated bogwera and bojale [long-abandoned circumcision rituals] as well as the signature Dikoma tribal singing' were revived after decades of suppression, and thus also feature in Motsepe's cultural origins.

It wasn't only culture. It was also politics. Khama's government had showed a 'reluctant inaction' towards assisting South Africa's liberation movements as Botswana was 'surrounded by states under South African influence and [was] economically dependent upon them'.[3] But, as South African president Thabo Mbeki noted at a gala dinner in 2012 in Gaborone, Linchwe had been active in supporting the ANC underground, offering an escape route through Botswana and even a hidden arms cache for use by MK cadres in a district he controlled there.

The artificial nature of the border between Botswana and South Africa meant that not only was it physically permeable, because it was sparsely patrolled, but it was also ideologically so. 'The lives of members of Bakgatla society transcended the demarcation in many ways, the deepest being kinship networks, family links and temporary flows and migrations.'[4] Separation didn't affect custom and tradition, as 'people on both sides ... [shared] cultural events, consulting each other and collectively making tribal decisions'.[5]

After Linchwe died, Motsepe was in a powerful bank of individuals, including then Botswana president Ian Khama, at Kgafela's coronation. Back in South Africa, drama was unfolding as a result.

When Linchwe presided, he'd had to nominate a deputy to occupy the Bakgatla ba Kgafela seat in Moruleng in the Pilanesberg area of South Africa, as the apartheid government wouldn't allow him to cross the border with ease. But John Molefe Pilane, the replacement regent or proxy, wasn't ready to give up power after the king died.[6]

That rift in the Pilanesberg community served as a signal to the Bakgatla ba Mmakau, who lived about 90 minutes away and were related to the people in Moruleng by way of family and close clan connections, of what could happen in their own village.

* * * *

The Motsepes had a very clear stake in decision-making in their community, having been part of the ruling house that had been in authority there for more than 125 years. The forebear of the family, the original Motsepe, who was born in the mid-1700s, was killed during raids under Mzilikazi in the 1820s. His people then fled to their more ancient grounds in the Waterberg area in the bushveld of what is now Limpopo.

History records that Manonwana Seamego, a son of the third house of Motsepe,[7] was chief when the Bakgatla ba Mmakau returned to Ga-Mmakau around 1840. He was succeeded by Moemise Motsepe, also a son of the third house.

In January 1921, seven elders from Mmakau – one of them a Mr EM Motsepe – prayed before embarking on a 72-hour, 80-kilometre trip on foot to appeal to the Catholic priest in Bantule location outside Pretoria to build a church for their villagers.

It was no coincidence that they arrived at their destination on the muddy outskirts of Pretoria on 6 January, the Christian day of the Epiphany: the men had planned it to coincide with the commemoration of the magi appearing at the crib of the divine child to deliver the gifts of gold, frankincense and myrrh. They themselves were pilgrims without treasures, but Father Camillus de Hovre was still glad to meet them.

The priest noted in his diary that the men 'had come from De Wildt [now known as Mmakau Village] to "find the True Church" in Pretoria, as they stated.'[8] He 'saw in this the Hand of Providence', as his bicycle would now come into good use.

Following this meeting, Father De Hovre cycled the country roads from what is Atteridgeville today to Mmakau several times to talk to the villagers before foundations were laid. Each round trip took a few hours, but the priest stayed a couple of days every time to get to know the people. Among them was the young Augustine Motsepe, later known as ABC, who was then about 5 years old.

To secure a holy site for the church, the priest tied a decree to a mulberry tree in the village. It read 'From Here We Shall Never Move'. When The Most Holy Redeemer Mission, the first Catholic church in Mmakau, was christened a few months later, the ample foliage gave shade to the parishioners in the summer months, and the tree's sturdy branches offered a place for children to play.

As it happened, the area wasn't only blessed by getting its own loving-built stone church from which 68 outstations, the first Catholic hymns and prayer book in Setswana, and a school that boldly defied Bantu Education would ultimately be created. Not long after The Most Holy Redeemer Mission was opened, the fortunate geographic basin – the Bushveld Igneous Complex – on which it was built was discovered.

* * * *

The leaders of the Bakgatla ba Mmakau had been a bulwark against the ruthless tide of colonial and white rule. They had even managed to accumulate some wealth for their people under 'communal land tenure'[9] although it was a fiction that the Bakgatla owned its resources, since such 'communal land' was held in trust by the state.

There were always myriad tensions. Patronage and clan nationalism were forged within apartheid's 'tribal' pockets, the bantustans, and the chiefs who were favoured by Pretoria's puppet governments in the homelands were often empowered while the people's actual rights were reduced.

Moemise Motsepe was succeeded by his sons, Sekwati Alfred and Malatse Matthews, but the death in 1974 of Malatse created challenges, as neither he nor his brother had surviving sons.

It was decided that the chieftainship would pass to the house of Kau, one of the four original dikgosi of the Bakgatla clans.[10] A relative, Richard Motsepe, acted unofficially until the appointment of Petrus Sephula 'Bazabaza' Rasepasa, a great-grandson of Kau, in 1975.[11]

It was when Petrus died, at the age of 73 after a long illness, in 2012, that Bakgatla intra-clan conflicts reared their head in Mmakau. While there was mourning, there were also arguments over succession. Tribe members under community leader Patrick Mmakau, a family member of Petrus, who considered himself the next in line to take over the chieftainship, contested the succession of the Motsepes under Sepoekane Motsepe, a relative of Patrice and his siblings. The people supporting Mmakau felt he could do a more powerful job of lifting the village out of poverty and representing their needs than an individual appointed simply because he was part of the royal family.

These debates in Mmakau directly affected the Motsepes, who were in the royal lineage from which a chief should be chosen. They had already tried to stave off a fight over who would rule Mmakau when they applied to the Nhlapo Commission set up by Thabo Mbeki in 2004 to address a number of traditional leadership disputes and claims, including theirs. The commission accepted evidence put before it by the Motsepes, and agreed in 2011, not long before Rasepasa died, that they should be the next in line for chiefly rule. But that angered the other side, and so the matter was taken before the Mafikeng High Court in North West, where a second decision was made in favour of the Motsepes.

In 2013 Patrice Motsepe arrived in person to give R5 million to the village. Bursaries were on offer for students to further their studies at 'traditional universities', and youth leader David Mokwena of the Mmakau Committee was elected to represent their interests at the Motsepe Foundation.[12]

In September 2017, Sepoekane Motsepe was designated the rightful chief of the Bakgatla ba Mmakau by officials from the North West government. But community members who'd rejected the Motsepes 'took to the streets in support of the Mmakau kraal, endorsing its legitimacy to royal status'. Villagers in their camp blockaded roads, wearing T-shirts printed with pictures of Patrick Mmakau, and '[accused] the Motsepes of using [Patrice Motsepe's] money to derail Patrick from becoming their chief'. Patrick himself said that 'no challenge' in court was necessary as 'the chief [was] endorsed by the community', not by the courts or a commission.[13]

By 2022, the destiny of Mmakau remained up in the air, the clan divided over who should be their chief, yet they all shared its early history.

PART III

Boardrooms and chambers

14

Trying his luck:
The birth of African Rainbow Minerals

In 1924, a farmer found a nickel-platinum deposit on his farm Maandagshoek. His discovery was confirmed by Hans Merensky, an accomplished South African geologist with a doctorate in mining from the University of Charlottenburg in Berlin. Merensky's name is now attached to the five-layer 46-centimetre-thick reef about the size of Ireland, with its geographic centre in Pretoria, which lies under the present provinces of North West, Limpopo, Gauteng and Mpumalanga. There are two others, the UG-2 Reef and the Platreef.

It wasn't known then, of course, that the Maandagshoek discovery, some four hours away from Mmakau, was just one aspect of a thick platinum reef on the eastern limb of the tremendous Bushveld Igneous Complex. This two-billion-year-old assemblage of rocks, which was formed by volcanic activity, represents at least 75 percent of the world's supply of platinum group metals. These deposits include platinum, palladium, osmium, iridium, rhodium and ruthenium, and their by-products, gold, silver, nickel, copper and cobalt, with a massive amount of iron, tin, chromium, titanium and vanadium.

Just under a century after the discovery was made, in 2001, Patrice Motsepe's African Rainbow Minerals (ARM) forged a joint venture with Anglo Platinum at Modikwa, near Maandagshoek, that would be the core of his formidable fortune. Today, there are at least 26 platinum operations in the Bushveld Igneous Complex, three of which – Modikwa, Two Rivers and Bokoni – are in the ARM stable.

Involved in Modikwa since 2001, and the development of Two Rivers since 2005, ARM bought the mothballed Bokoni platinum mine from Anglo Platinum in January 2022 with the intention of restarting the operation where more than 2 600 mineworkers had been left unemployed in 2017. ARM paid R3.5 billion to acquire the shares and 'committed to investing a further R5.3 billion over the next three years to redevelop [it] as a new mine ... [taking] nearly everybody by surprise'. Neither of the former operators had been able to make a go of it – the mine was 'a dog' – but Motsepe was convinced that new mechanised methods would succeed for him where others had failed.[1]

This unpredictability tied in with the disruptor in the billionaire. ARM had posted 'stellar results underpinned by the ongoing commodities boom' in September 2021. Its 'diverse suite of mining assets' was the reason.[2]

* * * *

Four origin stories seek to explain Patrice Motsepe's success. Each reflects South Africa's race and class entropy.

The first is that he's a 'comprador capitalist', or an oligarch who paid his way into favour with the new political elite.

The second is the 'patriotic bourgeois' notion – that, by virtue of conscience, he felt obliged to repay the party that led the struggle.

The third is that he was given a free pass into making a heck of a lot of money by the ANC, which used empowerment policies to pick and choose who would get to be both black and rich.

The fourth is that Cyril Ramaphosa – who became Motsepe's brother-in-law two years after Motsepe joined the mining sector – influenced big capital to favour him. Or the ANC to favour him.

Or something along those lines.

But there's a more plausible origin story that doesn't require reverse-engineering a destiny.

In 1979 Patrice matriculated from St Mark's in Mbabane, and the following year he enrolled at the University of Swaziland for a BA in law, which he earned in 1983. He then registered at Wits to do his LLB, which took four years.

Among his peers at Wits were Adrian Gore, who graduated as an actuary in 1986 and went on to found Discovery; Shabir Madhi, who graduated as a doctor in 1990 and went on to become a member of the World Health Organisation Strategic Advisory Group of Experts; and Mamokgethi Phakeng, who graduated with an MSc in mathematics and went on to become the vice-chancellor of UCT. Like Motsepe, none of these people had the kind of contemporaneous political connections that could immediately boost influence; none was a member of Umkhonto we Sizwe, or a detainee, or an activist; none was an alumnus of a school posh enough to market him; none had famous friends.

* * * *

Motsepe's first attempt to enter the extractives industry was in 1989, when, as a brand-new law graduate, he tried to buy small-scale mining operations from Gencor[3] and Anglo American – and failed. No one would lend him the money or buy shares in his nascent company. Banks, especially, weren't interested.

That was a heightened time in South Africa, which was soon to see the unbanning of the liberation movements and the release of Nelson Mandela by FW de Klerk. It was also when the Chamber of Mines, a 100-year-old organisation of mine owners, started coming to terms with the inevitable end of private ownership in favour of the state becoming the custodian on behalf of the people.

The ANC based its plans to maximise resources on that principle as laid out in the Freedom Charter, the 1955 statement of core principles of the South African Congress Alliance, which the ANC and other democratic forces had supported. Empowerment was predetermined.

So Motsepe would have participated in rigorous internal debates at Bowman Gilfillan, the company he joined on graduating, about what mining was going to look like in a democratic South Africa. This wasn't business as usual; it was planning how to operate in a new country.

Motsepe was rising at the firm – he'd been called a 'superstar' by his superiors – when he was recommended to the American Bar Association for selection for a prestigious two-year exchange programme in the USA. Based as a visiting attorney at McGuireWoods in Richmond, Virginia, in 1991 and 1992, he had the chance to develop case law about how to turn dormant mining enterprises into successful businesses. That was a whetstone for Motsepe, who was swept up in the possibilities as he 'read extensively ... collecting every single book [on the subject] he could lay his hand upon'.[4]

When Motsepe returned to Johannesburg in 1993, he was announced as the first black partner at Bowman Gilfillan, going on to represent mining companies 'while studying what made some mines succeed and others fail'.[5] A takeaway was that the successful ones were lean.

By 1994, Motsepe was ready to try his luck in business again. He threw everything into this second attempt, registering a company called Future Mining with which he started small as a contractor.

The way he got going was to 'ask the bosses what the worst job is on that mine and then ask if you can do it'.[6] Then he hired a team that would become skilled in gleaning dust, left over from blasting, from inside gold-mining shafts. It wasn't easy work. 'South Africa's gold mines are deep, hot and water runs everywhere,' one writer observes. 'They are slippery, uncomfortable places to work in, and they get deeper and hotter every year as the quest for gold burrows ever further into the earth.'[7]

The uptake on individual contracts went reasonably well, but Motsepe couldn't pique the interest of financial institutions, or even mine owners, for long-term agreements. He didn't have a proven history of running an operation, or working capital, and has described how he 'literally managed Future Mining' from his briefcase[8] – becoming known as 'the suitcase man' – doing the legwork and looking for contracts from mine to mine. He was persistent, and continued to research how to run his own operations using marginal shafts, all the while saving every extra rand to build up reserves.

Meanwhile, the 'big six' mining houses – Anglo American, Anglovaal, Gencor, Gold Fields, Johannesburg Consolidated Investments and Rand Mines – were at various stages of de-listing from the JSE. Having dominated mining for most of the 20th century, controlling the means of production, exploiting racial divides and creating South Africa's post-colonial capitalism, they'd become unsettled by regulatory uncertainty. Mergers with other transnational mining companies were under way, as were moves to international exchanges.

At the same time, serendipitously for Motsepe, the world had fallen out of love with gold by 1997, and AngloGold was looking to dispose of loss-making shafts at its huge Freegold mine at Welkom in the Free State and at Vaal Reefs near Orkney in North West province. Bidding for the shafts started at $8.2 million (about R30 million at the time).

This was a rare moment for an entrepreneur like Motsepe to invest in a major business, and an opportunity to test himself out personally. He tried to get a loan to finance the purchase of the shafts, but no bank would front him the money. 'The banks said,

"Are you mad?"' he recalled.[9] There were no financing models against which to examine a proposal such as his, without a portfolio of administering minerals.

Mining colossus Harry Oppenheimer himself had little faith that Motsepe would be able to make it work. Motsepe recalled, 'He was very polite, but he said to me, "What makes you think you are going to make money where Anglo has not?"' And this lack of confidence crossed racial lines, with National Union of Mineworkers boss James Motlatsi saying that Motsepe 'wanted me to support the deal, but I said it will be embarrassing to black people if Patrice cannot make money out of it'.[10]

But Motsepe had a drive to succeed and was determined to shoot his shot. He founded African Rainbow Minerals (ARM) with venture capital off the back of Future Mining, and presented a solid proposal to Bobby Godsell, Anglo's chief executive of gold and uranium. Godsell had previously come across Motsepe through his contracting work and had been 'impressed by his doggedness and resolution'.[11]

Motsepe said he convinced Godsell to take a chance on ARM 'because he knew [Future Mining] had done numerous contracts for them'. He drew attention to the disjuncture between Anglo's 'long-life, high-grade asset requirements' which would not necessarily suit some of its deposits.[12]

Godsell's version of events is slightly different; he said he 'wanted to help black South Africans get into the business'. 'I was seeking to create capitalists out of people who had no capital.'[13] And Godsell's reputation bears this out: he was critically involved in business-led discussions with the ANC in exile in the 1980s. But even he was unable to persuade South African banks to back Motsepe. It was either Anglo reached out, or there would be no way forward.

In a deal that went down in history as one of the most important for South Africa's post-apartheid business recovery, Motsepe and Godsell were able to work out terms affording Anglo a return on profits with a R500 000 loan to ARM. It was the kind of project-based financing secured against anticipated cash flows that would play out in numerous joint ventures to come.

Motsepe took on mining's disquieting legacy the moment he acquired the Orkney mine shafts, at which more than a hundred lives had been lost a few months after the first democratic elections in what came to be known as the Vaal Reefs Disaster.

On that day, 10 May 1995, 'Miners, who had just finished a day's work 1.4 miles (2.3 kilometres) below ground, boarded a two-floor elevator to take them back up to the surface at approximately 10.30pm. At the same time, an underground train was travelling in a tunnel that was supposedly blocked. The train lost control and crashed into a barrier, sending it down the mine and taking with it the elevator's conveyor system. The impact was so strong that the elevator, which can hold up to 100 people, was crushed to less than half of its original size.'[14]

National Union of Mineworkers' Motlatsi, traumatised, talked to reporters about the terrible scene, saying 'pieces of flesh were scattered all over ... as a two-floor mining elevator was crushed into a one-floor tin box ... As the incident happened during a shift change, more than 100 people were inside. It was a difficult task to recover and identify the individuals who died, as the disaster left miners unrecognisable. Upon crashing, the train also hit a cage used for inspections on the way down the mine shaft, but luckily, the occupants escaped and survived.'[15]

At least 316 children were left without fathers and there were 109 widows. AngloGold and the National Union of Mineworkers established a trust to care for the dependants of the deceased.

* * * *

Motsepe paid the $8.2 million back to Anglo within three years, but 'the first few months were frightening' as gold prices plunged, and Motsepe was forced to embark on 'some rather radical management initiatives, adopting a low-cost, lean, mean management approach' to running his mines.

For starters, he downsized the management staff by half and gave jobs to only 5 000 out of 7 500 employees at the Orkney mine, which was the most profitable.[16] He also rejigged work shifts so that the shafts would be productive 353 days a year, up from 276 days, and he 'slashed overheads by eschewing a home office in Johannesburg, three hours away, instead working out of a building in Orkney'.[17]

Labour laws were still being rewritten in South African when Motsepe launched his first subsidiary, ARMgold, in 1997, so he started out using his own management techniques and taking 'a radical approach to the pay structure of the miners in Orkney'.[18] 'Instead of the standard R1 000 a month in salary, Motsepe offered [them] a base salary of R750 plus a profit-sharing bonus that could double their pay.' This was 'a deal that is talked about at the mine to this day, not least because Motsepe involved the workers at a time when this was rare'[19] and it won him a lot of favour.

Within 12 months, the shafts had become profitable.

Neither the ANC, nor his brother-in-law, had had anything to do with it, nor with the creation of ARM, which had sealed the deal. And for Anglo, there was that Easter egg: a shining opportunity to unexpectedly get in front of a priority by the government to push black empowerment.

* * * *

ARMgold was the first black-owned company to list on the JSE Securities Exchange, and was the first new entrant on the Paris stock exchange's gold index in 15 years. Amid the bells ringing for that event, Motsepe said he'd waited until the time was right: 'International investors have realised that we are here for the long run. The listing has taken two years. We have never been rushed into a decision and certainly have no intention of changing that now.'[20]

In 2003, ARMgold went into a merger with Harmony Gold,[21] a South African enterprise founded in 1950 which became the biggest gold-mining company in the world; and in 2004, ARM went into another merger, with Anglovaal Minerals (Avmin), whose parent company had been established in 1933 as the Anglo-Transvaal Consolidated Investment Company Limited, with interests in mining, finance and industry. Avmin had previously been involved in ventures with Anglo American, both companies mining base and precious metals not only in South Africa, but also in the Democratic Republic of the Congo, Namibia and Zambia.

To that point the country's biggest mining concern after Anglo American, Avmin 'then quietly disappeared from the JSE Securities Exchange to make space for ARM',[22] and Motsepe would by 2004 represent the largest black mining interests in South African history as executive chairperson and controlling shareholder of a group whose market share was a massive R3 889 billion, even though its liquidity was 'quite small compared to that of other mining groups'.[23]

Harmony was exercising its mineral rights in the Kraaipan Greenstone Belt, an extraordinary expanse of 250 000 hectares in the Kalahari between Mafikeng and Vryburg. The mineral rights Motsepe accessed there through Harmony were to open-pittable (surface-mined) platinum and palladium metals that had been discovered by Anglo American in the early 1990s. Dated at over three billion years old, the Kalahari reef was different from Modikwa in Limpopo, where open-pit operations, which didn't require excavation or tunnelling within the 12 kilometres along which mining could happen, were expected to be effective only for between six and ten years before operations would have to go underground to find the minerals.

* * * *

In 2005, ARM went into two joint ventures with Platinum Australia Limited – including one for the Kalahari – in which Platinum Australia would do pre-feasibility studies at a cost of R53 million and provide a specialised metallurgical process, in exchange for the right to up to 49 percent of the profits from the project.

ARM and Platinum Australia needed between R500 million and R600 million to develop the mine, which was expected to generate a cash flow of R500 million a year and have an estimated profitability of 90 percent. It was thought that about 300 permanent jobs would be created.

Such was the success of this partnership that Motsepe was able to afford to buy the controlling shares in that other passion of his: Sundowns Football Club. It was a purchase that was to become an elemental feature of his life.

Motsepe's style of lean investments with clear organisational goals continued over the next two decades as ARM successfully divided into platinum and ferrous-metals divisions. This success would lead in 2015 to the launch of African Rainbow Capital (ARC), an investment vehicle that would diversify Motsepe's business interests.

By the 2020s, Motsepe had started to shun certain mining stocks – coal, in particular – in favour of disruptive industries such as insurance, IT and telecoms, and he showed no sign of tiring as he continued to grow his fortune.

15

'Here are the deals':
The fight for business

The National African Federated Chamber of Commerce and Industry (NAFCOC) comes with a significant biography. Founded in 1964 by black business giants Sam Motsuenyane (who would be the country's first ambassador to Saudi Arabia in 1996) and Richard Maponya, among others, its sole objective was to promote black business and black entrepreneurship. Its predecessor, the African Chamber of Commerce, had been set up in 1955 amid the surge of defiance campaigns. Both chambers emerged in Johannesburg, the centre of political and economic activity in the country.

One of the most important annual general meetings in NAFCOC's history took place in 1990 in Venda, which is now part of Limpopo but was still a bantustan in those days. At the time, it proclaimed that by the year 2000, a decade into the future, 30 percent of the equity of the companies on the JSE should be black-owned, 40 percent of all the managers in South Africa should be black, 50 percent of all directors of the companies on the JSE should be black, and 60 percent of the goods and services bought by businesses should be sourced from black businesses.

In September 2002, Thabo Mbeki opened NAFCOC's conference at North West holiday resort Sun City by congratulating Patrice Motsepe on having been elected the chamber's president, then headed straight into the bleak outcome over the preceding 12 years since that 1990 Venda gathering. 'It is obvious that we have not achieved any of the [1990] targets in this ... programme that is an important component ... of the transformation of our society,' he said. 'The fact that our economy is still not representative of the majority ... eight years after our freedom, points to the enormous challenges that we still face.'[1]

Certainly, the 1990 proclamation had been ambitious, but the business environment was still a blanket of whiteness that had stifled the chamber's progress, despite the hustling going on around industry bodies at the beginning of the 2000s. Among other vital organisations was the Black Business Council, an independent membership-based body founded in 1996 representing professionals, business associations and chambers. It intended to allow black businessmen to play a more central role in key national economic initiatives. There were others that sought the same outcome.

But there were more problems than a stalled agenda to change the white-dominated economy.

In 2000, NAFCOC's president Simon Mathysen had signed 'articles of association' to merge with the 'white' formation, the South African Chamber of Business, resulting in a unitary organisation, the South African Federated Chamber of Commerce. Many of NAFCOC's members were against Mathysen's idea, however, and wanted to contest the constitutionality of such a 'unitary' body in court.

Mathysen's position was that a memorandum of understanding had been signed in 1995 with the Afrikaanse Handelsinstituut, a white-dominated business organisation founded in 1942 that was actively involved in most major sectors of the South African economy, and that a pact with the South African Chamber of Business was no different.[2]

It wasn't going to be a short war, and it was time for Motsepe to step up. Although he was still young in the roughhouse world of business, he said he'd been 'a member of the NAFCOC culture too long to say no' to leading the 'rebels' who opposed Mathysen, and 'could under no circumstances sit still while NAFCOC [was] swallowed up by the more prosperous [South African Federated Chamber of Commerce].'[3]

'Our black businessmen made mistakes,' Motsepe explained. 'We focused too much on our business success in our companies and did not care enough about what was happening in NAFCOC … Unity in the organised business sector is of crucial importance. Goodness knows, we are lagging far behind in that respect. We should have started with this seven years ago, but a new business organisation meant to represent the entire business sector must have credibility.'[4]

Motsepe felt that a true umbrella body should rather be formed in which NAFCOC, the South African Chamber of Business, the Afrikaanse Handelsinstituut and the Foundation for African Business and Consumer Services (founded in 1988 to promote the development of black business in South Africa) should cooperate and act as one for the business sector.

Some members of NAFCOC believed, however, that the Afrikaanse Handelsinstituut should embrace black empowerment first, before they participated in a merger with it. But Motsepe, who'd already taken many by surprise with his strident entrance into NAFCOC politics, didn't see it that way. His view was that 'the reason for the merger is, in point of fact … to promote black empowerment … The process cannot take place the other way around'.[5]

Motsepe made a proposal at a pivotal NAFCOC board meeting in April 2001 for a lekgotla (meeting) to thrash out the meaning of a merger. 'We would explain to [all members who were unhappy about the proposed merger] that it would give exposure to businessmen who have more experience and knowledge than we have and that this could only be to our benefit.'[6]

His idea was unanimously accepted – by all but Mathysen, who chose to ignore the process, and went so far as to move NAFCOC's offices to the South African Chamber of Business headquarters without a full mandate. Motsepe then 'ordered Mathysen to vacate NAFCOC's head offices and hand over all assets'.[7]

Mathysen continued to present challenges, however. A 'shrewd businessman with interests in the liquor industry who had amassed huge wealth as an operator of luxury coaches', he was suspended by NAFCOC in June 2022 pending an investigation into cheques of R100 000 and R50 000 supposedly issued to him and the chamber's secretary-general.

Mathysen was undeterred. He tried to block the September 2002 conference at Sun City, arguing that he was 'still president'. When, on election night, he wasn't nominated, he left, threatening court action and to 'talk to my people'.[8]

It could have been chaos, but once Motsepe took over from him as NAFCOC president, there was a steadier focus.

When Mbeki addressed the conference, he reflected on how the chamber had been effective in its early days 'because it was led by credible and committed leaders of our people who correctly located the challenges of black business within the struggle for freedom'.[9] It was at that point that Mbeki introduced an 'African Renaissance' through the New Partnership for Africa's Development (NEPAD), a programme of the African Union, saying it was appropriate for NAFCOC to play a central role in its development at a 'time when the ... continent is experiencing its rebirth'.[10]

Mbeki chose Motsepe to announce on that occasion that government projects worth R2 billion had been set aside for members of NAFCOC 'as an agency for empowerment'. 'The government is standing ready with many opportunities that require massive investment and an appetite and muscle for investment, not only in the country but also the region and the continent,' said Motsepe, noting that 'never before had so many parastatals and corporates said: here are the deals, come and take them'.[11]

A unified Chambers of Commerce and Industry of South Africa (different from the South African Federated Chamber of Commerce of the Mathysen era) was already conceptualised as a 'change in the historic complexions' of those earlier business environments. Motsepe closed the 2002 NAFCOC congress having bought time by signing a two-year cooperation agreement with the South African Chamber of Business to lay the foundation for that umbrella body. That in turn meant signing a cooperation agreement with the Afrikaanse Handelsinstituut too.

Motsepe invited disgruntled individuals and groupings to participate, leaving analysts with the view that 'his personal credibility [had] helped bring together ... factions at loggerheads for the better part of ... two years' since Mathysen had acted without the full support of NAFCOC.[12]

Black Business Council chairperson David Moshapalo, in particular, hailed Motsepe's contribution 'as being driven by a desire to redeem an organisation he had known since childhood'. 'He has been generous with his time and resources,' Moshapalo said. 'There is a lesson in this for all of us – that plough-back time is now.'[13]

Reporting on the 2002 conference, one media outlet noted 'Motsepe's ability to relate both to small entrepreneurs and captains of industry' was his strength. 'At the [NAFCOC] conference, he [had] rubbed shoulders comfortably with representatives of hawkers and [then Rembrandt, now Richemont] chairperson Johann Rupert.' And he was, surprisingly, 'also a guest of honour at the [South African Communist Party]'s congress [that year]'.[14]

Motsepe had a tendency to make constituent forces feel like he was taking them into his confidence, and then to step back to allow others with the relevant capabilities continue with his agenda. In the case of NAFCOC after Sun City, deputies ran the organisation in Motsepe's stead, while together they tried to bed down a new, more powerful, black-led image.

This was reflected in the words of NAFCOC spokesperson Sipho Mseleku in October 2002, when he noted that 'it was apparent that white business chambers needed a new home', and 'NAFCOC believes the time has come for white business and the chambers ... to consider joining [our revitalised chamber]. Their contribution to NAFCOC would help to shape a new, non-racial business movement which will address the needs of South African business, both black and white'.[15]

* * * *

The Chambers of Commerce and Industry of South Africa, made up of the four major multisectoral business bodies – NAFCOC, the South African Chamber of Business, the Afrikaanse Handelsinstituut and the Foundation for African Business and Consumer Services – was established in October 2003.[16]

It's important to situate Motsepe's influence in that event. Business had been unable to cooperate after the end of apartheid because it was so divided, and that had prevented the sector from having an impact on government policy-making. White business tended to reflect positively on how hard it tried, but its exclusionary model waited on legislation for black participation. The ANC had also not created opportunities that were flexible or open enough to black and white business working together, and there was no way they would be able to succeed working apart.

After nearly a decade of ambiguity, Motsepe – for better or for worse, depending on your ideology – played a central role in finally bringing the sector together by 2003. That didn't mean the bonds didn't break, that it was a warm and welcoming space, or that the chambers were able to work effectively enough with government to build a national economy. But history shows that he drove a vision which has not yet been superseded.

Almost as soon as it was set up, the Chambers of Commerce and Industry of South Africa received an invitation from parliament to participate in the public hearings on the medium-term budget policy statement, focusing attention on employment and economic growth. Also known as the 'mini budget', this indicates how government intends allocating the upcoming national budget, and allows government departments to apply for adjustments to their budgets and/or request additional funds.

Top South African business mind Bonang Mohale[17] was among 127 individuals and organisations who were then invited by Mbeki to a meeting in the Kruger National Park to 'seriously work on business unity'. After that first gathering, Mohale recalled, 'a few of us were subsequently asked to reconvene a few weeks later ... to formalise the agreement ... [that] gave birth to Business Unity South Africa'.[18] 'Ntate Tlhopane Patrice Motsepe was elected the inaugural president. The Black Management Forum's Baba Bheki Sibiya (Sotobe) became its inaugural managing director with a measly budget of R7m, to be succeeded later by another Black Management Forum member, Baba Jerry Vilakazi.'[19] Futhi Mtoba was the first woman president and Nomaxabiso Majokweni the first woman CEO.

But Business Unity South Africa – which was created as a 'business advocacy group' off the back of those post-Sun City unitary movement events in 2003 – battled to foment a significant-enough transformation agenda. Even Motsepe was drawn to say it failed to 'address structural deficiencies'. The embedded nature of apartheid – which the negotiations between the ANC and the National Party in the early 1990s had failed to address, as these essentially favoured white control of the economy – had to be consistently confronted, and Business Unity South Africa had not been able to do that.

It wasn't only a fight for that fundamental change that went on, however. It was also a struggle for domination of the sector itself.

Motsepe was no longer Business Unity South Africa chairman in July 2011 when the Black Management Forum was among organisations that decided to cut ties with it. The forum – one of the bigger affiliates of the Black Business Council, which had been 'absorbed' under Business Unity South Africa's umbrella in 2003 – said its decision was based on the belief that there was 'no way black business could ... have its voice heard on transformation issues ... primarily because of a one organisation/one vote policy [in Business Unity South Africa] that saw only 10 votes going to black business out of 50 member organisations'. It said Business Unity South Africa's structure was 'fundamentally flawed', with the voice of black business 'permanently outnumbered and suppressed'.[20]

Jacob Zuma, who'd taken over as president of the country in 2009, presented a conciliatory face at a black business summit in Johannesburg in September 2011, saying that unity was 'paramount in ensuring the achievement of the transformation goals'. 'The time to differ, I think, is gone; it's now time to find one another.'[21] Nonetheless, Business Unity South Africa's CEO Majokweni and president Mtoba were 'reportedly asked to leave' the summit.

A decision was then made by the delegates present to revert to the original mission of the Black Business Council, and to see its name restored as a body independent of Business Unity South Africa, which would meanwhile continue on its own mission.[22] 'This process of revitalising the Black Business Council would be led by a team of the presidents of national organisations and black business stalwarts under Motsepe'.[23]

Having been so involved in the sector's organisational issues in the past, he was an obvious choice, and there were echoes of his reconciliatory approach in statements that, once the Black Business Council had come back into its own, it would then again engage with Business Unity South Africa. But Motsepe had become more successful as a businessman himself by the time the disintegration happened, and he was less diplomatic about seemingly endless rifts and shifts in the sector. Speaking to journalists in Johannesburg, Motsepe wasn't soft on his peers. He, in fact, 'rebuked corporate South Africa' in general, saying 'racial discord' had to end before the country could meet its 'enormous' socio-economic challenges.

Calling for an end to the standoff between the Black Management Forum and Business Unity South Africa, he pointed out that the discord couldn't have come at a worse time for South Africa. 'There is a growing feeling of frustration and despondency among black entrepreneurs and professionals, as well as among black youth and women and the organisations that represent them, about being ostracised and marginalised from participating and benefiting from the growth and development of our economy. These problems are separate from the enormous challenges of creating jobs and eradicating poverty, which confront us all.'[24]

Motsepe reflected on when Business Unity South Africa had been formed, with 'one of the key issues to bring those members who have historically been discriminated against and excluded to the centre of the economy. There was a clear recognition that uniting black and white business is in the interest of business. We cannot deal with the challenges of South Africa if black and white do not come together. It is crucial.'[25]

He regretted the growing chasm between rich and poor, he said, and made the point that South Africa's poverty crisis was also one of class, just as it had been under apartheid. 'For those of us who live in Sandton behind high walls, with overdrafts that are manageable, we can be oblivious and live in this world of success and comfort and not be aware that there are challenges. And those of us who have been reasonably successful, we have to lead that process of trying to make sure we espouse those grievances and that alienation of our people.'[26]

Insisting that all South Africans had to feel that they had a future 'whether they are black or white' and had to believe '[that they would] not be held back or discriminated against because they are the wrong colour', Motsepe said 'we need to make sure that ... our people feel that this is their country and that they can dig their roots deep and make sure that the challenges of job creation and poverty are dealt with.'[27]

* * * *

The billionaire has so rarely given private interviews that his personal views on the ongoing rifts in the business sector can only be assumed. But it might not have made sense for Motsepe to go on devoting as much of his time as he had in the past to pushing unification after ten years of effort had had such mixed results. That didn't mean he was no longer interested in leadership, however, and he accepted the role of chairman of the South African contingent of the new BRICS business council in Durban in 2013 at the formation's key fifth summit.

The BRICS business council consisted of 25 entrepreneurs from the five member countries – Brazil, Russia, India, China and South Africa – 'each representing key enterprises in their own country which have global influence in a certain industry'. Motsepe had to work closely with prominent black businessmen Sandile Zungu and Iqbal Survé,[28] and Business Unity South Africa's Nomaxabiso Majokweni and Transnet CEO Brian Molefe (who would later be at the centre of state-capture allegations), as well as top white businessman Stavros Nicolaou, the group senior executive of Aspen Pharmacare, which was at that time instrumental in developing the first generic antiretrovirals in Africa.

The Black Management Forum welcomed Motsepe's appointment. Its managing director Nicholas Maweni was hopeful about the power of the new BRICS entity, saying 'each member country would provide market access to its ... partners'. This was, at least, in theory.

China had invited South Africa to become a member of BRICS in 2010, with Zuma saying this represented 'an important element that Africa is part of the changing world, is part of the alternative voice, therefore it is important that we are a country that represents our continent'.[29]

About 100 South African delegates from business and government had gathered for Zuma's keynote BRICS speech that year, at an outdoor evening cocktail function in China. Among them were Motsepe, entrepreneur Robert Gumede and Baba Jerry Vilakazi, who was by then the outgoing chief executive of Business Unity South Africa, having previously been with the Black Management Forum.

South Africa's trade with its BRICS partners grew from 2011 after Zuma encouraged businesses to be 'aggressive' in taking on new opportunities in Brazil, Russia, India and China. By 2012, South Africa's total trade with its BRICS partners stood at R294 billion: Brazil was at R20 billion, Russia at R5 billion, India at R67 billion, and China – which was South Africa's largest bilateral trading partner – at R201 billion. Each had shown a marked increase from the previous year.

Progress was meanwhile being made to establish a BRICS Development Bank to cater specifically for the needs of the bloc. The dominance of the World Bank and the International Monetary Fund – key to the World Economic Forum environment to which Motsepe was strongly inclined, and which was mentoring him – were essentially being challenged.

By the time of the BRICS summit in South Africa in 2013,

Motsepe would surely have been aware that members of South Africa's black business community were talking among themselves about how to move forward as 'partners' to the government. Zuma would later be alleged to have protected private support networks within that community – and within the white business community – which undermined the state.

The angry side of Motsepe, which would surface from time to time, was seen more often then, especially when he seemed to suspect divisions were being created between black and white business to suit agendas that weren't good for him, or for the country if it was to stay onside with investors.

The BRICS summit provided scale for Motsepe. Links between Africa and Asia were cemented there, with the focus on a wide range of his own interests, including financial services and green economies.

* * * *

Motsepe was no longer the Black Business Council chairman or the BRICS business council South African chairman when NAFCOC congratulated him upon being selected by *Forbes* as one of its 100 Greatest Living Business Minds in 2017. NAFCOC said it was 'particularly proud [of] and inspired by [his] accolades and achievements'.

But behind that applause, the wrestling was still going on.

Business Unity South Africa had told the Black Business Council that year that it would no longer share seats with it at the National Economic Development and Labour Council (Nedlac), the vehicle, launched in 1995, by which government, labour, business and community organisations seek to cooperate, through problem-solving and negotiation, on economic, labour and development issues. The two entities could still not find a way to work together.

For its part, the Black Business Council had issued a smouldering press statement in which it said it would 'not extend the olive branch to white business forever'.[30] This was after a Nedlac meeting at which one of the Black Business Council's representatives was ejected for 'not having standing to be there'.

KwaZulu-Natal-born tycoon Sandile Zungu, Motsepe's former colleague on the BRICS business council, was elected president of the Black Business Council in 2018. The multimillionaire owner of Zungu Investments Company (and, later, the Amazulu football club), he was ingloriously portrayed in some media as being too close to Jacob Zuma. Motsepe's sister Bridgette Radebe – the owner of Mmakau Mining – was also appointed to the Black Business Council leadership that year.

In 2019, there was a rapprochement when the Black Business Council under Zungu and Business Unity South Africa, under its new president Sipho Pityana, held an 'exploratory' meeting 'at which both organisations discussed issues critical to business'. 'The two organisations [then] agreed on the need for a common platform for a business voice and ... appointed a committee, four from each ... to explore the modalities of how that can be achieved.'[31]

Unlike in the early 2000s, many in the South African business sector were jaded by then on the issue of the two entities trying to settle their differences. It could be said that the organisations had an abusive relationship – one that would always be ready to be raked over as a battleground.

By the time they were having their meeting in 2019, Motsepe appeared to finally be out of that arena, only touching base with both again in 2020 when they reunited for the cause of fighting covid-19 together with his companies and associated businesses.

16

From pillar to post: Empowerment and loss

African Rainbow Minerals (ARM) had a R5 billion valuation in 2002 when Patrice Motsepe became NAFCOC president, and he was planning an aggressive expansion phase.

That was a make-or-break year as the rand took a nosedive, the currency losing around five percent of its value when government's draft mining charter, calling for a dramatic shift in the ownership of South African mining assets, was leaked. The document proposed black control of all new mining projects and 30 percent black ownership in existing mining business by 2012. More than R50 billion was wiped from the value of the country's top mining stocks in three days. Few who travelled at that time will not remember paying R16 to the US dollar and R24 to the pound.

The plunge was symbolic of the scepticism that corporate capital had suppressed during the first years of democracy. 'Wealth redistribution' remained a fearful phrase for wealthy white people. But now South Africa's transformation threatened to crumble in front of the world – not because the ANC was failing or anarchy had consumed the cities, but because the government had at last announced its intention to set black empowerment rules.

Patrice Motsepe and Bobby Godsell stepped up, appealing 'for calm' and a 'quick solution to the crisis of confidence'.[1] Holding back a tide of disinvestment was essential for Motsepe as one of the most influential black businessmen of the time, and for Godsell, one of the most influential white businessmen. And while the optics of them standing together to fight it were not that important to the markets in 2002, they certainly created a durable image of a patriotic partnership.

If there was a plot to destabilise the government's plans by leaking the document, it didn't work. Irreversible change came when the department of minerals and energy promulgated the Mineral and Petroleum Resources Development Act of 2002, formally recognising the state as custodian. The mining futures that Motsepe and his colleagues had discussed at Bowman Gilfillan in the late 1980s and early 1990s were now coming to fruition.

The mining charter was a commitment to immediately put 15 percent of equity stakes under the ownership of 'historically disadvantaged South Africans', and 26 percent by 2014. Then minister of finance Trevor Manuel earmarked R10 billion for black economic empowerment in the industry for three years, with industry players expected to raise R100 million in support of empowerment ventures.

* * * *

When ARM became the world's fifth-largest gold miner in 2004 after its roughly R20-billion mergers with Harmony and Anglovaal Minerals (Avmin), Motsepe was on track to becoming South Africa's first black dollar billionaire. Producing and supplying gold to the global market, ARM and Harmony listed on the JSE, and Harmony also listed on the New York Stock Exchange and the London FTSE.

Motsepe's deals represented a massive uptick in his personal fortune and were also a pre-emptive strike for black economic empowerment, fulfilling the mining charter's equity requirements 'years ahead of schedule'. 'Instead of having to be concerned about putting in place various black economic empowerment initiatives over the next 10 years, they basically take the leap in the current year,' one media outlet explained. 'Once they have that in place, they can focus on the business going forward.'[2]

The black economic empowerment aspect of Motsepe's deal with Harmony was ratified in law, with the notarial certificate from Bowman Gilfillan, which represented Motsepe, describing ARMgold as 'controlled by historically disadvantaged individuals [under] Motsepe, the non-executive chairman of the merged company, [who would] play an active and extensive role in advancing ... long-term interests ... Historically disadvantaged individuals [would thus] hold approximately 26% of the issued share capital.'[3]

The merging parties, which noted that they had 'complementary management cultures and strategies', pipped to the post a similar transaction between ANC military veteran and former Gauteng premier Tokyo Sexwale's company, Mvelaphanda Resources, and top-six mining company Gold Fields. That would be the second such major empowerment agreement, with Mvelaphanda buying a 15 percent stake of Gold Fields' South African operation.

While many, if not most, sectors dithered, the mining and minerals arena was opening up to black economic empowerment, with Motsepe at the forefront.

He subscribed to the section of the BBBEE Act that defined a 'black-owned company' as being 50.1 percent economically owned by black people, with black people also exercising substantial management control of the company. This is different to a 'black-empowered company', which must be 25.1 percent owned by black 'interests', and with a significant number of black non-executive directors, although any micro-enterprise or company with a turnover of less than R5 million – later, R10 million – is exempt.

It's important to note that the Act refers to 'white' and 'black', black meaning blacks, coloureds and Indians who could claim, or whose parents could claim, South African citizenship as of April

1994, and Chinese people who were 'reclassified' black in 2008 after the Chinese Association of South Africa took the government to court (along with the 1994 citizenship rule).

Broad-based Black Economic Empowerment (BBBEE) codes allocating minimum targets of 40 percent in terms of ownership, skills development and enterprise development were gazetted in 2013 after an avalanche of complaints about a 'black economic empowerment elite' dominating through individuals' prior, or purchased, links to the ANC. Even Motsepe had been accused of being a member of that 'elite', although he strongly denied ever having been favoured for any reason except his own hard work.

The 'BBB' aspect, now including the words 'broad-based' in front of 'black economic empowerment', was intended to make it clear that all black people – women, youth, the disabled, the poor, those in rural areas – should benefit from economic empowerment, not only a select few, well-placed individuals. The annual reports for Motsepe's Ubunto-Botho Investments (UBI) would publish details about the 'broad-based' components of its black economic empowerment, although both he and UBI CEO Johan van Zyl described how years before the gazetting of the codes they went out as a team on roadshows to promote the widest empowerment possible. Motsepe was undeniably in the vanguard of that movement.

* * * *

Two decades later, the policy was still being pulled apart on talk shows, in society, in analyses and academic studies, and in inter-government dialogues, remarkably with no overwhelming end position in sight on its success or failure. *The Wall Street Journal* was, however, prepared to call black economic empowerment 'the world's most extreme affirmative action program'[4] as it noted, perplexed, that there was a virtual absence, or inability, or unwillingness, on the part of big capital to in fact ever defy the government and not do what the Act said.

The reason the most powerful financial media in the USA said this was because big capital was rarely bullied. In other parts of the world, it either did the bare minimum with regard to empowerment, or it did nothing, but in South Africa, it acquiesced to actual percentages and rules, presumably for reputation management. Not to have complied would have been seen to support white supremacy on the world's greatest stage for racial freedom. There was also, of course, the very real risk of financial sanctions by the state, and trade union action that would shut down production.

Thabo Mbeki's brother, intellectual Moeletsi Mbeki, was one of those who dubbed black economic empowerment 'crony capitalism' and 'an anti-competitive system'.[5] For Motsepe, what was 'critically important' was what empowerment meant to the poor: 'How do we translate empowerment into sustainability?' he asked. 'You will find that we're going to take more of an entrepreneurial perspective to empowerment because we've got to get people to be able to do things themselves.'[6]

This was within Motsepe's vision of 'wealth redistribution' – but it seems he was largely alone in this. In 2010, a year after the mining charter had been signed, economist and analyst Duma Gqubule was commissioned by the South African Mining Development Association to study ownership by 'historically disadvantaged South Africans' in the JSE's mining sector. A review of more than 90 percent of black economic empowerment transactions by value over the preceding decade established that the 'gross value of black shareholding in the JSE-listed top 25 mining companies was equivalent to 5.27%, or R98bn, of their market capitalisation. The combined market capitalisation of the top 25 mining houses had reached R1.8 trillion at the end of March 2010.'[7]

Within those top 25 mining companies, the report went on, 'a lion's share of the black wealth was concentrated in three JSE-listed companies, coal miner Exxaro, Motsepe's diversified mining and minerals company ARM, and platinum miner Impala'.[8] The black ownership of these firms accounted for 69 percent, or R66.8 billion, of total black mining ownership on the JSE.[9]

Gqubule's study confirmed the findings of a government-sponsored draft review, also in 2010, that 'the industry had woefully failed to meet its [BEE] ownership targets, [with] top JSE-listed miners [having] only transferred 5.27% of their wealth'.[10] A five-year draft assessment by the department of mineral resources (previously the department of minerals and energy) – which had set the 26-percent net-value target – found that black ownership of the mining sector was only at nine percent.

* * * *

Motsepe's ARM Mining Consortium (ARM MC) deal with Anglo Platinum at Modikwa was looking good for full production by 2004, with ore already stockpiled. The expenses of developing the mine were estimated at 'about R1.6 billion' and were shared between the two companies. Motsepe had been expected to put in R100 million himself, with a R650-million loan to be arranged for the remainder. But there were delays, and the contract got sticky, creating an issue with the bank that was advancing money for the project.

ARM's CEO Andre Wilkens explained that Motsepe 'therefore put in R300m initially after selling ARMgold shares, and then a further R200m to give the banks comfort for the R700 million loan'. Interest payments still outstanding on the loan before the capital amount would start to be paid off were about R600 million. Wilkens admitted '[our] team might have thought better of it if they had known beforehand what they were getting into'.[11]

In terms of the deal, a separate percentage of the profits would be held on behalf of the Maandagshoek farm communities around whom the mining operations would take place. The older people from the Maandagshoek community talked about how 'an Anglo representative' had visited their area in 1994, and '[made] promises' to them. (This was a decade before Motsepe struck his deal with Anglo – he'd only established his first company, Future Mining, in 1994.)

Chief Sonias Vilakazi of the Matimatsatsi community, who lived in Maandagshoek, explained that later when Motsepe and other entrants into mining in the area struck joint ventures with established companies like Anglo, there was a lack of clarity about what the mines would mean for the people. 'We called the community and agreed with them that the mine can start ... Because we didn't know anything, we asked them what are we going to get. They said we don't have land and the land belongs to them. We said because we are the residents we need to get something from the mine. They said they will develop the company for us like Section 21.'[12]

Then 'workers [presumably employed by the companies] began taking farmland by force to begin constructing the mine'. 'Moreover, although the companies began bringing machines and developing the mining site, they did not keep promises such as building roads, providing electricity, or offering well-paid local jobs. The only fulfilled benefit was water infrastructure.'[13]

Around the time that ARM MC and Anglo Platinum were thrashing out their deal, the government was crafting the Mineral and Petroleum Resources Development Act and the Traditional Leadership and Governance Framework Act, two acts that were not so much progressive as 'developed in concert with one another to enable politically connected business and traditional leaders to use their homeland antecedents and their political connections to cut themselves into South Africa's most significant source of wealth, the mining industry, on terms that exclude the poor black people who own the land on which mining takes place'.[14]

So the political backdrop was intense. As a lawyer, Motsepe would have had to pay that special attention.

Researchers have disputed that there was meaningful consultation from the side of the mining companies in Maandagshoek, and questioned why many mine employees were not from the surrounding community, but from outside it, and why was there such high unemployment in the village itself.[15] They pointed out that there was a lack of basic services to the people, who seemed to have believed that a mining company could assist them with that. They also explained that the traditional authorities seemed confused about the meaning of land being held in 'trust' for the collective, as the mine owners seemed to claim it.

It wasn't even the traditional authorities' job to allocate land for development. 'That [was, in fact] the right of the occupants, whose ownership [was] confirmed in the Constitution and in at least one crucial post-apartheid law – the Interim Protection of Informal Land Rights Act of 1996. ... This law [remained] in force because of government's failure to introduce a comprehensive law to deal with communal land [but it was] widely abrogated by traditional leaders, who [signed] mining deals without consulting those whose land rights are affected.'[16]

The axis between 'the collective', being the people, and mine owners like Motsepe and the state, was hazardously strained.

After a few years of unresolved strife, a Maandagshoek Development Committee was formed in 2006 under community leader and activist Emmanuel Makgoga. Among the problems the committee raised were water contamination, and damage to ground and surface water sources. Nelspruit-based human-rights lawyer Richard Spoor represented them pro bono.

That year, the police were called as community members protested about the continuing infringements on what they said were
their indigenous land rights. 'They demanded to negotiate new
terms for accessing their lands as well as compensation for past and
current damages and environmental rehabilitation'.[17]

On a particularly shocking day, 'the police beat and shot at
the demonstrators with both live and rubber bullets, hospitalis-
ing 26 people, including a baby'.[18] The traditional leaders were
arrested. So were Makgoga and others, and hundreds of people
then marched against that brutality. But the standoff continued
for months.

In early December 2006, the community built blockades out of
stones on a mine road, set fire to some of the company's equipment
and refused to allow workers to start drilling. A number of people
were then arrested and held behind bars until they were finally
given bail on New Year's Eve.

Five weeks later, on 8 February 2007, more than 5 000 people
gathered outside the Limpopo premier's office in the provincial
capital, Polokwane, under the banner of the Maandagshoek Development Committee, chanting, 'Naga ke a rona! The land is ours!'
(Their actions might have reminded Motsepe of demonstrations
against corporate raids in Mmakau in the 1980s.) They had turned
their cries against injustice and human-rights violations into a peti-
tion addressed to minerals and energy minister Buyelwa Sonjica
and Limpopo premier Sello Moloto.

* * * *

In the absence of government-built infrastructure, ARM MC and
Anglo Platinum built a R65-million road from the Modikwa village
to Limpopo's main provincial freeway, the R37 between Polokwane and Burgersfort, in 2011. Motsepe believed there was 'an

obligation' to do so. Construction took 14 months and about 400 jobs were created, with most of the employed from the seven communities around the mine.

ARM MC and Anglo Platinum described the new road as 'a wonderful example of creating shared value', and hosted an opening event in partnership with the local municipality, with the guest list including Julius Malema, who was then still the ANC Youth League president, new Limpopo premier Cassel Mathale, King Thulare III of the Bapedi nation and paramount chief KK Sekhukhune. (Motsepe's 'New York-based shareholders' had expressed 'reservations', he revealed; they 'felt building roads was a government responsibility'.)[19]

Nevertheless, the relationship between the mine bosses and the community hadn't improved much – and this wasn't helped by a finding in 2016 of the South African Human Rights Commission that 'mining companies paid only for the land and were offering below what [was] considered to be appropriate ... causing systemic economic displacement and impoverishment'. The Commission noted that for 'compensation to be meaningful, it should account for a loss of life, loss related to communal and individually held tenure or title as well as loss incurred for production value gained from the land, whether that production value is linked to traditional ways of life or more commercial enterprises'.[20]

In March 2017, Motsepe sounded 'a dire warning over the "highly politicised" interaction between the mining sector and the local communities where mines [operated], saying this situation [had] become critical'.[21]

His analysis, during an ARM interim results presentation in Sandton, marked a watershed and would go down as one of the most important of his career. He reflected both angrily and sadly on the parlous political and economic state of South Africa post-

Zuma and set himself in a space somewhere between business and the people – which may, in fact, have been where he'd considered himself to be all along.

He said that mines could expect no help from the South African government in dealing with communities who were being advised by political activists who 'can't even fasten their shoelaces', and that he would shut a mine down rather than agree to 'unreasonable demands' involving threats and campaigns. He had no patience with 'politically motivated community action ... aimed at interrupting mine operations', he said. 'This is important. If we don't work together and make the mine successful, then we are going to close the mine.'[22]

This was 'against the specific background of ARM's troubled Modikwa mine ... which [had] been hit by technical problems and [localised] civil unrest'. Motsepe's operations there had been the target of many union- and community-led protests related to wages, employment and sharing value. Motsepe indicated this was, nonetheless, an industry-wide morass and that problems had been accumulating over more than 15 years.

His concern was such that he had recently 'paid a visit to Modikwa to attend a mass meeting with workers and talk to the local communities'. 'I needed to sit down and listen personally to what employees and community members had to say,' he said, revealing that he'd learnt that they wanted 'more equity; they want dividends to flow from that equity even when dividends should not be paid because you are investing for the future.

'They want more contracts and tenders to be awarded to locals and they want more senior positions to be occupied by locals.'[23] Motsepe, who himself had never applied for or received a government tender,[24] continued, 'We have to engage very seriously with the communities, in particular because the capacity of the business constituency in this country to influence policy-making is zero at best.'[25] The business community must understand, he said, 'that the politicians will throw us in front of any bus or any train that comes along if their choice is between the votes they get from the communities and the business community that we represent, which is seen to have made lots of money.'[26]

Motsepe took the picture back to when he was still a student conceptualising a time when workers and communities would have the vote, and businesses – especially mining – would find a way to work with the people for their mutual benefit. 'But we are now living in a democracy. We are learning the new rules.'

Among those 'new rules' were how labour in South Africa was treated.

* * * *

A year after that speech, Motsepe was having to consider the effects of growing violence around his mines. The most destructive was an arson attack that took place in 2018 during protest actions. Six people were left dead after a bus transporting Modikwa mine employees from the neighbouring Ga-Maroga village caught fire. Five people were charged with murder and malicious damage to property. The joint partners in the mine strongly condemned what they called a 'senseless attack' which had caused loss and grief to many families and their community.[27]

Eighteen months later, hundreds of protesters marched to Modikwa, this time calling for the resignation of the general manager. Community members also handed a memorandum to the local municipality.

Other, even more specific, hardships were taken up on a national platform when communities approached the Human Rights Commission[28] in December 2021 about the uncompassionate relocation of their community's graves. The people wanted the

Commission 'to investigate after numerous requests for the mine to speak to them'.[29]

John Pilane, a local resident living near Motsepe's Nkomati mine between Barberton and Machadodorp, talked about the 'continual fight for compensation ... for graves that were exhumed, and homesteads and cattle kraals that were demolished to make way for [a dumping site]'.[30] The Nkomati mine was a joint venture with Norilsk Nickel, whose biggest shareholder at that time was Russian oligarch Vladimir Potanin.

Pilane claimed that 'dozens of families who used the land for growing crops, grazing cattle and a graveyard [had been convinced by the mine] to allow it to remove ... graves' in 2008. Of the approximately 50 families who'd entered into agreements with Nkomati mine, some said they'd never received compensation, while others said that the mine 'gave them R2 000 for only the exhumation and relocation of each grave'.[31] The families had moved 30 kilometres away, Pilane said, and now their cattle were dying, their land was no longer conducive to farming and there had been no development in the area.

The people had been 'sent from pillar to post ... with the mine representatives [promising] that they would urgently attend to our problems, but they have not'.[32]

* * * *

There were also the human losses through accidents that harmed the people. The deaths of five miners who worked at Harmony Gold's Kusasalethu mine near Carletonville, who were trapped and then succumbed underground in 2017, were also used for political ends.

About 3 000 miners managed to escape unharmed when a tremor caused sections of the mine to collapse and parts of the structure to cave in, burying the unfortunate men three kilometres below the surface. They were remembered as 'brave warriors who died in battle', with Jacob Zuma's minister of mineral resources Mosebenzi Zwane describing their deaths as 'horrible and unacceptable'.

When Zwane addressed a memorial service at the mine, he targeted Motsepe, who was in attendance as the Harmony Gold chair, saying, 'You can do what you are doing at Sundowns and pay mineworkers decent salaries', emphasising that communities around the mine were still living in poverty.[33]

National Union of Mineworkers' health and safety national chairperson Peter Bailey noted that 'every mineworker who died had an average of 10 dependents'.[34] The ill effects of poverty had indeed worsened through South Africa's post-apartheid 'resource curse' – a term describing the situation where countries with an abundance of natural resources had less economic growth, less democracy or worse development outcomes than countries with fewer natural resources. Discussions all over the world about the 'resource curse' inevitably spiralled into arguments about benefits to mine owners, and how these were derived through workers, and thus that workers should be treated well.

When Motsepe got his chance to speak at the service, he conceded that 'this country and the whole of the economy was built by the sacrifices of mineworkers'. Noting that Kusasalethu wasn't profitable, he nonetheless insisted that 'the money and profits of the mines were not more important than the lives of people'.[35]

And there were other incidents that haunted Motsepe, such as the cases of manganese poisoning at ARM-owned Assmang's Cato Ridge, Durban, smelting factory. This occupational illness is difficult to diagnose, although the symptoms are similar to those of Parkinson's disease. The company addressed this issue in its annual report in 2008, noting that four cases of manganism were identified in 2006, followed in 2007 by a further six cases. 'As a result, compensation was applied for on behalf of 10 employees to the Compensation Commissioner.'[36]

Assmang said it had 'developed a more comprehensive medical surveillance programme for manganism [including] examination by a movement disorder specialist and a neuro-psychologist', but that some of the workers 'who were initially diagnosed with manganism should be medically re-examined by specialists qualified in the field'.[37]

Then, in 2008, a furnace explosion resulted in the deaths of six people, who were among nine who suffered severe burns. A memorial service attended by employees, family members and management was held at the factory, and Motsepe flew in from Johannesburg to 'assess the situation'. 'Workers at Assmang need the reassurance that the incident is being taken seriously at the highest level. Outside observers will note that Motsepe takes a responsibly humanitarian approach to the disaster and hasn't resorted to the mudslinging and buck-passing we've come to expect from many in authority when things go wrong.'[38]

* * * *

In March 2020, amendments to the Mineral and Petroleum Resources Development Act came into effect, expanding obligations for mining companies to consult with communities. Mining-rights holders were required to 'contribute towards the socioeconomic development of "labour sending areas" [local municipalities in which a majority of mineworkers reside] in addition to areas in which they operated'. In other words, the amendments stipulated that mining-right holders would 'be required to demonstrate steps to uplift areas from which they sourced workers (historically and currently), not just where they operated'.[39]

Motsepe could justify his companies' right to exist within this framework by claiming that without the capital they generated, he wouldn't be able to give back via empowerment mechanisms or philanthropy. That was the classic anti-Marxist argument. But in South Africa, 'conscientious capitalism' was still a new idea.

Motsepe had been a disruptor from the time he approached Godsell – who represented white capital – for a loan. Motsepe's timing was spot-on. By the 2000s, when he'd proved he could run a business, and when black economic empowerment was a certainty, Motsepe had styled his deal-making as a willingness to partner with white capital to benefit them both, and help raise South Africans out of poverty. White businessmen who'd operated during apartheid weren't used to that, but Motsepe prophesied that such a spirit of ubuntu would build the economy.

The joint venture at Modikwa entrenched the notion that the communities around a mine would benefit directly when that mine made money. It was, however, something of a cautionary tale. The deal, announced in 2001, seemed to ensure that Anglo Platinum gained direct empowerment credentials via the ARM Broad-Based Economic Empowerment Trust, which held the communities' percentage of profits. Anglo Platinum believed this to be so, and claimed this in 2011 about its empowerment holdings.

But ARM made a clarification. It turned out that the Trust owned shares directly in ARM MC, and therefore did not, in fact, form part of the 2001 joint venture in the way it was understood by Anglo Platinum.[40]

It's complicated to grasp, but it may make more sense when considered against a reminder given to the government during an industry briefing on black economic empowerment to the minerals and energy portfolio committee in 2003. There was a flaw in the Companies Act in terms of which the balance sheet of a subsidiary couldn't be used to support a black economic empowerment venture if that balance sheet was owned by the holding company. It was noted at the time that 'this has obvious implications for joint ventures with the mining giants' and needed to be addressed.[41]

In the case of the joint venture at Modikwa, ARM was the holding company that owned the ARM MC balance sheet. ARM MC contained the Trust. Since ARM was a black-owned company, it, not Anglo Platinum, could have claimed a full empowerment quotient, allowing the Trust then to represent its 'conscientious capitalism'.

17

The changing order:
Capital diversified

When *Forbes* first announced that Patrice Motsepe was a billionaire, in 2008, it felt irresistibly drawn to say that 'his wealth can't just be explained by good business nous'. 'His political connections made the difference.'[1] The magazine dipped into the simmering rage around black economic empowerment. 'For all the adulation, in South Africa such success comes with a price: being labelled an oligarch. Even many blacks have complained that the country's 1994 transformation ... has benefited only the elite few.'[2]

But for some businesspeople, there were two sides to that story. In 2016, Motsepe took a swipe himself at the response to government's empowerment policies. 'I hear stakeholders say we incurred costs on black economic empowerment,' he said, 'and you cannot expect us to incur that cost again.'[3]

He was referring to the contentious 'once empowered, always empowered' principle, which had seen the Chamber of Mines take legal action on whether the existing charter obliged them to get new black partners if their old ones sold their shares, no matter the inducements on the table. The Pretoria High Court found in 2018 that the charter was in fact only 'an instrument of policy', not law, and that there would be no need to 'top up credentials' if black economic empowerment and, later, BBBEE requirements had been satisfied before.

Motsepe had nonetheless looked to retain the precepts of the original mining charter in his companies, and had also taken on the energy of some of the white-owned companies that had been willing to be partners in the early 2000s. An example of this was the Bakubung Initiative, a groundbreaking, multi-stakeholder consultation in 2000 in North West and the brainchild of mining and finance industry figures who'd met with government and World Bank representatives to 'find ways to [support] new entrepreneurs'. Key to the plan had been the establishment of a fund of up to R1 billion to tap into 'white skills' for mentorship.[4]

It seemed sometimes that the boardrooms of Motsepe's companies were the only places where he could manifest what he idealised as best practice for South African businesses. In 2018, for instance, he praised the 'world-class South African management team' of ARM, which he described as 'fully integrated and fully representative of all languages and colours'.[5]

His ARM boardroom by then hosted black and white representatives of Anglo Platinum, Assore, Glencore, Impala Platinum, Norilsk Nickel Africa, Vale and Zambian Consolidated Mines. Outside were mostly black communities whose interests were represented under the ARM Broad-Based Economic Empowerment Trust, and via philanthropy through his Ubuntu-Botho Investments (UBI) and the Motsepe Foundation.

It was that satisfaction, that 'enjoyment' of the work of philanthropy, to which Motsepe was referring when he initially turned down SAFA's bid to have him as its candidate to run for CAF president: he'd created the space of which he had dreamed when he was a young businessman.

Motsepe noted that 'the confidence in South Africa of hardworking black and white South Africans is not unfounded' and was 'based on the exceptional people that South Africa has and that I'm privileged to interact with'. But he also added that, 'In whatever humble way we can, we have to engage and say the things that are correct even though they may not be popular.'[6]

* * * *

When Motsepe established his Ubuntu-Botho Investments (UBI) consortium in 2003 and took an initial eight percent stake in Sanlam,[7] his purpose was to build the very black-controlled capital that had been touted at the NAFCOC Sun City conference in 2002. And while taking a stake in Sanlam, a company that exemplified white Afrikaner – not black – business, might have seemed antithetical at first, Motsepe saw it as giving him the best possible means of expanding.

He didn't hesitate to do things the way he wanted to do them, and he had clear reasons for choosing a company profoundly linked to apartheid-era capital. He was determined that his boardrooms would defy race expectations, believing that when white entrepreneurs and black entrepreneurs got their heads around working together, they could make magic.

He was also inspired by Sanlam's enduring history of successful financial empowerment, even though this had been empowerment for white Afrikaners, and especially the white Afrikaner working class. The company had been established in 1918 as a reaction to the isolation felt by Afrikaners when English-speakers dominated society, and it had indeed brought value to its wartime clients.

Thus, Motsepe was attracted to it from a parallel historical point of view. There was no other company that had contributed so much to Afrikaner growth and upliftment at a time when English-speaking capitalists dominated and Britain was still in control.

Motsepe examined Sanlam's core methods and set out to replicate aspects of those in the service of black empowerment, saying he 'wanted to learn and partner with them so that we [can] make a contribution to the upliftment of all South Africans'.[8]

He deliberately courted connections with white Afrikaner business leaders, and although this was controversial to those who thought he should shun them because they'd been rewarded by apartheid, it was a positive signal to those who couldn't see South Africa succeeding without their involvement. Motsepe believed he could convince white partners 'of the huge benefits for them in the growth and success of a black middle class', and insisted that the more black entrepreneurs were created, the more they, in turn, would 'encourage [other] black people to start, run and own ... businesses'.[9]

Meanwhile, Sanlam's empowerment status once it went into business with UBI immediately enhanced its competitiveness. A wider reach of clients impressed other potential stakeholders, and it saw its market value grow on average R10 billion per annum.[10]

* * * *

The same was certainly true for Motsepe and his family. Thirteen years after the deal was struck with Sanlam, he had such a high level of wealth that he was able to build African Rainbow Capital (ARC), a 100-percent subsidiary of UBI. Johan van Zyl would leave his position as group CEO of Sanlam to join Motsepe as a co-CEO at ARC and CEO of UBI, which by then had a 14.5 percent stake in Sanlam.

In 2016 Motsepe, then deputy chair of Sanlam, had been asked to take the chair there when the incumbent, Desmond Smith, announced he would retire the following year. Motsepe instead had nominated Van Zyl. 'Patrice was the board's choice, but the board respects his decision and recommendation that Johan, a consummate leader, is well positioned to take over as chairman,' said Smith.[11]

Van Zyl's name would be affected by controversy, however. In December 2017, the CEO of the global furniture retailer Steinhoff, Markus Jooste, resigned in disgrace after auditors flagged accounting 'irregularities' in its books in what would turn out to be the biggest fraud in South African corporate history. The Stellenbosch-headquartered group's share price plunged by over 95 percent and billions were wiped from its market value. Van Zyl, a director and a member of the supervisory board at Steinhoff, quit in April 2018 in the week of a tumultuous annual shareholder meeting in Amsterdam. He was publicly condemned for his 'complete failure to take responsibility, and (his) total lack of any remorse'.[12]

But when Motsepe hired Van Zyl, that lay in the future.

Their partnership grew exponentially as they also put their weight behind UBI's empowerment trust by engaging with broad-based shareholders, including trade unions. Two of UBI's entities were wholly owned by Cosatu affiliate the National Education, Health and Allied Workers' Union, and SADTU Investment Holdings, whose beneficiary communities were the more than 256 000 members of the South African Democratic Teachers Union.[13]

A mighty R3 billion of the value created by the Sanlam and UBI black economic empowerment partnership over the first 10 years between 2003 and 2013 went to projects linked to about 700 shareholders, including religious groups, entrepreneurs, small and micro business owners, women's entities and youth groups. Several business leaders who were identified as being able to make a direct impact on empowering small business were also among the beneficiaries, as were some non-executive directors from Sanlam and senior black Sanlam staff members.

In 2015, Sanlam enabled UBI – which held about 292 million shares (or 13.5 percent of the entire issued share capital) – to pay a special dividend of R830 million to shareholders. UBI's related companies included ARM, ARM MC, Mamelodi Sundowns Football Club, African International Entertainment Enterprises, African Rainbow Energy and Power (AREP), African Rainbow Minerals

Platinum, ARM Coal, Chloorkop (Sundowns' training ground), Goedgevonden Coal and Sanlam Life Insurance, among others. Future Mining remained on the list, too.

Sanlam had meanwhile collected stakes in 30 African countries, Lebanon, Saudi Arabia, India, Malaysia and the UK, and had interests in the USA, Australia, Burundi, Lesotho and the Philippines, becoming one of the 50 largest internationally active insurance groups in the world.

When Johan van der Merwe, the former Sanlam Investment Management CEO, was named co-CEO with Van Zyl at ARC in 2016, Motsepe's vision seemed to take proper focus. It also worked well for the 'two Johans', who went on to draw their own headlines.

After Motsepe's investment in Sanlam grew tenfold, he established African Rainbow Capital Investments (ARCI) in 2017 under Van Zyl and Van der Merwe. ARCI – which would focus on boosting black participation in the economy – made R5.5 billion in investments in the first year, with R2 billion of that going into financial services ventures.

It listed on the JSE with a market value of about R8.5 billion, with R2 billion in cash for future purchases. The Public Investment Corporation, Sanlam Private Wealth and GIC Pte Ltd, Singapore's sovereign wealth fund, would take up R2.1 billion of shares and another R1.9 billion would go to 'selected investors'.

The co-CEOs were doing well enough in running the company that they were able to make 'R192m [themselves] ... by betting big on the [company's] share price', buying about 62 million ordinary shares of ARCI each in September 2020. 'At R2.75 per share, the two Johans paid R185m each for these shares. At the end of trading on Friday 18 June 2021, ARC's share price was R4.18. The shares they [had] bought [were] therefore worth R281.1m – each.'[14] The men thus each made R96.2 million from the transaction.

* * * *

The year 2020 had been a test for ARCI, and Van Zyl and Van der Merwe, when the company attracted all the wrong attention for sending out 'a poorly conceived rights issue notice' in which it announced it 'wanted to raise R750m by issuing new shares, and selling them to existing shareholders – but [adding] that 27% of the money [would] be used to pay fees to the managers of its investment fund'.[15]

Many shareholders, who had initially seen ARCI's share price lose value in a poor economy as the company slowly tried to create opportunities for the young enterprises it was adding to its portfolio, baulked at paying these managers R205 million. The company quickly had to change tack, saying it would settle the management fees from internal resources.

Scepticism remained, however, and many financial-media outlets suggested the problem lay in 'the rather convoluted group structure of Motsepe's various investment entities'.[16] In the end, it was UBI that had to fork out R126 million to buy ARCI shares when investors holding almost a fifth of the company 'did not want to take [those] up'.

There was, however, no denying that ARCI had made significant acquisitions, of which the most exciting, in 2019, were the new digital bank, TymeBank, and the mobile network operator, Rain. And the new stock exchange A2X had come in too after new legislation opened up the market, with the goal to disrupt the JSE by taking away its trading market share through lower fees – much like TymeBank had set out to do in the banking world.[17] A2X's 33 listed securities included Sanlam and Standard Bank. Its total value traded since it arrived in 2017 was at R2.3 billion, meaning it was a good investment for ARC, which took a 20 percent stake in 2019.

ARC expanded again in 2021, going into business with financial-services firm Alexander Forbes, which then went on its own hunt to expand its offering through an operational footprint in Namibia, Botswana, Zambia, Uganda, Nigeria, Zimbabwe and the Channel Islands. The Alexander Forbes Group was the largest multi-manager in South Africa, with more than 1.3 million customers and R310 billion in assets under administration and management.

Motsepe's ARC Health was primed for social influence in 2021, with Motsepe hoping it would play a role in reforming the private healthcare sector 'as well as the public healthcare system, to consolidate government spending with a special focus on legislated compensation for injuries and other related costs'.[18]

Motsepe saw ARC Health acting as a catalyst to ensure a sustainable National Health Insurance, taking his lead from Harmony, which had been in that realm since 2004 when it announced a joint venture with Network Healthcare Holdings (now Netcare).

Motsepe's other investments in health by 2021 were with Afrocentric Investment Corporation and the National Health Care Group, an ARC subsidiary centred on access to primary care for uninsured South Africans. Its tech dipped into contracting models involving more than a thousand doctors, pharmacies and other providers.

In December 2021, Sanlam announced its own strategic intent to 'significantly expand its presence' in private healthcare with products and partnerships under Sanlam Health Solutions.

That same year, in alignment with ARC's ambition to establish an ecosystem of fintech-related business, a consortium that included ARC 'swooped up fintech firm Crossfin in a deal valued at R1.5bn'.[19] It was 'one of the largest private equity-led investments in South Africa's fintech sector', with Crossfin engaged in payments technology, smart funding and broader fintech.

ARC deal executive Charmaine Padayachy expressed a view drawn from the Motsepe script: 'Crossfin has a capable management team in place that we are confident will continue to add significant value.' She called it an innovator and 'pioneer'.[20]

By 2021, ARC owned a 50-percent stake in London-based private equity firm ARCH Emerging Markets Partners and was raising funds and opening offices in various African countries. Its momentum was steady.

* * * *

In January 2020, Motsepe was invited to join the World Economic Forum's board of trustees, along with Kristalina Georgieva, managing director at the International Monetary Fund. 'Both have a track record of thought leadership and long-term success in their field which will contribute to strengthening the Forum's platform for public-private co-operation,' said a press statement.[21]

Other members of the board included president of the European Central Bank Christine Lagarde, governor of the Bank of England Mark Carney, former American vice-president Al Gore, cellist Yo-Yo Ma, president of the International Committee of the Red Cross Peter Maurer, Queen Rania al Abdullah of Jordan, and Min Zhu, president of the National Institute of Financial Research for the People's Republic of China.

This was a world of influence to which few South Africans were invited. Under Motsepe's plan to immerse Africa in opportunities, it was a foremost posting.

Johan van der Merwe, who was somewhat defensive that year when ARCI's listed market value was trading at a huge discount to its intrinsic net asset value, noted that ARCI wasn't adding 'more building blocks'; rather, it was enhancing those that already existed, even if it had its problems. 'People think we suck these values out of our thumbs,' he said, 'and think we as management [are the ones who] put [just] any value on it [while] this is scrutinised and the auditors have to sign off on these values'.[22]

When Motsepe took up his seat as a World Economic Forum trustee, he was embracing the vicissitudes of a changing capitalist order. With his taste for disruptive companies, he understood the nature of the new game – as did some other billionaires around the world, including a few who'd signed the Giving Pledge like him. More traditional investors, who wanted accurate values, were less keen on young unlisted companies, such as the ones Motsepe fancied.

Motsepe was undeterred. Instead of always demanding the financials, he saw where there was underlying value, and recognised that this could make for greater competition. He repeatedly urged the medium- to long-term game – as he'd noted back in 2013, after shares in platinum producers dropped following violent strike action that shut down mines, 'You cannot be affected by short-term desolations and short-term periods of volatility [and] uncertainty.'[23]

18

Mobilising energy:
All colours green

Motsepe's ambitions to expand his businesses in Africa had experienced challenges. His gradual development into becoming a global competitor was more successful, but this was deliberately slow as he carefully considered each option available to him.

He seemed to properly refine his trajectory on the continent and internationally when clean energy gained momentum in the early 2020s as scientists' warnings over decades turned into real-life climate crises, and other billionaires started getting directly involved in green new deals.

* * * *

Motsepe's African ventures began to take shape in 2010 when ARM and Brazilian company Vale announced a joint venture to develop the Lubambe underground copper mine situated about 500 kilometres north of the Zambian capital of Lusaka.

Three years later, Motsepe explored investing in Guinea's iron-ore industry after the government in Conakry announced revisions to its mining code. Although reticent about the history of insidious corruption in Guinea's mining industry, Motsepe was presented an opportunity to buy at a discount. But there was a reason why other investors had been put off: massive investment would be required in transport and infrastructure simply to get the product to where it needed to be, and although this was a plague common on the continent, Guinea's returns felt rather too far away, so he didn't pursue that deal.

Instead, Motsepe continued concentrating on Lubambe, but its profitability was reducing as the company burned working capital trying to get the mine properly underway. ARM CEO Mike Schmidt called it 'a bleed situation'. Then the Zambian government threw a curveball: it decided to change its tax regime, and declared that the state-owned Zambia Consolidated Copper Mines was forthwith to receive 20 percent in royalties accrued by foreign companies mining there.

Motsepe was either angry or disheartened enough to request a 'heart to heart' in Lusaka with state officials to discuss such a significant change years after construction had started under a different understanding. 'This is not the time to slap on increased royalties,' he said in 2015. 'These are times when we should work together. When things are good and we make good money as an industry, we are prepared to review those royalties. But set the rules before we start and let's set them up in a manner that's good for you as government as well as us. Don't change the goal posts mid-stream. That's a no-no.'[1]

Lusaka decided not to listen, and announced that its royalties decision held. So ARM exited its investment, which had started out as a R6 billion project to develop Lubambe, selling its stake for about R1.5 billion to a private equity group.

Motsepe's attention seemed to turn after that to becoming a global competitor, specifically via a strategic investment Harmony had made in 2008 with Australian company Newcrest Mining in Papua New Guinea. The copper that had been found in its Wafi-Golpu gold prospect there was a major attraction.

The Harmony board under Motsepe's chairmanship had rejected direct and indirect offers for that asset, purchased for about R30 billion in 2011, as it believed 'disposal at [an] early stage of

170

development would not enable the full potential value'. That steadfastness paid off, and by 2022, Harmony was looking at making a profit in the southwestern Pacific nation.

Another international option had come about in 2011, when Motsepe went into talks with Indian industrialist and philanthropist Ratan Tata about financial services in India and minerals in South Africa, where the Tata Group was already a major foreign investor. That contact had come about through the India-South Africa CEOs Forum launched in 2006 under Mbeki and Indian prime minister Manmohan Singh. The forum was revitalised to boost business cooperation in August 2010, when Jacob Zuma held official talks with Singh at Hyderabad House in New Delhi while on a state visit.

While visiting Tata, Motsepe said South African businessmen felt 'very comfortable in India'. 'It's like home, and the same can be said about Indian businessmen in South Africa. We have got close to 2 million South Africans of Indian origin. We also speak very emotionally about the time Gandhi spent in South Africa. Those are very special, emotional relations.'[2]

Motsepe said he was 'confident of investing several hundred million dollars in India in the short term in financial services' in 2011,[3] but that seemed to really take place via Sanlam, which already had a 'wealth management' joint venture with Chennai-based conglomerate the Shriram group, and another with Delhi-based SMC Capital.

* * * *

By 2015, Motsepe was becoming interested in developing connections around the world through clean energy. The zeitgeist had shifted dramatically in that decade as the world lurched towards a dangerous edge with the environment under horrific pressure.

There was global support, with some signatories of the Giving Pledge having radiated into a clean energy grouping of their own that year. AREP's holding company Ubuntu-Botho Energy Holdings was cited as the only African company in partnership with the international investor-led fund Breakthrough Energy Ventures,[4] an initiative started by Bill Gates which aimed at zero emissions.

This grouping of philanthrocapitalists made a significant impact in 2015 at the historic 21st Conference of the Parties (or COP21) in Paris, where 196 of the world's leaders gathered for the most important climate negotiations the world had seen. The United Nations Framework Convention on Climate Change would have to reach an international agreement to limit greenhouse gas emissions and hold planetary warming below 2°C above preindustrial levels. As Facebook's Mark Zuckerberg put it, 'We won't be able to make meaningful progress on other challenges – like educating or connecting the world – without secure energy and a stable climate'.[5] The negotiations brought about the Paris Agreement, a legally binding international treaty, on 21 December 2015.

The 28 investors who attended were collectively worth an estimated R5.5 trillion (basically, the same as South Africa's gross domestic product – the size of the economy). Drawn from both the developed and the developing world, they included Gates, Zuckerberg, Tata, Britain's Richard Branson, China's Jack Ma, India's Mukesh Ambani, China's Neil Shen, Gulf prince Alwaleed bin Talal, Nigerian industrialist Aliko Dangote and Motsepe.

They had 'found a social outlet for their wealth'. 'Their aim [was] to push for a shift away from the production paradigm of 18th to 19th centuries' industrial revolution, and to create a more sustainable future driven by clean technologies.'[6] Gates saw business and government as essential partners as the climate crisis gathered frightening momentum.

This fitted in perfectly with Motsepe's belief that the two should work together. The South African government had its own priorities, however. The presidency under Zuma issued a statement ahead of COP21 in which it asserted South Africa's 'special responsibility' as the current chair of the Group of 77 and China – a coalition of developing countries that promoted its members' economic interests and created an enhanced joint negotiating capacity in the United Nations – and an active member of the African Group of Negotiators on Climate Change, established at COP1 in Berlin in 1995.

South Africa would have to advance 'the collective and shared interests of developing countries in the negotiations for the Paris Agreement', which necessitated defending their legal rights, 'including to receive the support they require to make the transition to a low carbon economy and to adapt to the reality of a climate that is already changing, and the loss and damage that is associated with this', Zuma said.[7]

Over the next six years, it became clear that without that support, developing countries like South Africa weren't going to meet the dreams of COP21.

Then came a breakthrough.

In the opening days of the COP26 international climate conference in 2021 in London, a financing deal was announced between South Africa and a consortium consisting of France, Germany, the UK, the USA and the European Union which 'aimed to support South Africa's just transition to a low carbon and climate resilient economy and society. Essentially a just transition is one where no one is left behind'.[8]

The multibillion-rand Just Transition Transaction (JTT) 'coal retirement' mechanism made international headlines, proposed as a way for South Africa – the 14th-largest contributor to global greenhouse emissions – to rapidly reduce nearly half of its emissions, and eventually end these.

The partnership intended to mobilise an initial R131 billion over the following three to five years, some of this in the form of grants and some in concessional debt finance, which was cheaper than commercial debt. Without this mechanism, it was believed, the country would be 'unlikely to deliver its full power sector decarbonisation potential'.[9]

Seizing the moment, Motsepe's AREP announced it planned to 'expand the pool of funding available for renewable energy developments in South Africa' in 2021, just as the country was also accelerating its plans to expand and diversify its energy base through government's Renewable Energy Independent Power Producer Procurement (REIPPP) programme. AREP already had a strategic stake in renewable energy solutions provider the SOLA Group, which had a portfolio of wind, solar PV and biomass investments in South Africa, which were part of the REIPPP.

Motsepe would have to reconcile a coal deal he'd made in 2005 as the black economic empowerment partner of the South African coal division of diversified Swiss-headquartered miner Xstrata Plc. And ARM had acquired even more of that company in 2006, with an agreement that a new coal mine should be built.

AREP's vision was, however, starting to dominate Motsepe's thoughts in 2021, and he wanted it to go further than just South Africa, planning to supply affordable electricity that could play a key role in Africa's economy.

The human resources Motsepe envisaged were networks of entrepreneurs and 'entities that have a history of empowering women, youth, rural and urban communities'. In terms of the 'private' power sector, AREP was working with 'several companies' on 'bespoke energy solutions'.[10]

In October 2021, a consortium named Ikamva ('the future' in Xhosa), led by global company Mainstream Renewable Power, was granted preferred bidder status for 12 of its projects under the

REIPPP programme. AREP was part of the Ikamva consortium's 100-percent African team of over 100 professionals.

Ikamva would deliver six onshore wind projects and six solar projects, including the first REIPPP project in KwaZulu-Natal. The wind and solar energy projects would produce about 4 500 gigawatt hours of green electricity each year, helping to avoid nearly five million tonnes of carbon dioxide emissions – the main driver of global heating – each year once fully operational.[11]

Although Mainstream owned 100 percent of the projects awarded in 2021, it announced that, at financial close, when it would have completed its work, ownership would transfer to an equity consortium, with 2.5 percent to 'community trusts'.

But an even more significant partnership unfolded in the 'just transition' space in 2021, when AREP and Absa launched their renewable energy investment platform, African Rainbow Energy, with Absa's target financing involving 'more than R100bn for environment, social and governance related projects by 2025'.[12] Absa had the track record, having already funded 33 projects representing approximately three gigawatts, which amounted to 46 percent of the total projects closed in South Africa by that time. Its renewable-energy loans amounted to R20 billion at 31 December 2020.

African Rainbow Energy would end up with approximately R6.5 billion of gross assets, covering 31 renewable assets, by 2022, 'making it one of the largest and most diverse independently owned energy businesses in South Africa'. It would be able to provide investors with exposure to utility-scale, industrial and commercial clean-energy investments, allowing it to 'seek [other] bankable projects in Africa'.[13]

* * * *

The billionaire showed that he would only do what he thought was best when he described his plans around coal, undoubtedly one of the most important issues in the world, in 2021.

Motsepe had been 'very excited' about prospects for ARM's coal business in 2013. Its production had increased sales to Eskom – the utility then generating more than 90 percent of South Africa's power – by 21 percent to 2.28 million metric tons,[14] and Eskom, which used coal for more than 80 percent of generation, was building what it was then hoped would become the world's third- and fourth-biggest plants.

But that excitement was gone, even though a 2021 report by the Council for Scientific and Industrial Research showed that 'coal continued to dominate the South African power supply, contributing 81.8% to the total energy mix in first half of 2021. Contribution from renewable energy sources totalled almost 11% (solar PV, wind, hydro, concentrating solar power, others) and zero-carbon energy sources, 14.3% (renewables and nuclear)'.[15]

ARCI would now be cleaning up its 50 or so investments, and coal mining was on the way out of its portfolio.

'The next 18 months, we think, signals a step change,' Van Zyl said at the company's results presentation in 2021. 'After a period of sustained growth acquisitions, it is really about pruning and capital allocation to assets that we think have more legs.'[16] ARC had 'decided to go lighter on mining assets', with the company intending to wind up certain operations partly because of environmental, social and governance concerns around coal mining.[17]

This gave Motsepe the edge in terms of the image he wanted to present. He wasn't an old-school businessman, but a philanthro-capitalist of the new world order. He wasn't attached to the ways he'd done business in the past.

There was, though, another aspect to all of this. In 2021, some of ARC's other 'cash-hungry assets' were 'expected to turn the corner', including its Elandsfontein phosphate mine on South Africa's west coast. Fertiliser is a lucrative business in Africa, and Elandsfontein contained 'quality phosphate rock' suitable for producing phosphoric acid, diammonium phosphate, monoammonium phosphate and single superphosphate, which are all critical to the modern plant nutrient industry.[18]

The background was that, in 2021, emerging African phosphate explorer and developer Kropz Plc had received a loan of R200 million from the ARC Fund to enhance the Elandsfontein project. Listed on the London FTSE and headquartered in London, the company would be majority-owned by Motsepe, who would have an 82.7-percent controlling stake in it. This was just as Kropz – which already had phosphate mining and exploration projects in West Africa – moved to become South Africa's second-largest source of phosphate rock for making phosphoric acid.

When Russia's agricultural products, which had made it a global producer, were banned in March 2022 after its invasion of Ukraine took horrifying effect, other sources of fertilisers had to be found. Elandsfontein was likely to 'enjoy advantageous freight rates to Brazil and the important markets in India, Australia and New Zealand' if it was a supplier.

But there was a catch. The ARC Fund would have to estimate a financial shortfall of around R135 million 'regarding the commissioning and ramp-up of Elandsfontein before first revenue could be achieved in the first quarter of 2022'. This was because the Elandsfontein operations passed through a significantly special area – the 'biodiverse and climate-change-resilient corridor which was earmarked for inclusion in the West Coast National Park'.[19]

A court case was inevitable, with the arguments representing some of the extreme moral, social and political challenges that would likely affect Motsepe's global energy and power acquisitions into the future.

It was already complicated before he'd bought shares. Kropz's mining right had been granted in January 2015, for an initial period of 15 years. The water-use licence was awarded in April 2017, also for 15 years. But the West Coast Environmental Protection Association believed its activities would disturb the nearby Langebaan lagoon, an extremely sensitive nature ecosystem, so it had applied to the department of forestry and water affairs' water tribunal to stop Kropz. This meant production couldn't commence at Elandsfontein until a decision was made by the courts.

Finally, in 2021, an urgent interdict application was filed in the Western Cape High Court by the environmentalists. Kropz, in turn, claimed there would be 'irreversible environmental damage done to groundwater if it was forced by legal action to stop pumping water from the Elandsfontein aquifer'. The company's spokesperson Michelle Lawrence said Kropz 'had [in fact] spent more than R6m on groundwater studies and the Elandsfontein aquifer was being responsibly managed'.[20]

When the company won, CEO Mark Summers said, 'The way is now clear for us to expedite production, creating desperately needed job opportunities for the local community, paying taxes and royalties and rewarding investors, local and international, who have supported us through this extended challenge of scientific evidence against human emotion.'[21]

Painful arguments such as this, which centred on the true impacts of capital even when business owners said they were doing their best to minimise danger to the environment and to people, looked set to deepen, and Motsepe would almost certainly find himself troubled by those debates as he expanded his portfolio.

* * * *

Throughout, Motsepe continued to use disruption to try out different angles. In January 2022, for instance, ARC backed Sun Exchange, a South African solar-panel and battery-storage project based at Nhimbe Fresh, a Zimbabwean fruit and berry producer, which was described as 'the biggest crowd-funded project in Africa'.[22]

It had raised about R21 million, initially through more than 1 900 individuals in 98 countries purchasing solar panels which would then be leased out to customers – and there were plans to expand in Africa. 'The approach [allowed] individuals to make a contribution to reducing climate-warming emissions with relatively small investments while still receiving a competitive rate of return. It also helped fill chronic electricity [shortages].' Soon, there were 35 000 investors from 180 countries with nearly R100 million raised.[23]

And there was a supposed additional attraction in the disruption: venture capital funds could invest and use blockchain technology. 'Individuals or other investors [buy] solar cells at $5 to $10 each, then lease them back – with investors being repaid over 20 years in either Bitcoin or rands'[24]. About 60 percent had apparently elected to be paid in the cryptocurrency.

Motsepe's views on this after the crash in cryptocurrency prices in May 2022 isn't known.

PART IV

Coming to the party

19

The post-liberation gospel: Keeping the ANC afloat

In February 2022, South Africa's Independent Electoral Commission dropped a bombshell. In accordance with the new Political Party Funding Act, donations had to be disclosed, and it was made known that Patrice Motsepe had spread his companies' funding across the country's five biggest parties, instead of serving just the ANC, as he always had previously.

Those deposits by Motsepe had coincided with the October 2021 local government elections, whose outcomes indicated dramatic shifts and disappointing results for the former liberation movement. Only its mighty stronghold, Limpopo – heartland of Cyril Ramaphosa, a mother-tongue Tshivenda speaker – was unaffected.

The ANC got R5.8 million from Motsepe, although it's not clear whether this was used to bail out its bankrupt Johannesburg headquarters, Luthuli House, in September 2021. There were rumours the party was broke, and owed SARS more than R100 million in tax, but this was denied by its treasurer-general Paul Mashatile, who said the ANC only had 'cash-flow problems'.[1] Still, it seemed that Ramaphosa, Motsepe and a small group of other wealthy ANC loyalists were essentially keeping the party afloat. 'Ramaphosa, in his personal capacity, made two separate donations of R166 000 and R200 000 [at the end of August],' a media report revealed.[2]

Motsepe's other donations were striking. Presumably for the first time[3] he gave money to the Economic Freedom Fighters (EFF), even though the party's leader Julius Malema had long castigated the businessman for his capitalism, his support of the ANC and his antagonism towards nationalisation. In 2018, on the occasion of the EFF's fifth anniversary celebrations, for instance, Malema had accused Motsepe of being 'a state capture threat' and claimed that Motsepe's interests in the state were being championed by Ramaphosa and Jeff Radebe.

'South Africa is a democracy. South Africa did not elect Patrice Motsepe as president,' Malema had railed. 'Patrice Motsepe must know his place. He must sit down; we are not Motsepe's people. Patrice is the brother-in-law of [Ramaphosa and Radebe]. They are capturing South Africa.'[4] 'We want to warn Patrice Motsepe, we are watching you the same way we watched the Guptas.[5] Stop doing what you are doing; it is unacceptable. South Africa does not belong to the Motsepe family.'[6]

Shortly before Motsepe's donation to the EFF was made known in 2022, Malema 'hinted that Motsepe was nothing less than an imposter pretending to be a billionaire'. This happened during cross-examination at the Equality Court, where Malema was testifying in a hate-speech case. 'I am not sure Patrice Motsepe is a billionaire,' Malema said. 'Sometimes I have [a] suspicion that [he is] an imposter.'[7]

Malema was, however, notably quiet about the R1 million his party received from Harmony Gold and the R1 million it banked from ARM. The two companies also each donated R2.1 million to South Africa's official opposition party, the Democratic Alliance, while smaller parties received between R200 000 and R300 000 each.

* * * *

The ANC's Reconstruction and Development Programme policy framework of the 1990s was touted as 'the result of many months of consultation within the movement, its alliance partners and other mass organisations in the wider civil society'.[8] In Mandela's words, '[It] was not drawn up by experts – although many, many experts have participated in that process – but by the very people that will be part of its implementation.' Those 'experts', crucially, included many white capitalists and corporatists representing outside Western interests.

Touting the Freedom Charter as a blueprint, the programme went through several drafts and incorporated numerous comments and proposals until it was regarded as enough of a manifesto to sell the ANC to the people for sufficient votes in 1994.

The ANC presented itself as humbled by having to introduce the Reconstruction and Development Programme under far-from-ideal circumstances – it had to share power with the National Party for the first three years in government – but said it believed it could do it. After all, it had the support on the ground that would help it succeed.

Then, rather more quickly than expected, the ANC indicated in 1996 that, with the best of intentions, the socioeconomic challenges were just too enormous, and it would have to access increasing amounts of capital from the markets which, it appeared, were more than happy to deliver at 'favourable' rates. That meant the Reconstruction and Development Programme was done and dusted without ever having been implemented, or even tested.

That was the moment at which the ANC's neoliberals outwitted the socialists and promoted 'growth' – 'the measurable increase in the output of the modern industrial economy'[9] – over development – 'a marginal effort of redistribution to areas of urban and rural poverty'.[10]

This sleight of hand saw the new macro-economic policy framework, Growth, Employment and Redistribution (GEAR), which was unveiled under Trevor Manuel, with Mandela and Mbeki's backing. The 'trickle-down' theory was quickly in charge, with the market to decide how to deal with poverty, jobs and inequality while it also took care of 'growth' and investment. Entrepreneurs like Motsepe who supported the ANC bought into the GEAR 'adjustment'.

In 1999, when Thabo Mbeki became president, he was looking for new partners favourable to the ANC. The access of such business partners to the upper echelons of the ruling party – and, in turn, their networks – would be incomparable, but their financial support would be required.

Motsepe was on the executive of the Chamber of Mines at that time, and the World Economic Forum had named him a Global Leader of Tomorrow, so it's no surprise that Mbeki identified him as a potential partner.

Motsepe was also the product of a new set of international trade rules which had come about in January 1995 when the World Trade Organisation said governments should be mindful of the actual people affected by global commerce. Those who were not, would not benefit from the subsidies and tariff reductions that were designed as incentives.

A founding member of the World Trade Organisation, South Africa was bound to these new international human-rights obligations, and so the ANC had to appear as if it was fixing the country's moribund economy by showing it was employing a range of protections for its people. But the ANC revealed over the next three decades that compliance was not necessarily a part of its mindset.

* * * *

In 2009, when Julius Malema was still president of the ANC Youth League, he'd insisted Motsepe was an enemy of the radical economic change described in the Freedom Charter of 1955. Malema had called for the 'nationalisation of Motsepe himself, as well as other wealthy black business leaders'. He said he believed that 'the transferring of ownership of mines from private hands to the state should not be seen as a complicated process', noting that government had 'already formed a state-owned mining company that is exploring for coal'.[11]

In response, Motsepe said he would support nationalisation or socialism 'if it benefited the people of South Africa'.[12] But he had a caveat, which he revealed a couple of years later. 'When I was asked to comment on nationalisation … I said that it is important that we ask all South Africans to make [an] input on the issue. Many of us have spent many years within the ANC dealing with this issue. I have said on numerous occasions that nationalisation's track record is very poor.'[13]

Motsepe would strike out equally at business in an interview with *Forbes* in 2011. 'Business should be caring about the welfare of their fellow citizens, just like it cares about share growth, competitiveness and the next dividend. But you must understand the culture of business in South Africa. For a very long time, business was growing and succeeding without regard for the needs of the people. When I sit with business colleagues, I recognise that there are things they don't understand. These are good people, mind you, but they were not brought up in a culture of having an obligation (to listen to the poor).'[14]

Motsepe said it was as vital for business 'to win over the hearts and minds of the people' as it was for politics, and that 'captains of industry [should reach] out to communities in the same way they go out to the market to convince potential shareholders to invest in their businesses'.[15]

Writing in 1997, the ANC's Pallo Jordan had said, 'The emergent black bourgeoisie should involve the elaboration of certain standards of conduct and a business ethic that will speed the realisation of the postponed goals of the national liberation movement. Such an element will constitute a "patriotic bourgeoisie"'.[16]

This is a central component in the Motsepe story, with academic papers trying to untangle how that seemingly graceful description, 'the patriotic bourgeoisie', pertains to him. There has been such a grouping in South Africa since 1948, when the National Party government promoted white 'ruling class unity' as much as white nationalism.

In June 2014, two American academics examined Motsepe's role in South Africa, finding that his philanthropy was 'an appropriate response to growing social economic and political inequalities' in South Africa. An institution like the World Economic Forum provided 'a platform for recognition of capitalist success while receiving absolution for capitalist accumulation by means of donation'.[17] But this didn't answer the question of whether Motsepe's generosity would 'speed the goals' of the national liberation movement.

The idea of the 'national democratic revolution' being pursued in 'phases' was how the ANC got its left wing on board when it was negotiating with apartheid's National Party at the Convention for a Democratic South Africa in the early 1990s. That 'phased' revolution has been the source of much uncertainty in South Africa since then. What it seemed to say was that the ANC would amass capital by way of a conventional free market, and initially forgo the public ownership that had been central to its programme while it was banned. That accumulation would continue until it had reached such a point of capitalism that the party could revert to the plan for a socialist state. Some in the ANC dubbed that Leninism, some called it Marxism, but it was believed to mean deferring, not denying, the transition. Basically, it was kicking the can down the road.

Western investors had insisted the ANC move away completely from socialist-style public ownership of assets or income equality if it was to secure their support. So the ANC softened its communist-leaning economic policies of the 1960s, 1970s and early 1980s, and accepted an internal ideological impasse which dampened the power of its alliance partners, the South African Communist Party and Cosatu. A divide widened, and most people on the left began to give up on the ANC ever watering its red roots again as it approached the 30th anniversary of South Africa's freedom in 2024.

Motsepe isn't on record expressing left-wing views or having socialist intentions, however, and it's unlikely he would 'speed the goals' of government planning over private ownership. He hasn't veered from the position that the private sector and government should be partners, and since he's in South Africa, that, in effect, means a majority black government should operate side-by-side with black and white business.

Many in the ANC preached a post-liberation gospel of neoliberalism, but that didn't seem to sit well with Motsepe, either. His increasing philanthrocapitalism indicated that he believed South Africans needed support as much from the private sector as from government. Those who were poor and without privilege would not simply be able to be consumers, and it would be unjust to expect everyone should get what they deserved from the free market. His philanthropy showed he believed the wealthy should give back to society.

Motsepe's funding of the ANC was in keeping with the view that strong cooperative links between business and government would only serve to increase wealth. This sounds, to an extent, like an oligarchy, although Motsepe preferred the more humanitarian American philanthrocapitalists' model, that the more money he made, the more money he could put back into society to change its course.

20

Guests of the president:
The patronage years

Politics had long tried to touch Motsepe, in sometimes curious ways, as was the case in May 2012 when he made headlines without breathing a word. Without any warning, Motsepe became part of the biggest story at that time in the country, as a political campaign pushed by a Zuma faction that would become known as the Radical Economic Transformation forces moved forward with force.

Motsepe's Twitter 'fan account' was the surprise lever, and the catalyst for a fight that went onto the streets all over South Africa was a painting by South African artist Brett Murray in his exhibition, *Hail to the Thief II*, at the Goodman Gallery in Rosebank, Johannesburg. The artwork, 'Spear of the Nation', which was created in the style of Bolshevik Russian posters of the Lenin era, depicted the president with his penis exposed.

In Europe or the USA, such an artwork might attract critical attention for how it captured the zeitgeist, or how it exposed the modalities of violent political protest, in shaping some irony for the piece. South Africa is, however, a conservative, patriarchal country with a poor public-education system, meaning its liberating constitution protecting freedom of speech served for nought in the over-reaction to the painting.

The purpose of *Hail to the Thief II* was to examine corruption and decadence in the Zuma era, and while there were many who acknowledged Murray's aesthetic, the president's supporters wanted Murray punished, even 'stoned to death'.

City Press, which published a photograph of the painting on its website, took extreme flak. Some members of the ANC called for boycotts of the newspaper and lashed out personally at the editor, Ferial Haffajee. The pressure on her to remove the painting from the website became ever more immense.

This is where 'Motsepe' came in. 'Don't expect a painted woman to remove a photo of a man with exposed penis, it helps her get through lonely nights,' read the tweet, posted by @PatriceMotsepe on 25 May.

Haffajee thought the tweet had been posted by Motsepe, and as they had a connection through having attended university together and being peers of the democratic public space, she reacted. 'The tweet that broke this camel's back was one by Patrice Motsepe, the businessman and soccer baron whom I have known since university and with whom I thought I had a congenial relationship ... It must have taken great anger to get a man I know to be of elegance and wit to get to such a point.'[1]

Then came the 'latest news in the ongoing Spear of the Nation saga': the tweet hadn't been sent by someone she'd known since university – but rather by his fan account.[2] Three days later, Haffajee tweeted, 'Patrice, the real, called to say @PatriceMotsepe is a fake. His lawyers are onto it. My apologies – it was being RT'd as if the real guy.'[3]

No further comment came from Motsepe. But the point about his impact had been made, with or without him.

* * * *

In March 2010, Motsepe had been named in *The Times* of London's 'Court Circular' column as having visited Queen Elizabeth at Buckingham Palace as part of a South African business delegation weighted towards supporting Jacob Zuma as president.

South African media said the 213-person-strong group was 'an eclectic mix of small entrepreneurs, mid-level executives from bigger companies and representatives of civil society ... [but it was] thin on captains of local industry – other than resource tycoons Patrice Motsepe and Lazarus Zim, Investec managing director Bernard Kantor, Thebe chairperson Vusi Khanyile, ArcelorMittal chief executive Nku Nyembezi-Heita and Netcare boss Richard Friedland.'[4]

Motsepe had always got attention when he appeared at ANC events. Without a history of understanding party funding during apartheid, when it was corrupt on a global scale, some South Africans assumed donors were also friends of the leaders. That assumption was costly for Motsepe when it came to Zuma, as he ran the risk of being associated with corruption linked to the former president in later years.

Still, it wasn't easy to ignore the R500 000 he paid to sit next to Zuma at a banquet for its elective conference in 2012 in Mangaung, Free State. 'Other business people [spent] between R25 000 and R350 000 to mingle with ANC heavyweights', and it wasn't only individuals among the 750 guests. 'Major private sector companies booked and paid for their seats [in advance] ... They included Absa, Standard Bank, FNB, Nedbank and Cell C.'[5] But Motsepe would inevitably be singled out.

He'd also been at the Gallagher Convention Centre near Johannesburg earlier that year, where a fundraising gala dinner opened the ANC's four-day policy conference. Zuma was said to have been in a lively mood as he addressed the more than 500 guests who included 'business people, party hacks, ministers, government officials [and] diplomats', as well as 'Indian, Chinese, Russian and Brazilian delegates' who had been at a BRICS colloquium held earlier.[6]

Motsepe and Moloi-Motsepe were at the top table, which was decorated with a huge ANC flag. Others at the table were Anglo

Platinum CEO Neville Nicolau, Graham Briggs from Harmony, and Mike Schmidt, Jan Steenkamp and Steve Mashalane from ARM. When pressed on how much ARM had forked out for seats at the table, organisers said they were 'guests of the president'.[7] Sponsors of the event included Emirates, Alexander Forbes and Nissan.

Some of the names of attendees at that gala dinner would appear again at the Judicial Commission of Inquiry into Allegations of State Capture, Corruption and Fraud in the Public Sector including Organs of State, better known as the Zondo Commission or the State Capture Commission, from 2018 onwards. Witness after witness there either implicated others or was implicated in 'preferred bidders' debacles, or in allegations of 'tenderpreneurship' and 'supply-chain mismanagement'. Hundreds of people and entities had gained entry to vaults of free money through massaging political favour during the R1.5-trillion mawing of the economy during Zuma's administration, and they were not all part of the black economic empowerment 'elite'.

But media analysts were clear that Motsepe, 'while instrumental in supporting the ANC and at the centre of power, [was] quite apart from the coterie of rich business associates', which included Sandile Zungu and Iqbal Survé – who had sat with Motsepe on the BRICS business council – as well as Black Business Council supporter Robert Gumede and Vivian Reddy, who the Motsepes knew from social events, such as then police minister Nathi Mthethwa's wedding. Also ubiquitous on such a list were the notorious Gupta brothers, Ajay, Atul and Rajesh, 'who [kept] Zuma afloat financially and [enjoyed] his patronage in return'.[8]

* * * *

In December 2015, Zuma delivered a rambling speech at a gala evening of the African Business Leadership Programme which was hosted by Motsepe and included on its guest list business leaders from at least ten African countries.

This was the night that Zuma precipitously fired his finance minister Nhlanhla Nene, replacing Nene with a little-known member of parliament, David van Rooyen, who was believed to be sympathetic to a faction of the ANC linked to the president.

An 'impromptu alliance' of ANC leaders and 'captains of industry' was assembled under Ramaphosa and the party's secretary-general, Gwede Mantashe. The business delegation included Bobby Godsell, Sanlam CEO Ian Kirk, Barclays Africa Group CEO Maria Ramos, Goldman Sachs' South Africa head Colin Coleman, Investec Bank's global CEO Stephen Koseff, FirstRand CEO Johan Petrus Burger and Imperial Holdings CEO Mark Lamberti. They presented a document itemising how, 'if Nene's sacking stood, the rand would continue its plunge, foreign investors would flee, the cost of borrowing by the state and state corporations such as Eskom and Transnet would become exorbitant, and inflation would soon hit the poorest people hard.'[9]

Once there was an unequivocal view, 'envoys' Zweli Mkhize, the ANC's treasurer-general, and Jeff Radebe, who was then minister in the presidency, confronted Zuma, who took 'less than an hour' to rethink the crisis he'd created. A new finance minister – Pravin Gordhan – was appointed, and Van Rooyen would forever be known as 'Weekend Special'.[10]

The day after that, however, Zuma was being 'commended' for his 'act of leadership' by the ANC's national working committee.

Motsepe wasn't happy. He gave politicians a tongue-lashing the following year, as even ARM's earnings had plunged. 'Speaking at the presentation of his company's financial results for the year to June, he said "politicians should not change rules midway".'[11]

* * * *

Within months of his election as president of CAF in 2021, Motsepe was the prize of a small group of lobbyists agitating for his consideration as an outsider for ANC president at the party's elective conference to be held in December 2022.

At the time of the announcement of this in December 2021, the divide between the rich and the poor in South Africa was catastrophically deep, those impacts threatening the future of the already-weakened ruling party. Institutional reform was being readied to allow independent candidates to contest national, provincial and local government elections after a Constitutional Court ruling against mandatory partisan affiliations in 2020. But there was a catch to Motsepe being backed to run for office, even assuming he wanted to: his supporters still wanted the ANC in power, only under him.

The group of 'concerned ANC members' who dubbed themselves the Unity 2022 Forum were mooting a changing of the guard. They argued that ANC support 'would dip below 40% in the 2024 national and provincial elections if the party [did] not change its face or president', and to avert this, Motsepe should become the next leader because he was a 'neutral figure'.[12]

The chair of the forum, Emmanuel Makgoga,[13] said, 'The ANC is in big trouble, and everyone can see that.' He and his group 'strongly' felt that Motsepe could 'rescue the sinking ship',[14] although Makgoga admitted that the group had not yet informed Motsepe of their intention.

Motsepe certainly had the capacity to draw supporters. Back in 2018, he'd attracted a small army of young fans when Sundowns had hosted Barcelona in Pretoria. That had made him 'a national hero on the streets of Twitter', with South Africans tweeps dubbing him the 'real president of South Africa'.[15]

But the ANC constitution doesn't allow an outside run on the office of party president. It stipulates that a person must have been a member in good standing for at least ten years before they can even be nominated for election to its highest decision-making body, the national executive committee. Details of whether Motsepe is an ANC member or not aren't known.

The ANC might, in any event, have scratched Motsepe off any list it had of possible leadership contenders in the future after he gave money to its rivals in 2021. He knew that information would go public. He didn't make the decision lightly. Hence, we could deduce that Motsepe may one day start his own political platform.

21

Perilous optics:
Looking into the future

The question of Motsepe's loyalty to the ANC has been central to his enigma – and never more so than when Cyril Ramaphosa became ANC president.

After Jacob Zuma was pushed to resign as ANC chief in early 2018 and the country's then deputy president Ramaphosa was sworn in, there was a rapid shift of gears. Ramaphosa took a 58-person business delegation, which included Motsepe, to Davos in Switzerland. Motsepe attended as ARM's executive chair, accompanied by his head of investor relations, Jongisa Magagula, and CEO Andre Wilkens. Moloi-Motsepe was there, too, representing the Motsepe Foundation as its executive chair.

The theme of that year's World Economic Forum annual meeting in Davos was 'creating a shared future in a fractured world'. 'Economic prosperity and social cohesion are not one and the same' was the message. Leaders had to 'rededicate' themselves to developing a shared narrative to improve the state of the world.[1]

And there was a different pressure on the South African team at that 2018 iteration: to 'turn global opinion of a junk status South Africa by pushing the story of economic stability and policy certainty'. The government under Ramaphosa was being situated as the custodian of another 'new' South Africa – the first one having been in 1994 – which would recover from the Zuma era and build a strong state.

* * * *

It's often mentioned that Motsepe and Ramaphosa are brothers-in-law in biographical information about Motsepe; articles critical of Motsepe, or fearful of the power he was amassing, even weaponised that fact.

Ramaphosa and Motsepe have been family since 1996, when Ramaphosa married Motsepe's eldest sister, Tshepo.[2] Two years before the wedding, Ramaphosa and Motsepe were both pursuing a future in business. With ten years in age between them, they had in common law degrees and an interest in mining – Motsepe from the point of view of buying mines, Ramaphosa originally representing labour as the first general-secretary of the National Union of Mineworkers in 1982, and then – after negotiating on behalf of the ANC at settlement talks with the apartheid regime – as a shareholder and board member, often the chair, of companies that traded in commodities such as metals or oil.

You couldn't miss Ramaphosa in the early 1990s. He was ubiquitous in his capacity of chair of the National Reception Committee, which coordinated the activities that followed Nelson Mandela's release – something that 'played no small part in elevating his profile, leading to speculation that he might be destined for greater things'.[3] Ramaphosa wasn't only in the support group around Mandela as he left Victor Verster Prison hand in hand with Winnie Mandela on 11 February 1990; he was standing next to Mandela when the newly released leader made his first public appearance on the balcony of the Cape Town City Hall.

The next year Ramaphosa became the ANC secretary-general at the party's national conference in Durban. 'With the ANC headed for the passages of power then, he was a man on the rise – smart, silver-tongued, passionate.'[4]

Ramaphosa was a member of parliament after South Africa's first democratic elections, and ANC secretary-general. He left politics in 1997 to move into business, first joining New Africa Investments Limited[5] and becoming its deputy chairperson. (He would also be chair of Anglo American and South African Breweries.) In 1999, he set about establishing his own company, Shanduka Group, as a black-owned investment holding company, building up a diverse portfolio of listed and unlisted assets, and serving on the boards of some of Shanduka's investees and other companies.

Nelson Mandela was among those who encouraged Cyril Ramaphosa's 'cadre redeployment'[6] to find donors – and become a donor to the party himself once he became rich, too – in 1996. The ANC knew its greatest chance of survival was to get its own boots into boardrooms to muster up cash reserves for itself in the private sector, and Ramaphosa was far and away its best cadre.

* * * *

In 2019, President Cyril Ramaphosa announced that the embattled state-run electricity utility, Eskom, would be unbundled into three separate state-owned entities – generation, transmission and distribution.

Motsepe had long struggled with Eskom's power cuts. He'd first expressed his anger about this publicly in 2015, saying that the power utility had 'let all of us down very badly'. Eskom had created mistrust between government and mine owners, he said, and he urged the state to 'intervene seriously to establish [it] as a competitive, cost-effective, reliable provider of electricity'.[7]

Lack of consistent power supply had placed his ferroalloys operation in Machadodorp on 'care and maintenance'. In comparison, his company ARMferrous was proceeding on schedule and on budget with Sakura, a ferroalloys project in Malaysia, where the power supply was reliable and where the government there and

Motsepe had agreed on a two and a half percent annual increase. Sakura also bought ore at market prices, which allowed it to reduce the ore more profitably. As ARMferrous's chief executive Andre Joubert pointed out, 'If you project that forward, in five years' time and ten years' time, and every year that goes past, Sakura just goes lower and lower on the cost curve'.[8]

After Ramaphosa's announcement about Eskom in 2019, Motsepe called a rare press conference to clarify issues around what he termed 'a major and serious perception problem', denying 'rumours that he would benefit in any way from [any Eskom-related] sale'. It was largely the EFF and its followers who had 'darkly gestured' at Motsepe on Twitter as a potential beneficiary of the unbundling, but the fact remained 'that it was legitimate – and indeed necessary – to keep an eye on the business activities of the President's former colleagues, friends and family members'.[9]

Motsepe was the first to admit that his links to political power in South Africa had sometimes seemed 'too close for comfort'. He conceded that at the press conference, saying 'relatives in very high positions in government justifiably [raise] perceptions of favouritism or improper conduct.'[10]

And it wasn't only perceptions of nepotism through relatives that had to be managed. Brian Dames, a former CEO of Eskom, was now the CEO of Motsepe's African Rainbow Energy and Power (AREP), and he had been included on Ramaphosa's Eskom Sustainability Task Team in December 2018.

'The optics of Ramaphosa selecting the boss of his brother-in-law's private energy company to advise Eskom on how to fix its energy problems [were], to say the least, strange'.[11] Acknowledging the conflict of interests, Dames resigned from the task team not long after he was appointed.

Motsepe showed that his investment in clean energy predated both Ramaphosa's and energy minister Jeff Radebe's appointments.

Further, he recorded that he had 'never supported the privatisation of Eskom or the sale of any of its assets, [meaning that AREP] would not be part of the sale of any entities or assets of any part of Eskom'. AREP's share of the department of energy's REIPPP amounted to less than 10 percent of the government's total investment.

* * * *

Around the same time, another family member, Motsepe's sister Bridgette Radebe, wife of Jeff, found herself at the centre of a political row between Botswana and South Africa, with her name linked to former Botswana president Ian Khama, who was the second child of Seretse Khama, first president of Botswana.

Like her brother, Radebe had business interests and family in Botswana, and when Gaborone-based media alleged she may know something about funding opposition to President Mokgweetsi Masisi, there were echoes in the highest reaches of the two governments. Masisi had succeeded Ian Khama as Botswana president in 2018, after Khama's ten-year presidential stint had come to an end. But Khama then said that appointing Masisi as his successor had been a mistake, and left the ruling Botswana Democratic Party to found his own party.

Botswana newspaper the *Sunday Standard* initially reported in April 2019 that 'Radebe, together with [aspirant Botswana presidential candidate] Samson Guma Moyo and [Botswana businessman] Shadrack Baaitse, [were] supposed to meet with Khama and a delegation at Victoria Falls on the northwestern border of Zimbabwe … not far from the Botswana border'. A rumour was created that discussions were planned there about money for Masisi's political rivals. Khama issued an immediate denial.[12]

Motsepe was embroiled in the brouhaha by the *Sunday Standard* when it suggested he was being investigated over links to alleged plans to fund the Botswana opposition's campaign.[13] Motsepe took no time at all to say he would sue for injury to his reputation, resulting in the newspaper being gagged.

The *Sunday Standard* had based its allegations on a meeting that Motsepe had apparently had with Khama at OR Tambo International airport in Johannesburg in April 2019. Motsepe's office didn't deny the meeting, but pointed out that he and Khama 'are old family friends' and 'shared strong family ties dating back to when both their fathers were at university'. The statement also took the opportunity to clear the air about the money: 'Dr Patrice Motsepe did not pay or contribute a single cent for political purposes or in connection with the presidential elections in Botswana. The allegations that he pledged [any money] to any political party or persons, or that he was involved in or was party to smuggling money into Botswana, are absolutely false.'[14]

But it was a battle that Motsepe was fighting on several fronts. He was also forced to take court action against South African politician Andile Mngxitama of socialist movement Black First Land First. 'At a press conference in May 2019, [Mngxitama] had accused [Radebe] of attempting to influence the politics in Botswana's ruling party. [Patrice] Motsepe then took issue with Mngxitama having alleged that his sister had ambitions to take over the diamond industry in Botswana and that she and Motsepe had together been involved in an alleged plot in the country to that end.'[15]

Mngxitama was ordered by the Gauteng High Court sitting in Johannesburg to refrain in May 2019. 'In his ruling, [the judge] also ordered Mngxitama to remove all injurious statements or references relating to or regarding Motsepe published on [the Black First Land First] website.'[16]

EFF leader Julius Malema then entered the fray in June 2019 when he tweeted that he believed there was 'a plot to remove the current Botswana government by some members of a powerful South African family'.[17] This revitalised memories of how Malema had been accused of calling for regime change during Khama's time in power in Botswana in 2014; he'd been disciplined by the ANC in the same year, with Botswana denying him a visa to enter the country.

Motsepe didn't take action against Malema, although he said that his family 'did not want to get involved, and have no interests, in the politics of Botswana or the development of any political party'.[18]

Bridgette Radebe hired Cherie Blair, a British barrister and wife of former British prime minister Tony Blair, to investigate the allegations against her; Blair found them null and void. Radebe also had the endorsement of South African former public protector Thuli Madonsela, who supported that finding. A press conference to that effect was held in August 2020.

By 2022, the matter seemed to be in the past for Patrice Motsepe, who shared a stage with President Masisi at the *Forbes* U30 Africa Summit held in Gaborone in the April. In his role as CAF president, Motsepe said they'd 'had a very good discussion'. 'We were exposed to the collaboration and assistance that the Botswana government is providing for the development and growth of football in Botswana [and] I want to thank [him] for his support and commitment.'[19]

22

Stakeholder theory: Disruption as a process

The World Economic Forum's first in-person annual meeting for more than two years took place in the Swiss hamlet of Davos in May 2022. Unlike in the past, when it had been held in January and 'the snow made it a winter wonderland, Davos [was] blooming in springtime. The drive from Zurich airport [was] a visual delight for visitors, with lush meadows and flowers, waterfalls and lakes'.[1] But if that sounded welcoming, it wasn't so to all.

'Davos', as that meeting has come to be known, is a very pricey and highly exclusive event. Unless you're an activist and plan to make your voice heard to the rich and powerful on a range of issues they don't necessarily want to ventilate outside, for free, you won't get in. Tickets cost R440 000 for individuals invited as company representatives, or, if you're a top-level forum member, your attendance is covered by your annual fee of about R9 million.

Patrice Motsepe is a member of the World Economic Forum's Board of Trustees, so it's unknown if or what he paid for his access, as that information is not publicly available. What's clear is that he buys into the forum's mission, which has been entrenched for 51 years, and is based on 'stakeholder theory'. This 'proposes that while a private sector entity's aim is to increase profits for its shareholders, it is incumbent upon the organisation to view the rest of society as having a stake in the company's actions ... Stakeholders such as ... the local and global community are to be considered in making key decisions'.[2]

Motsepe has articulated this position many times: he's a servant of the country who wants to give back to it, as he's been gifted support in his life. Hard work, not handouts, are the way to succeed. And the private sector should play a significant role in the economy, but this will only succeed if all South Africans – black and white – work together as equals.

* * * *

In May 2022, Patrice Motsepe was one of the world's wealthiest people. He'd achieved that through his own intellectual sweat, and refusal to stand down, and by surrounding himself with others who were very good at the jobs he was unable to do himself.

His ambition was to always set himself apart, and in 2021, in South Africa, he'd continued to do so by spread-betting his donations across the political spectrum. This meant that he was no longer backing the ruling party, the ANC, but rather backing 'democracy' – a government and its stakeholders interacting – as a concept.

'Democracy' is also the byword of the World Economic Forum, but it's far from victorious. Democratisation suffered reversals in 2021, with the percentage of people living in a democracy falling to well below 50 percent and authoritarian regimes gaining ground.[3] South Africa itself is considered a 'flawed' democracy, in which elections may be fair and free and some basic liberties honoured, but there are 'issues in the functioning of governance'.[4]

This sets a stage for Motsepe, who celebrated his 60th birthday in January 2022. If Elon Musk is 'maverick', Bezos the 'boyfriend', Ma a 'geek', the best single-word description of the richest black South African is 'disruptor'. And if, as American business consultant Clayton M Christensen notes, disruption is a process rather than an event,[5] Motsepe may be in the early stages of this process.

He's now a vice-president of FIFA, a global industrialist and an international philanthrocapitalist. Those worlds have certain features in common, but perhaps prime among them is the motive to make a profit. Motsepe, with his appetite for disruption, would be unlikely to remain satisfied at having proven that he can, indeed, make a profit and also plough some of that back into society to try and make a difference.

So perhaps Patrice Motsepe is biding his time, deciding the best way out of the tried (and untrusted) methods to date to influence and shape policy and markets, to approach the only really big prize left for him to take: the president's office in South Africa.

Epilogue

There's no such thing as 'lost glamour' in South African politics. We've had charisma, but we've never done 'glamour'. Our political beat was serious, and mystique would have been off-key.

But Patrice Motsepe's instinct has been to play that off-key beat to his advantage. Just when people thought they had a handle on him, he stepped to the side or the centre, or out of view.

* * * *

Take his boardroom. The African Rainbow Minerals (ARM) corporate head office in Chislehurston isn't in a glinting high-rise like other capitalist enterprises down the block in Sandton, Johannesburg, although you'll need an invitation to lightly crunch a stray leaf underfoot up the stairs to the entrance.

Small, secluded Chislehurston is one of the few suburbs in South Africa where there are similar numbers of black and white residents, most of them superbly wealthy. Commercial space is let for about R70 000 a month; average house sales are in excess of R10 million.

The late-afternoon sun shines up the leather chairs while the clock ticks. The boardroom opens on to a balcony where, doubtless, numbers of people with sway over power have watched Johannesburg's showy sunsets.

Culturally priceless Black Consciousness lithographs circle the main table. Similar pieces to these – black South African masters whose work typically fetches far less than white artists on auction

– have attracted a R6-million to R7-million price tag on auction at Bonhams in London.

I've been given an interview with Motsepe after months of to-ing and fro-ing, with this biography now in its final stages of completion. So far, he's a construction of research and curiosity to me. We've never met.

His discreet personal assistant pops in to say the chairman has been delayed and will be there in a few minutes.

The door soon bursts open and three men in dark suits and dazzling smiles make an entrance mid-banter. Two must be body-guards. Before I've had a chance to take it all in, they've greeted me, swept through the room and are gone, closing the door behind them. This takes less than a minute.

The third man is Motsepe – tall, friendly – offering his elbow in the classic covid-19 greeting, asking about refreshments and step-ping right into the moment before he sits down without taking off his jacket. Make no mistake, he's immediately a presence.

* * * *

In an interesting twist in his 60th year, Motsepe was the guest of honour at the South African National Editors' Forum (SANEF) annual general meeting in July 2022. Invited to describe his views on democracy through his extensive travel in Africa, which has exposed him to dozens of journalists, Motsepe grappled with a formal space he rarely takes up: he doesn't often talk closely with the media – if ever. He admitted as much during that unusual event, which was covered live on the national broadcaster. But addressing SANEF had clearly buoyed Motsepe, whose medium is less speech-making than stream-of-consciousness.

His first point of conversation for this interview in his offices in Sandton was that invitation from SANEF.

'*The Star*, the *Post*, *The World*. I mean, did you read the *Rand Daily Mail*?' This was the message he'd put forward to the editors, too. 'These were not only papers. You could be *proud* of them.' Motsepe asks how I feel about South African newspapers today. After a brief diversion along that rocky route, he wonders if some legacy titles haven't morphed into little more than 'a leverage to political access'.

Regarding our interview, Motsepe says people advised him not to open himself up to a lone journalist, but he quips that he's 'comfortable' with it. The time-limit is, however, specific. This is likely partly to do with Motsepe's draining schedule and partly to do with his presupposed narrative.

To get a word in edgewise will be tricky. He's skilled at that: being the raconteur who doesn't quite allow dialogue to develop.

Motsepe repeats something he said to SANEF – 'You know, I nearly went into the media … A group of us, Tokyo [Sexwale] and others' – and then he laughs, physically waving away the idea as if it's as momentarily offensive as a smoke cloud. He quickly remarks that some print titles in South Africa have become so toxic that he wouldn't touch them.

It's plain when you compare off-the-cuff comments Motsepe makes on various public platforms – business, philanthropy, football – that he has decided on singular messaging, for now. He avows non-racialism. He admires the creativity and talents of South Africans to survive under the harshest of circumstances. He believes that without job creation, the country is doomed.

Motsepe seemed tired at the SANEF AGM. His voice was dysphonic, scratchy, as if he had used it non-stop over several days and had also not got enough rest. The thing is, he doesn't use social media or write op-eds, preferring almost exclusively to communicate orally. It's unusual in an age of increasing distance between capital and the masses, and it must be a strain.

In this interview, he comes across as lighter. It feels opportune to ask Motsepe right at the beginning when he's going to have a conversation with South Africa about his political ambitions. After all, he spread his funding generously between major parties during the campaigning period for the local government elections in 2021.

What was that about?

He laughs. 'We've been doing that all along. It's just come out now [because of a change in the law around donor transparency], but for the past 20 years, [we've given] money to all political parties. The principle was, you know, we give money to everyone. It's in the public domain now and democracy requires that but, in fact, it was always like that. It's the best thing that can happen. It will keep everybody on their toes.'

Central to this is Motsepe's question to himself about how he could contribute back at the dawn of South Africa's democracy in 1994. He was his own person, with his own capacities, and he wanted to add value in the way that he could do best. For example, since he was not going to be a trade unionist but a mine-owner, he could support trade unionists in their work. This could be through harnessing empathy or financially, or both.

'People will say, you've got to be careful man, and I understand that, but it is also part of the promises I've made. Take Helen Zille. She sat here at this table ...' Motsepe pauses. He knows it might not go down well that he's had heart-to-hearts with the former leader of the Democratic Alliance (DA). Zille had anti-apartheid credentials, but also left a mixed legacy through her autocratic tendencies, hurtful, idle tweeting and acontextuality. And that he spent time talking to Zille isn't an indication of anything: Motsepe has been carefully creating his network since the late 1980s, meaning he's had a lifetime of relationships, friendships, bonds and links to people across the ideological spectrum – a position different to that of most capitalists. It would be foolish to label him too narrowly.

He says what's on his mind anyway: 'She is a good person deep down. It frustrated her that the ANC sort of took credit for what she thought were the DA's policies. But in my view, that's good for the country. In the end, people were having the same ideas about how to move South Africa forward.'

* * * *

Strong beliefs were instilled in Motsepe when he was a young child. His father, ABC Motsepe, was raised in the analytical practice of fellow students at Fort Hare who included ANC leaders Oliver Tambo and Govan Mbeki (father of Thabo Mbeki). The intellectuals whose ideas swirled in his father's imagination about a future South Africa were anti-imperialists and internationalists.

Named after Congolese independence leader Patrice Lumumba, Motsepe is proud of having had those revolutionary influences and regrets how ongoing discrimination conflicts with that vision. This applies to blacks from different language backgrounds, as well as to other races; he has even commented at public events that there are, for instance, too few white footballers in the big South African teams and the national team, Bafana Bafana. 'The greatest countries in the world are countries where there's been an assimilation, a coming together, a recognition ... that I can learn so much from [another person].'

Motsepe specifically mentions the impact that Gomolomo Mokae, a medical doctor, writer and political commentator, had on his development. Mokae is from Ga-Makopane, near to where Motsepe grew up in Pretoria.

A Black Consciousness advocate whose intentional multilingualism in public spaces is but one way he inhabits being African, Mokae had a marked impact on Motsepe.

'He is a very, very good example of a person who has been

steadfast,' Motsepe enthuses. He's especially proud that Mokae was taught by his father, ABC Motsepe. 'He's a great person; a top, top doctor. He was just wonderful.' Anyone who's met Mokae would have come away with two key elements: joviality and accomplishment – a bit like Motsepe.

He switches to Oliver Tambo, and emphasises that his family was close, and remains close, to the Tambo family, and that he would never abandon the ideals of 'OR'.

'It's not just about how important Oliver Tambo was. Yes, he was very unique, absolutely unique. But it's a deep personal and family obligation to keep his legacy alive.'

Tambo, who was a freedom fighter from his youth and the president of the ANC from 1967 to 1991, was virulently against a one-party state. He was also the voice of authority at the liberation movement's 1985 Kabwe Conference, where it was agreed the armed struggle should be stepped up since the apartheid regime's structural violence was continuing unabated. Tambo's instruction was to avoid civilian casualties.

Throughout, however, Tambo met with as many South Africans seeking reconciliation as he could at the ANC's headquarters in exile in Lusaka, Zambia. These included Afrikaner academics and businessmen, white corporate leaders, young black and white activists, representatives of workers and the left, global allies.

This was a tradition Motsepe admires.

* * * *

Motsepe's earliest memories play colourfully in his mind.

This is more than anecdotal. He seems to regard central characters from then as establishing his story today.

He goes back to when he started school at the age of 5, sent to a Catholic mission in Aliwal North in the footsteps of his older sisters Bridgette and Tshepo, to be educated in the way his parents wanted.

Most of the teachers were German nuns and priests, and Motsepe was motivated by the high benchmark they set for their charges.

'You get 80 percent, and the sisters are disappointed. You should be getting 95 percent. So you learn from them [as elders].'

Immediately, he makes the comparison with his own elders: 'Then you also learn from the African culture, for instance, that when your parents get old, you show them respect. You don't put them into some home. [Honestly], they make us better people.'

Motsepe is good-humoured when he relates how he was treated when he arrived at St Joseph's school.

'Of course, in the past there would be schools for blacks, Africans, coloureds, Indians and whites, and this mission school was for coloureds, so when we went there, they [said], "Look, as soon as [we] see your sisters, we can see they are the result of mixed marriages, but – Patrice?"

'I was much more black [in complexion] than I am now.'

It is the teachers' compassion towards the children in their care that he carries most profoundly.

'You know, the beauty is the love I experienced there, because a lot of the students there had parents [who were in interracial marriages] and, you know, this was a place created in the name of religion that brought us all together. Those experiences, of having those German and Irish teachers who give you so much love and so much commitment, shape you.

'I also think about Sister Majella Quinn and that culture [in my own village as a child], and that helps me to think we'll get over the racial issues.' Sister Majella is still resident in Mmakau, where she continues her community work as a Catholic nun.

The 'racial issues' to which Motsepe refers are not as benign in his private discourse as he makes them sound on podiums where he talks to these. He feels the ANC made an error in not appealing to white voters or, latterly, to Indian and coloured voters. He questions the party's allegiance to its non-racialism. 'I come from an absolutely rural family background, and I fully understand [why the ANC has concentrated on black South Africans], but the issue for us has to be about creating jobs, education, [decent] pay.' The ANC has to 'occupy the moral high ground, but it should also reach out to everybody,' he says.

In this interview, he situates himself firmly as a 'child of apartheid', and when asked about the criticism he has fielded from Economic Freedom Fighters leader Julius Malema, he briefly ponders if Malema's party 'is pulling us in this direction' – using 'racial issues' to ensure divides remain between South Africans.

But he doesn't pursue it. Instead, he says 'it should be about values – what you believe in, what you stand for – and if there's something wrong with the values, interrogate them, but you can never build a philosophy, a policy or an ideology at the heart of which is segregation, discrimination, alienation, division'.

'Some of the smartest people don't look like you. You simply need to be a better person. All of us have got a limited time, you know, and you can make your contribution only in such time or we're a disaster, we're too old.'

Motsepe is getting closer to a more definitive explanation for his early decision to widely fund democratic ventures, while remaining closest to the ANC for the longest time.

'It's not a secret any more that communism and socialism have not worked. Countries must create opportunities for their people, but of course the basis has to be democracy, free speech, free and fair elections, which allow you to realise your dreams. You can't have leaders putting their own impediments on you – that because you belong to this tribe or you speak that language or because you have the wrong colour, you can't get those opportunities.

For the last few years, I think, [we've been having] some political problems, but … you know, the voters speak. There must be some attempt to bring everybody together and let the people decide in terms of who they believe in.'

* * * *

Motsepe mentions major commercial projects between Limpopo and Mpumalanga's black and white farmers arbitrated by the Motsepe Foundation in partnership with AgriSA, the South African agricultural industry association. Worth at least R70 million, these were announced at the end of June 2022 after the foundation was able to unlock loans under similar repayment conditions to which Motsepe himself was able to acquire his historic loan via Bobby Godsell for his first mining operations in the 1990s.

The farming projects are expected to maintain over 1 500 jobs, impacting nearly 6 000 households.

Motsepe is over the moon about it – but it follows more than two years of on-off criticism of him, after he first spoke at a conference in Bloemfontein about a multibillion-rand fund to assist black farmers. He said on that occasion that land was a 'deeply emotional issue' and that 'you will never be able to take the politics out of [it]'. Then, averred his critics, he went quiet.

The fact is that building viable scaffolding for such projects takes time, and he won't be forced into doing anything half-heartedly.

'This country belongs to [the farmers] as much as it belongs to me,' he explains, noting that there also have to be 'guarantees' for white farmers to stay on the land, and not go and live in the towns or, worse, emigrate, which can happen if they have simply been compensated. His posture is that white farmers be properly 'encouraged to stay' because the option to leave is also 'not in the interest of the black communities'.

* * * *

Steeped in the theories of African decolonisation from his parents' era, Motsepe's views expanded as he grew up around people of his own generation who joined Umkhonto we Sizwe in the 1980s. Some developed, like him, into highly successful businesspeople over the 1990s and 2000s, their eventual berth as capitalists brokered by the ANC which – through no fault of its own – was the last movement on the continent to win freedom. Motsepe has especially warm memories about Nkululeko Sowazi, founder of Tiso Blackstar and chair of investments holding company Kagiso Tiso Holdings, with whom he went to school. Sowazi, who is today one of the wealthiest South Africans, was among tens of thousands of ANC recruits who fled abroad on the instruction of the leadership in the late 1980s, and who came home in the early 1990s.

In 2003, Sowazi's Tiso Capital was in a partner consortium to manage Two Rivers Platinum, which is today within the ARM stable.

The men first knew each other in boyhood in eSwatini.

'I loved Swaziland,' Motsepe says, about completing primary and high school and doing his undergraduate degree in the kingdom. He went to the University of Swaziland (now the University of eSwatini) before he decided on Wits for his LLB.

'All of the top professors whose books we read, whose books were prescribed, were there [at Wits].'

'[Esteemed scholar] Carole Lewis became a judge. World class, world class. Professor Michael Katz. World class.'

* * * *

The business aspect of Motsepe's life is the golden thread. He grins when he talks about the 'family enterprises – they made me what I am'.

Involved in rebuilding the old shopping centre that the Motsepes once owned and ran in his home village of Mmakau, he reflects on the people there who 'always have the passion to try and make a difference'.

'We have to create circumstances of hope and aspiration. I have been so privileged, immensely privileged. My father taught me that I should never stop working.'

He goes back to those childhood pictures.

'You know, I once came home from boarding school – I think I was 7 or 8 – and I said to Daddy, the children at school, most of my friends, get taken on holiday.' The Motsepe children had never been on holiday – when the other kids got the weekends off, the Motsepes were 'standing behind the counter'.

His father occupies 'a very big space', Motsepe says, and it's an opinion echoed by many leaders of the previous generation who hold ABC in the highest esteem. An example is former president Kgalema Motlanthe, who has spoken about the impact ABC had on him as an educator and an entrepreneur who never gave up.

'I had a beautiful unfair advantage,' says Motsepe, 'because, I'll tell you, [my father] taught me things at a young age that [matter, such as] always be part of the community. At times my school fees weren't paid and [yet he] would pay the fees of the students in the community. It was everything to him that people were educated.'

It's a tradition Motsepe has carried on in his own life, with the Motsepe Foundation paying for thousands of students to attend universities.

'When you are young, you don't understand it, and you [could] go through life and believe it's all about yourself. But you realise that's not correct, and you grow. If your community and your country doesn't grow, you're also retreating.

'It's so wonderful to listen [to other people]. We get inspired as well as people getting inspired by us. There's so many good people who say they will not give up on their country, and have that very real objective to build.'

Motsepe sees South Africa as a pivot on the continent. This is not so much a default as his unwavering belief. He doesn't despise people who emigrate, but he's confused about their inability to see the 'gifts' so evident in the country.

'[We have] to tell each other, this is not like any other country in Africa. We've got a real possibility at the moment to bring about generational multicultural and multilingual change, and these are in fact large things, but because they are somehow so difficult to put across, they [can feel like] small things.'

Enlivened by this will to 'South Africanise', Motsepe opens this out to the role the country has to play in the race against the climate crisis. 'Bill Gates calls me and says, "Listen, we're putting this Breakthrough Energy [grouping] together,"' he says, and before he knows it, 'I'm going to the COP21 in Paris.' That buzzed his brain into all kinds of new arenas.

Gates, who drew Motsepe in as one of the world's 28 high-net-worth individuals to be part of the initiative, identified Motsepe as an ally in the global south early on. Motsepe and Moloi-Motsepe were by that time already part of the billionaire's Giving Pledge.

For that, says Motsepe, Gates called him and said, 'We want a few families that will commit on a philanthropic basis,' and since the Motsepe Foundation was already active, with the couple's mindset tuned to contribute, Motsepe could agree to it immediately.

'At the beginning, it was $50 million. It's now $100 million.'

He pays tribute often to the everyday people who routinely deliver for their families and communities, against the odds, as compared to the macro-scope of being a signatory to the Giving Pledge. 'My message is, it doesn't matter. The way that I actually see it, it doesn't matter even if I give $100 million, there's an old lady who's got a grant, she's got R1 300 every month, and she gives some of her grants to her grandchildren or others, and because she does that for some time, she can't even pay for meat, she can't pay for vegetables. So those are the real heroes, because she makes a sacrifice. I give a big amount, but I'm still fine. My wife and children are still okay, you know. So those are the heroes we should celebrate.'

He circles back to Gates's environmental intentions, and says that too is 'part of our deep, deep commitment'. To an extent, Motsepe was primed to join capital's suddenly vigorous energy consciousness because of his childhood experiences: drought and heat, especially, affected survival in the area where he grew up.

Surprisingly, he seems star-struck when he talks about working closely with Leonardo DiCaprio and Matt Damon in their ecological endeavours. The three men met in the 2010s. Motsepe and Damon – whose focus is on water – were on the same programme at the Philanthropic Roundtable of the Victor Pinchuk Foundation in Davos in 2014.

'When it comes to Leonardo, initially I thought that's [just] Hollywood, but I was so impressed,' he says, pointing out that DiCaprio has recently drawn attention to the critically endangered mountain gorillas in Rwanda. The Oscar winner also supports the Virunga National Park in the Democratic Republic of the Congo, which is facing unprecedented threats.

He talks about the 'incredible experience' of seeing the gorillas, then adds, 'But that is about wildlife, and [we're also learning about how to get involved in protecting] life in the oceans, which is a good part of what they do.'

The spotlight on the environmental damage from Motsepe's mines will be unrelenting as he gains an increasingly larger space in energy provision in the future. He says he's trying to face that head-on because 'mines and many other industries [are big polluters]'.

'Making sure that [we] know this target of [limiting warming to] 1.5°C must be 'at the heart' of business, he says. High standards should be set from the moment a business plan is drafted.

It's encouraging that there are now 'so many initiatives' to claw the planet back to sustain human life. But to Motsepe's mind, 'the ones that are doing the incredible work' can be found at the World Economic Forum. He believes he benefits from being 'part of that process', where the attention is on climate change and 'how they are going to contribute' to maintaining standards around emissions. It's centred on excellence – the summit being the same for all, 'to make the world a better place'.

His thoughts turn to other billionaires who he believes are also giving this their best shot – like Johann Rupert, because 'he's with the heart and soul of Africa'. He won't hear a bad word about Rupert. He even tilts his hat at Rupert's father, Anton Rupert, despite the mangle of arguments against them.

* * * *

Camaraderie, shared goals – these are drivers for Motsepe. Those were what saw him go into co-owning the Blue Bulls with Johann Rupert so they could find common ground – in this case, behind the H-shaped uprights.

Motsepe relates a story that he also told at the SANEF meeting, about when the Springboks won the Rugby World Cup in 1995.

'That evening, I had to go to Soweto because I had to give my aunt money … there was some kind of a family event.' And there were people out on the streets, shouting and dancing, which was not the conventional reaction in the place where he was born.

'Rugby is not something that blacks in that part of the world had anything to do with. Look at what sports has done. It's brilliant.'

The reaction to the victory overturned Motsepe's expectations, and he keeps searching for more opportunities for that to happen.

He lights up remembering how he came up with the name Business Unity South Africa when he was involved in the negotiations for a new chamber in the early 2000s. He says he was on his way back from the airport and saw a sign for Unity College – and 'I said, "I've got it!" I wanted something that gave us that feeling about being united, everything is united. Positive, optimistic.' These are among Motsepe's favourite words.

Unexpectedly, he asks why I wanted to write a biography about him. He isn't an activist – he's never claimed that title – and he embraces integrity; try find dirt on him, and you could be digging for a long time. 'There are more exciting and more interesting things for people to read and learn about,' he says.

He talks about *A Life Too Short*, the biography of Chris Hani that Beauregard Tromp and I completed in 2009, and which was also published by Jonathan Ball.

'We have an everlasting obligation to these people … It's weird in South Africa that the exceptional person that was Nelson Mandela is almost more appreciated outside this country,' says Motsepe.

'Hani, too, was exceptional. We have to explore this more and more because we're a country that struggled with where we were, ideologically.'

He pauses, because this is a sore point. His generation of black leaders who moved into corporate boardrooms have been targeted as sell-outs. But of what? His cross-funding has always included workers' federations, not to polish his image, but for fairness.

'I had to address about 10 000 mineworkers in the 1990s, because we were buying these mines that were old, unprofitable, marginal, and were going to be closed. A part of my issue was always to talk to the mineworkers, but more importantly, to hear from them, because you learn so much from people's own statements of what their life is like.

'As the management [I wanted to know] what are the problems, what did we do wrong, what must we improve on, you know, because those things are key to me. So then, they [can also] ask you questions and give you their comments.

'In management, the best ideas on how to make the mines more profitable' often come from the mineworkers, and so, as they presented it, 'the plan was, we would pay them all based on performance. If we make more money, we share the money with them. That's a basic principle of bonuses.'

He adds, 'You know, you were talking about me being a mentor, and what I must say to you is that there are millions of mentors. At times, people credit me with good ideas when they were not my ideas; those were the ideas I had the privilege of getting exposed to in a meeting with other people who are either smarter or more educated, and sometimes even ordinary.

'There are so many good, exceptional people, and what we should try and do is just keep encouraging as many as possible to pursue their dreams because they also encourage and motivate us.

We all go through times in our lives when you know things will work out and when you're pretty motivated, and then we go through times when something we've been struggling with is just not succeeding, and you need to have courage. This is part of the culture.'

* * * *

That night, Motsepe is flying to the UK. He's hoping to be able to spend time after the trip with one of his sons at Harvard, a premier institution, but the nightmare of trying to get a visa for the US, with its post-covid backlog, has hindered that. If that is a taste of the glamour that South Africa has been lacking in its leadership, it's fairly slender.

Motsepe is, instead, surprised not only that he's 'interesting' enough for a biography, but also that anything much could be uncovered about him. He says he's dedicated to keeping a closed and private world, but he's gracious. It's been a friendly encounter.

A few days after this interview, I have a chance meeting with a prominent left-wing academic and activist, who brings a lovely story to light.

In the early 1990s, when Cosatu and the SACP still occupied offices on the verge between the Johannesburg CBD and Braamfontein, he had a key post within those organisations. From an upper floor, he would often see a shiny new sports car arrive and park in the street, and its occupant, a beautifully suited young black man, step into the building.

When he asked around about this visitor, he learned it was Patrice Motsepe, there to see compatriots in the National Union of Metalworkers and the National Union of Mineworkers. After spending some time in the building, Motsepe would jump into his car again and zoom away – until the next time.

That, of course, is the bizarre nature of this. You can never quite put your finger on what it's all about. The only certainty is that the next chapter about Motsepe is coming, and only he knows what stories it will tell.

Patrice Motsepe's shareholdings[1]	
Sports franchises	Mamelodi Sundowns Blue Bulls
Ubuntu-Botho Investments	Sanlam
African Rainbow Capital	Alexander Forbes Colourfield INfund Solutions Khumo Capital Lima Mbeu Portfolium QED Sanlam 3rd Party Asset Management A2X Alternative Prosperity Bravura Constellation Capital EdgeGrowth Ooba Sinayo AI Fund TymeBank TymeGlobal African Rainbow Life EBS International LifeCheq Rand Mutual Holdings Capital Legacy Indwe Afrocentric National Health Services Smart Health Investments Acorn Agri & Food RSA Subtropico ARC Real Estate

	ARC Property Development
	Barlow Park
	Majik
	Val de Vie
	MetroFibre
	Rain
	Autoboys
	Bluespec
	Capital Appreciation
	EOH
	GemCap
	Humanstate
	Afrimat
	GAM
	Kropz Group
	Last Mile Fund
	ARC Investments
	ARCH Emerging Markets Partners Limited
	Fledge Capital
African Rainbow Minerals	Modikwa
	Two Rivers
	Nkomati
	Khumani
	Beeshoek
	Nchwaning
	Gloria
	Cato Ridge
	Cato Ridge Alloys
	Sakura
	Machadodorp
	Participative Coal Business
	Harmony Gold
African Rainbow Energy and Power	African Rainbow Energy and Power

References

702. 29 March 2022. 'ANC is tax compliant, the R102-million Sars debt is an old story – Mashatile'. https://www.702.co.za/articles/441880/anc-is-tax-compliant-the-r102-million-sars-debt-is-an-old-story-mashatile

Absa. 6 August 2021. 'African Rainbow Energy and Absa launch investment platform'. https://www.absa.co.za/media-centre/press-statements/2021/african-rainbow-and-absa-launch-a-renewable-energy-investment-platform/

Adams, S. 6 March 2008. 'The Prince of Mines'. Forbes. https://www.forbes.com/forbes/2008/0324/088.html?sh=12ea68ad3afe

African Rainbow Minerals. 2008. Annual Report. https://www.arm.co.za/archive/files/annual/2008/default.htm

Alaka, J. 26 April 2022. 'CAF President urges African businesses, governments to invest in football'. Premium Times. https://www.premiumtimesng.com/sports/football/526063-caf-president-urges-african-businesses-governments-to-invest-in-football.html

Al Mouahidi, K. 4 March 2021. 'Election to the CAF: the clarification of Jacques Anouma from Côte d'Ivoire'. MedAfricaTimes. https://medafricatimes.com/22667-election-to-the-caf-the-clarification-of-jacques-anouma-from-cote-divoire.html

Amanze, J. n.d. 'Motsepe, Cuthbert Alban Ramasodi'. Dictionary of African Christian Biography. https://dacb.org/stories/botswana/motsepe-cuthbert/

AP News. 13 October 2021. 'French football league opposes plans for biennial World Cup'. https://apnews.com/article/soccer-sports-europe-france-fifa-3c9fe2f628fddde1c2381533f0b2e93d

Associated Press. 19 May 2021. 'Saudi Arabia formally proposes World Cups every two years'. ESPN. https://africa.espn.com/football/fifa-world-cup/story/4389476/saudi-arabia-formally-proposes-world-cups-every-two-years

Bailey, S. 31 July 2002. 'Godsell, Motsepe call for empowerment calm'. AllAfrica. https://allafrica.com/stories/200208010502.html

Baleka, M. 12 March 2021. 'There is so much to admire about Patrice Motsepe, says Norman Arendse'. IOL. https://www.iol.co.za/sport/soccer/africa/there-is-so-much-to-admire-about-patrice-motsepe-says-norman-arendse-bbcd073e-715a-4c4b-9623-337e3ba5ffef

Baloyi, C, Khoza, N and Ndebele, S. 12 March 2021. 'Motsepe told: prioritise African unity, TV rights deal'. SowetanLive. https://www.sowetanlive.co.za/sport/soccer/2021-03-12-motsepe-told-prioritise-african-unity-tv-rights-deal/

Barnard, M. 2015. 'The Motsepe Ethic: An exploration of the role of the BEE power elite'. Research Report, University of the Witwatersrand. https://wiredspace.wits.ac.za/jspui/bitstream/10539/18389/2/the%20motsepe%20ethic%20final%20sub.pdf

Basson, A. 5 March 2010. 'Crony capitalists on JZ's coat-tails'. Mail&Guardian. https://mg.co.za/article/2010-03-05-crony-capitalists-on-jzs-coattails/

REFERENCES

Battersby, J. 24 December 2015. 'Brilliant: John Battersby unpacks Nenegate, Jacob Zuma's greatest blunder'. Fin24. https://www.news24.com/Fin24/brilliant-john-battersby-unpacks-nenegate-jacob-zumas-greatest-blunder-20151224

BBC Africa. 6 April 2022. 'Afcon 2023: Ivory Coast progress "reassures" CAF president Patrice Motsepe'. https://www.modernghana.com/sports/1150136/afcon-2023-ivory-coast-progress-reassures-caf.html

BBC News. 24 January 2020. 'Patrice Motsepe's "Africa loves Trump" comment divides opinion'. https://www.bbc.com/news/world-africa-51235485

BBC Sport. 31 March 2022. 'FIFA did not propose biennial World Cup'. https://www.bbc.com/sport/football/60937907

Billebault, A. 13 July 2021. 'Football: Heads have been rolling ever since South Africa's Patrice Motsepe arrived at the CAF'. The Africa Report. https://www.theafricareport.com/107602/football-heads-have-been-rolling-ever-since-south-africas-patrice-motsepe-arrived-at-the-caf/

Bishop, C. 2017. *Africa's Billionaires: Inspirational stories from the continent's wealthiest people.* Penguin Books.

Blignaut, M. 10 July 2018. 'Move over Cyril! Patrice Motsepe dubbed SA's new president after booking Beyoncé'. Briefly. https://briefly.co.za/14098-move-cyril-patrice-motsepe-dubbed-sas-president-booking-beyonce.html

Bloomberg News. 26 February 2013. 'Motsepe: Mining assets are a good buy'. IOL. https://www.iol.co.za/business-report/companies/motsepe-mining-assets-are-a-good-buy-1477329

Bloomberg. 27 January 2022. 'Bitcoin-paying South African solar company plans expansion'. BusinessTech. https://businesstech.co.za/news/energy/553494/bitcoin-paying-south-african-solar-company-plans-expansion/

Bond, D. 28 October 2011. 'FIFA criticised after TV rights handed to Sepp Blatter's nephew'. BBC. https://www.bbc.com/sport/football/15497214

Brummer, S. 28 January 2000. 'Granite mining scars Bakgatla village'. Mail&Guardian. https://mg.co.za/article/2000-01-28-granite-mining-scars-bakgatla-village/

Burger, S. 3 November 2021. 'Ikamva consortium to build 1.27 GW of new wind, solar in South Africa'. Engineering News. https://www.engineeringnews.co.za/article/ikamva-consortium-to-build-127-gw-of-new-wind-solar-in-south-africa-2021-11-03

BusinessTech. 18 January 2018. 'Here's the full list of South Africans going to Davos in 2018'. https://businesstech.co.za/news/business/219819/heres-the-full-list-of-south-africans-going-to-davos-in-2018/

BusinessTech. 1 September 2020. 'Patrice Motsepe on encouraging investment – and why he won't leave South Africa'. https://businesstech.co.za/news/business/430494/patrice-motsepe-on-encouraging-investment-and-why-he-wont-leave-south-africa/

Buthelezi, L. 2 November 2020. 'Battle of the stock exchanges: A2X's plans to take JSE's market share. Fin24. https://www.news24.com/fin24/markets/battle-of-the-stock-exchanges-a2xs-plans-to-take-jses-market-share-20201102

Buthelezi, L. 14 September 2021. 'Motsepe's African Rainbow Capital to exit Metrofibre and coal mining as it "prunes" portfolio. News24. https://www.news24.com/fin24/companies/motsepes-african-rainbow-capital-to-exit-metrofibre-and-coal-mining-as-it-prunes-portfolio-20210914

CAF Online. 10 December 2016. 'Billiat out to make the Sundowns shine'. https://www. cafonline.com/news-center/news/billiat-out-to-make-the-sundowns-shine

CAF Online. 23 April 2021. 'President Motsepe takes his office at CAF headquarters'. https://www.cafonline.com/news-center/news/caf-president-dr-patrice-motsepe-holds-key-meetings-in-cairo

Cantwell, L. 2015. 'Chiefly Power in a Frontline State: Kgosi Linchwe II, the Bakgatla and Botswana in the South African Liberation Struggle, 1948–1994'. *Journal of Southern African Studies*, 41(2)

Cape Argus. 22 December 2008. 'Motsepe slates coach Michel for no-show'. https://www. iol.co.za/capeargus/sport/motsepe-slates-coach-michel-for-no-show-596739

Cele, S. 29 July 2018. 'SA does not belong to the Motsepe family – Malema'. City Press. https://www.news24.com/citypress/news/sa-does-not-belong-to-the-motsepe-family-malema-20180729

Channel24. 26 March 2017. 'Dr Precious Moloi-Motsepe celebrates a decade of fashion with AFI'. Yahoo!News. https://uk.news.yahoo.com/dr-precious-moloi-motsepe-celebrates-decade-fashion-afi-074809389.html

Chauke, A. 22 September 2011. '"Racial discord bad for business": Motsepe'. TimesLive. https://www.timeslive.co.za/news/south-africa/2011-09-22-racial-discord-bad-for-business-motsepe-/

Chikamhi, E. 7 February 2022. 'Zimbabwe: Proposed African Super League excites Dynamos'. AllAfrica. https://allafrica.com/stories/202202070169.html

Chukwu, S. 13 March 2021 'Motsepe cannot shake off FIFA influence, but he can succeed with CAF governance reform'. Goal. https://www.goal.com/en-za/news/motsepe-cannot-shake-off-fifa-influence-but-he-can-succeed/1q1rtp85mp5rk1uol62jq1lxjz

Cilliers, C. 9 June 2019. 'Malema promises to speak about "powerful SA family" in Botswana "plot" against government. The Citizen. https://www.citizen.co.za/news/south-africa/politics/2141020/malema-promises-to-speak-about-powerful-sa-family-in-botswana-plot-against-government/

City Press. 25 April 2010. 'Miners fail to meet BEE targets'. Fin24. https://www.news24. com/fin24/miners-fail-to-meet-bee-targets-20100425

Claassens, A. 2019. 'Mining magnates and traditional leaders: the role of law in elevating elite interests and deepening exclusion 2002-2018'. Mistra. https://mistra.org.za/wp-content/uploads/2019/10/Aninka-Claassens_-Working-Paper_Final.pdf

CNBCAfrica. 16 May 2021. 'Rwandan President praises new mindset for African football'. https://www.cnbcafrica.com/2021/rwandan-president-praises-new-mindset-for-african-football/

Cobbett, E and Friesen, E. 2014. 'Motsepe's Gift: or how Philanthropy serves Capitalism in South Africa'. *Selected Themes in African Political Studies: Political Conflict and Stability*. Springer.

Cobley, AG. 1986. '"On the shoulders of giants": The black petty bourgeoisie in politics and society in South Africa, 1924 to 1950'. Thesis. University of London. https://eprints.soas. ac.uk/33865/1/11010655.pdf

Collins, N. 7 January 2017. 'Goodbye Dolly! Why South Africa's shining talent must go to Europe, before it's too late'. Neal and Pray. http://neal-collins.blogspot.com/2017/01/goodbye-dolly-why-south-africas-shining.html

Conn, D. 16 March 2017. 'Issa Hayatou deposed after 29 years as CAF president by Ahmad Ahmad'. The Guardian. https://www.theguardian.com/football/2017/mar/16/issa-hayatou-caf-president-ahmad-ahmad-madagascar-fa-fifa

Cotterill, J, Massoudi, A and Blitz, R. 10 February 2015. 'Dalian Wanda buys Sepp Blatter nephew's sports rights agency'. Financial Times. https://www.ft.com/content/92157ce8-b070-11e4-a2cc-00144feab7de

Creamer, M. 9 December 2009. 'Mine nationalisation okay if good for South Africa – Patrice Motsepe'. Mining Weekly. https://www.miningweekly.com/article/mine-nationalisation-okay-if-good-for-south-africa-patrice-motsepe-2009-12-09

Creamer, M. 16 March 2015. 'ARM's Motsepe urges serious govt intervention on Eskom let down'. Polity. https://www.polity.org.za/article/arms-motsepe-urges-serious-govt-intervention-on-eskom-let-down-2015-03-16

Creamer, M. 7 September 2018. 'ARM mulling "very exciting" growth opportunities – Motsepe'. Engineering News. https://www.engineeringnews.co.za/article/arm-mulling-very-exciting-growth-opportunities-motsepe-2018-09-07/rep_id:4136

CSIR. 5 August 2021. 'CSIR releases power sector statistics for first-half of 2021'. https://www.csir.co.za/csir-releases-power-sector-statistics-first-half-2021

Daniel, L. 3 May 2021. 'President Ramaphosa's Ankole cattle just sold for R2.7 million – with bull "Mufasa" voted best'. Business Insider SA. https://zambezinews24.com/president-ramaphosas-ankole-cattle-just-sold-for-r2-7-million-with-bull-mufasa-voted-best/

Davis, R. 22 February 2019. 'It is perfectly legitimate to scrutinise Ramaphosa's business buddies during his presidency – here's why'. Daily Maverick. https://www.dailymaverick.co.za/article/2019-02-22-it-is-perfectly-legitimate-to-scrutinise-ramaphosas-business-buddies-during-his-presidency-heres-why/

De Ionno, P. 18 June 2000. 'R500m proposal for the fostering of junior mining sector'. IOL. https://www.iol.co.za/business-report/companies/r500m-proposal-for-the-fostering-of-junior-mining-sector-794324

Dillon, K. 4 February 2020. 'Disruption 2020: An interview with Clayton M. Christensen'. MITSloan Management Review. https://sloanreview.mit.edu/article/an-interview-with-clayton-m-christensen/

Ditlhobolo, A. 1 October 2020. 'Pitso Mosimane's top 10 moments as Mamelodi Sundowns coach'. Goal. https://www.goal.com/en/lists/pitso-mosimanes-top-10-moments-as-mamelodi-sundowns-coach/12hwn1mxp1prp1ngshougaey23

Dolan, KA. 16 November 2011. 'Africa's 40 Richest: 2011'. Forbes. https://www.forbes.com/sites/kerryadolan/2011/11/16/africas-40-richest/

Drum Digital. 22 February 2013. 'Minister of police Nathi Mthethwa weds'. News24. https://www.news24.com/drum/News/minister-of-police-nathi-mthethwa-weds-20170728

Dube, M. 5 December 2021. 'Motsepe's mine in reparation row'. Mail&Guardian. https://mg.co.za/news/2021-12-05-motsepes-mine-in-reparation-row/

Duda, T. 5 April 2017. 'Op-Ed: Communal land belongs to the people, not to the chiefs'. Daily Maverick. https://www.dailymaverick.co.za/article/2017-04-05-op-ed-communal-land-belongs-to-the-people-not-to-the-chiefs/

Du Plessis, C. 26 June 2012. 'Zuma in jovial mood at glamorous ANC fund-raising event'. The Witness. https://www.news24.com/amp/witness/archive/Zuma-in-jovial-mood-at-glamorous-ANC-fund-raising-event-20150430

Du Plessis, C. 29 November 2019. 'Court stops Botswana paper from publishing negative stories about Patrice Motsepe'. Daily Maverick. https://www.dailymaverick.co.za/article/2019-11-29-court-stops-botswana-paper-from-publishing-negative-stories-about-patrice-motsepe/

Economist Intelligence (EIU). 13 May 2022. 'Democracy Index 2021'. https://www.eiu.com/n/campaigns/democracy-index-2021/

Edwards, P. 14 January 2021. 'How CAF went from stopping Hayatou's pension to honouring him'. BBC. https://www.bbc.com/sport/africa/55654829

Edwards, P. 8 March 2021. 'Motsepe to become CAF president as Ahmad appeal fails'. BBC Sport Africa. https://www.bbc.com/sport/africa/56323524

Ehlers, A. 2015. 'The Helpmekaar: Rescuing the "volk" through reading, writing and arithmetic, c.1916-c.1965'. *Historia*, 60(2)

eNCA. 18 April 2018. 'DA welcomes Johan van Zyl's resignation from Steinhoff board'. https://www.enca.com/money/da-welcomes-johan-van-zyls-resignation-from-steinhoff-board

Engineering News. 14 April 2011. 'Seize Brics opportunities – Zuma implores SA business'. https://www.engineeringnews.co.za/print-version/seize-brics-opportunities-zuma-implores-sa-business-2011-04-14

Engineering News. 8 April 2020. 'Amendments to the Mineral and Petroleum Resources Development Regulations'. https://www.engineeringnews.co.za/article/amendments-to-the-mineral-and-petroleum-resources-development-regulations-2020-04-08

Environmental Justice Atlas. n.d. 'Anglo American Platinum Modikwa Mine in Maandagshoek, Limpopo, South Africa'. https://ejatlas.org/conflict/modiwa-platinum-mine-in-maandagshoek-limpopo-south-africa

Eyewitness News. 26 January 2022. African football boss blames closed gate for Cup of Nations tragedy'. https://ewn.co.za/2022/01/26/african-football-boss-blames-closed-gate-for-cup-of-nations-tragedy

Fakude, E. 4 December 2019. 'Five reasons Pitso will stay with Downs'. Kickoff. https://www.kickoff.com/news/articles/south-africa-news/categories/news/premiership/five-reasons-pitso-mosimane-wants-to-renew-his-mamelodi-sundowns-contract/668795

Fakude, E. 14 December 2020. 'Diouf: Downs among biggest in the world'. Kickoff. https://www.kickoff.com/news/articles/south-africa-news/categories/news/premiership/el-hadji-diouf-explains-attendance-at-mamelodi-sundowns-50th-anniversary-event/691113

Fashion4Development. n.d. 'Agents of change: Dr Precious Moloi-Motsepe' http://www.fashion4development.com/dr-precious

Faver, D. 29 April 2022. 'Rulani's challenge To Chiefs, Pirates: We need stronger rivals'. Soccer Laduma. https://www.soccerladuma.co.za/news/articles/local/categories/mamelodi-sundowns/rulani-mokwena-s-challenge-to-chiefs-and-pirates/

Fin24. 10 October 2002. 'Motsepe is Entrepreneur 2002'. News24. https://www.news24.com/fin24/motsepe-is-entrepeneur-2002-20021010

Fin24. 20 June 2004. 'Exciting future awaits Motsepe'. https://www.news24.com/fin24/exciting-future-awaits-motsepe-20040620

Fin24. 8 September 2011. 'Motsepe to chair black business body'. https://www.news24.com/Fin24/Motsepe-to-chair-black-business-body-20110908

Fin24. 19 December 2016. 'Motsepe turns down Sanlam chair position for Van Zyl'. https://www.news24.com/Fin24/motsepe-turns-down-sanlam-chair-position-for-van-zyl-20161219

Football Ghana. 21 October 2021. 'CAF president Patrice Motsepe defends why World Cup every two years will help Africa'. https://footballghana.com/caf-president-patrice-motsepe-defends-why-world-cup-every-two-years-will-help-africa

Forbes. 2 May 2018. 'Forbes releases 2018 list of the world's most powerful people'. https://www.forbes.com/profile/gianni-infantino/

Francis, J. 27 May 2013. 'Cannes amfAR Gala: We rub shoulders with Leonardo DiCaprio, Jessica Chastain and more at the star-studded charity night'. Fashion. https://fashionmagazine.com/flare/celebrity/amfar-gala-2013-cannes/

Francsjeux.com. 8 March 2021. 'With Patrice Motsepe, Gianni Infantino secures the voices of Africa'. https://www.francsjeux.com/2021/03/08/with-patrice-motsepe-gianni-infantino-secures-the-voices-of-africa/74036

Gibbs, H. 23 February 2021. 'Cosafa backs Patrice Motsepe's "business acumen" to help CAF in tough period'. IOL. https://www.iol.co.za/sport/soccer/africa/cosafa-backs-patrice-motsepes-business-acumen-to-help-caf-in-tough-period-1eb105c2-5780-4964-8db6-2770671c2bf8

Gibbs, H. 7 December 2021. 'FIFA's love affair with CAF is fuel for world football bust-up'. IOL. https://www.iol.co.za/sport/soccer/africa/fifas-love-affair-with-caf-is-fuel-for-world-football-bust-up-b7e8ef94-4685-43bf-8c05-c19ee6adb3a2

Gleeson, M. 22 December 2013. 'Obituary: Zola Mahobe – Soccer boss who lived large on loot'. Sunday Times Lifestyle. https://www.timeslive.co.za/sunday-times/lifestyle/2013-12-22-obituary-zola-mahobe-soccer-boss-who-lived-large-on-loot/

Gleeson, M. 7 December 2016. 'Second-chance Sundowns hit Club World Cup ahead of schedule'. Reuters. https://www.reuters.com/article/ozasp-uk-soccer-club-mamelodi-idAF KBN13W0L0

Gordon, D. 28 July 2009. 'Daughter of exile traces the pulse of Y-Generation'. Business Day. https://www.hci.co.za/2009/07/28/daughter-of-exile-traces-the-pulse-of-y-generation/

Gosling, M. 18 October 2017. 'Mine hits back over West Coast aquifer'. GroundUp. https://www.groundup.org.za/article/west-coast-mine-says-stopping-it-pumping-out-aquifer-will-only-cause-more-harm/

Gower, P. 8 March 2021. 'TuksSport and Mamelodi Sundowns form a partnership to scientifically enhance the game of football'. University of Pretoria. https://www.up.ac.za/football/news/post_2957159-tukssport-tukssport-and-mamelodi-sundowns-form-a-partnership-to-scientifically-enhance-the-game-of-football

Guest, R. 23 December 2004. 'The World's Most Extreme Affirmative Action Program'. WSJ. https://www.wsj.com/articles/SB110376334634607918

Gumede. N. 17 March 2022. 'Mosimane slams Motsepe, likens his CAF leadership to that of Hayatou'. Phakaaathi. https://www.citizen.co.za/sport/soccer/local-soccer/3052262/mosimane-slams-motsepe-likens-his-caf-leadership-to-that-of-hayatou/

Gundan, F. 30 December 2014. 'South African billionaire Patrice Motsepe spends 68-million rands on Cape Town luxury retreat'. Forbes. https://www.forbes.com/sites/faraigundan/2014/12/30/south-african-billionaire-patrice-motsepe-spends-68-million-rands-on-cape-town-luxury-retreat/

Haffajee, F. 28 May 2012. 'The Spear is down – out of care and fear'. City Press. https://www.news24.com/news24/columnists/ferial-haffajee/The-Spear-is-down-out-of-care-and-fear-20120528-2

Haffajee, F. 28 May 2012. @ferialhaffajee. https://twitter.com/ferialhaffajee/status/207042839174062080

Harden, B. 11 April 1988. 'Chief Linchwe gets his way'. The Washington Post. https://www.washingtonpost.com/archive/politics/1988/04/11/chief-linchwe-ii-gets-his-way/03f14b57-7a5f-407d-bfd0-b25ece0a42cb/

Harris, JF, Eder F and Heath, R. 22 January 2020. 'Trump roars and Davos shrugs'. Politico.com. https://www.politico.com/news/magazine/2020/01/22/donald-trump-davos-102147

Hartley, R. 12 November 2017. 'How Ramaphosa nearly became Nelson Mandela's deputy'. Sunday Times. https://www.timeslive.co.za/sunday-times/news/2017-11-11-how-ramaphosa-nearly-became-nelson-mandelas-deputy/

Hendricks, A. 29 July 2019. 'The new football champions of Stellenbosch'. New Frame. https://www.newframe.com/the-new-football-champions-of-stellenbosch/

Hlongwane, S. 31 January 2013. 'South Africa's only black billionaire donates half his fortune to charity'. The Guardian. https://www.theguardian.com/world/2013/jan/31/south-african-billionaire

Hughes, A. 28 September 2018. 'Founder of African Fashion International partners with Global Citizens Festival'. WWD. https://www.yahoo.com/lifestyle/founder-african-fashion-international-partners-132238855.html

Impey, S. 8 June 2020. '"We didn't sign Siya the rugby star": How Roc Nation is building the Kolisi brand'. SP. https://www.sportspromedia.com/analysis/siya-kolisi-roc-nation-springboks-rugby-world-cup-south-africa-coronavirus/

I-Net Bridge. 20 January 2013. 'Patrice Motsepe donates half his wealth'. BusinessTech. https://businesstech.co.za/news/trending/30852/patrice-motsepe-donates-half-his-wealth/

IOL. 27 November 2000. 'NAFCOC drafts plan for SACOB unity pact'. https://www.iol.co.za/business-report/economy/nafcoc-drafts-plan-for-sacob-unity-pact-784852

IOL. 17 May 2002. 'Empowerment hits gold'. https://www.iol.co.za/business-report/economy/empowerment-hits-gold-778604

IOL. 3 October 2002. 'SA Chamber of Business gets new CEO'. https://www.iol.co.za/news/south-africa/sa-chamber-of-business-gets-new-ceo-95505

IOL. 13 October 2003. 'NAFCOC members' R2bn windfall'. https://www.iol.co.za/business-report/economy/nafcoc-members-r2bn-windfall-773885

IOL. 11 October 2004. 'Motsepe says he lost R500m on Modikwa platinum mine'. https://www.iol.co.za/business-report/companies/motsepe-says-he-lost-r500m-on-modikwa-platinum-mine-759355

IOL. 21 September 2011. 'Unity of black, white business crucial: Motsepe'. https://www.iol.co.za/business-report/economy/unity-of-black-white-business-crucial-motsepe-1142092

IOL. 26 February 2013. 'Motsepe: Mining assets are a good buy'. https://www.iol.co.za/business-report/companies/motsepe-mining-assets-are-a-good-buy-1477329

IOL. 9 September 2016. 'Motsepe slams policy uncertainty'. https://www.iol.co.za/business-report/companies/motsepe-slams-policy-uncertainty-2066115

IOL. 13 September 2017. 'Protesters claim Motsepes use cash to get control of tribe'. https://www.iol.co.za/pretoria-news/protesters-claim-motsepes-use-cash-to-get-control-of-tribe-11194748

IOL. 20 April 2019. 'BBC, BUSA will work together to help the economy'. https://www.iol.co.za/business-report/economy/bbc-busa-will-work-together-to-help-the-economy-20907940

Itano, N. 14 November 2003. 'South African mines in a 3-way deal'. The New York Times. https://www.nytimes.com/2003/11/14/business/south-african-mines-in-a-3-way-deal.html

Jacobs, C. 14 April 2019. 'Condé Nast International Luxury Conference where the fashionably late and truly fabulous gather'. Sunday Times. https://www.timeslive.co.za/sunday-times/lifestyle/fashion-and-beauty/2019-04-14-cond-nast-international-luxury-conference-where-the-fashionably-late-and-truly-fabulous-gather/

Jacobs, S. 21 January 2014. 'Mr Big Bucks and the Mamelodi Sundowns'. The Far Post. https://roadsandkingdoms.com/2014/mr-big-bucks-and-the-mamelodi-sundowns/

Jordan, ZP. 16 December 1997. 'The National Question in post-'94 South Africa (abridged)'. African National Congress. https://www.anc1912.org.za/50th-national-conference-the-national-question-in-post-94-south-africa-a-discussion-paper-in-preparation-for-the-50th-national-conference-abridged/

Josselsohn, D. 8 August 2003. 'Agreement to merge between African Rainbow Minerals and Exploration (Pty) Ltd and African Rainbow Minerals Gold Ltd and Harmony Gold Mining Company Limited'. Notarial certificate. https://www.sec.gov/Archives/edgar/data/1023514/000120561303000189/exhibit4_14.htm

Kagan, J. 24 October 2021. 'World Economic Forum: WEF'. investopedia.com. https://www.investopedia.com/terms/w/world-economic-forum.asp

Kaizer Chiefs. 7 January 2017. https://www.kaizerchiefs.com/news/congratulations-sundowns-motaung/

Kickoff. 20 August 2013. 'Analysing Motsepe's decade in charge'. https://www.kickoff.com/news/articles/south-africa-news/categories/news/premiership/patrice-motsepes-lack-of-success-at-mamelodi-sundowns/545365

Kickoff. 10 April 2015. '"Mazembe can't afford SA players"'. https://www.kickoff.com/news/articles/world-news/categories/news/caf-champions-league/mazembe-boss-moise-katumbi-discusses-sa-players/558126

Kickoff. 24 October 2016. 'Mosimane ends Motsepe's wait'. https://www.kickoff.com/news/articles/world-news/categories/news/caf-champions-league/mamelodi-sundowns-patrice-motsepe-credits-pitso-mosimane-after-champions-league-triumph/573647

Kickoff. 13 January 2017. '"Motsepe was misinformed on Dolly"'. https://www.kickoff.com/news/articles/south-africa-news/categories/news/psl-transfer-news/patrice-motsepe-was-misinformed-on-keagan-dolly-sundowns-made-9-changes-to-contract-in-disputed-buyout-clause/575781

Kickoff. 13 January 2017. 'How Sundowns won Dolly DRC case'. https://www.kickoff.com/news/articles/south-africa-news/categories/news/psl-transfer-news/how-mamelodi-sundowns-won-psl-drc-keagan-dolly-contract-dispute-case-patrice-motsepe/575670

Kickoff. 17 January 2017. 'Downs set for internal investigation'. https://www.kickoff.com/news/articles/south-africa-news/categories/news/premiership/mamelodi-sundowns-set-for-internal-investigation-into-keagan-dolly-contract-mistake/575868

Kickoff. 11 May 2018. 'Sundowns boss hails importance of Barca visit'. https://www.kickoff.com/news/articles/south-africa-news/categories/news/mamelodi-sundowns/mamelodi-sundowns-president-patrice-mots/589324

Kickoff. 29 November 2021. 'Motsepe wades in on standard of African refs'. Chronicle. https://www.chronicle.co.zw/motsepe-wades-in-on-standard-of-african-refs/

Kickoff Lifestyle. 6 May 2021. 'Motsepe confirms R145m donation'. https://www.kickoff. com/lifestyle/categories/community/patrice-motsepe-foundation-donates-r145m-to-fifa-caf-pan-african-school-championship/698759

Koka, M. 13 August 2020. 'I wasn't willing to sacrifice family for career: Dr Precious Moloi-Motsepe'. SowetanLive. https://www.sowetanlive.co.za/news/south-africa/2020-08-13-i-wasnt-willing-to-sacrifice-family-for-career-dr-precious-moloi-motsepe/

Koubakin, R. 2 March 2021. 'CAF election: African football is at a crossroads'. DW. https://www.dw.com/en/caf-election-african-football-is-at-a-crossroads/a-56720175

Kubheka, T. 14 December 2015. 'Patrice Motsepe brings early Christmas to Soweto children'. Eyewitness News. https://ewn.co.za/2015/12/14/Patrice-Motsepe-brings-early-Christmas-to-Soweto-children

Kunti, S. 25 February 2021. '"African football must become the best in the world": Billionaire Patrice Motsepe lays out his plan to become continent's soccer boss'. Forbes. https://www.forbes.com/sites/samindrakunti/2021/02/25/mining-billionaire-patrice-motsepe-launches-manifesto-to-run-african-soccer/

Kunti, S. 16 March 2021. 'Motsepe backs Veron to hit the ground running at CAF and tells TV it is time to pay Africans'. Inside World Football. https://www.insideworldfootball.com/2021/03/16/motsepe-backs-veron-hit-ground-running-caf-tells-tv-time-pay-africans/

Kunti, S. 7 February 2022. 'More African Super League talk as Motsepe says it will be FIFA run and privately funded'. Inside World Football. https://www.insideworldfootball.com/2022/02/07/african-super-league-talk-motsepe-says-will-fifa-run-privately-funded/

Lambley, G. 22 October 2021. 'Patrice Motsepe backs idea for Soccer World Cup every 2 years for "benefit of African football"'. The South African. https://www.thesouthafrican.com/sport/soccer/patrice-motsepe-backs-idea-for-soccer-world-cup-every-2-years-for-benefit-of-african-football/

Laurence, P. 30 September 2010. 'Bridgette Radebe, the ANCYL and nationalisation'. Politicsweb. https://www.politicsweb.co.za/news-and-analysis/bridgette-radebe-the-ancyl-and-nationalisation

Lerman, S. 5 February 2011. 'Downs coach steps down after death threats'. Sapa. https://www.timeslive.co.za/sport/soccer/2011-02-05-downs-coach-steps-down-after-death-threats/

Liebenberg, J-L. 2006. 'Critical evaluation of the late-restitution process (from the land-owner's perspective): The case of Krelingspost, North West province, 2005. Urban Changes in Different Scales: Systems and Structures. International Geographical Union.

Madisa, K. 14 June 2019. '"He's a family friend" – Motsepe defends meeting with Botswana's Ian Khama'. SowetanLive. https://www.sowetanlive.co.za/news/south-africa/2019-06-14-hes-a-family-friend-motsepe-defends-meeting-with-botswanas-ian-khama/

Mahlaka, R. 18 April 2021. 'Forbes 2021 billionaires list: During the pandemic, the very rich got very much richer – even in South Africa'. Daily Maverick. https://www.dailymaverick.co.za/article/2021-04-18-forbes-2021-billionaires-list-during-the-pandemic-the-very-rich-got-very-much-richer-even-in-south-africa/

Mahlakoana, T. 'Motsepe's lawyers head to Botswana to address political meddling claims'. Eyewitness News. https://ewn.co.za/2019/06/13/motsepe-s-lawyers-travelled-to-botswana-to-address-political-meddling-claims

Mahlangu, JK. 25 February 2019. @kennydior. https://twitter.com/kennydior/status/1099994119668158464?lang=en

Mail&Guardian. 1 October 2002. 'Black business has a bold new face'. https://mg.co.za/article/2002-10-01-black-business-has-a-bold-new-face/

Mail&Guardian. 8 August 2013. 'A rendezvous for great design'. https://mg.co.za/article/2013-08-08-00-a-rendezvous-for-great-design/

Mark, J. 22 November 2021. 'SAFA say referee complaint is valid, confident ahead of FIFA response'. The Citizen. https://www.citizen.co.za/sport/soccer/local-soccer/2913441/safa-referee-complaint-valid-confident-fifa-response/

Masilela, J. 13 December 2015. 'Memories of village boy called Tlhopane'. Sunday Independent. https://www.iol.co.za/sundayindependent/memories-of-village-boy-called-tlhopane-1959581

Masilela, J. 1 November 2018. 'Retired Bela-Bela educator Cisco Maphokga also played in the Soweto Derby'. The Post. https://diepos.co.za/52435/retired-bela-bela-educator-cisco-maphokga-also-played-soweto-derby/

Matshe, N. 21 December 2007. 'Motsepe, Igesund in tense crisis meeting'. IOL. https://www.iol.co.za/capeargus/sport/motsepe-igesund-in-tense-crisis-meeting-582877

McKay, D. 31 August 2020. 'Cash behind ARM's decision to overrule chairman Motsepe on Harmony's R3.5bn rights issue'. Miningmx. https://www.miningmx.com/news/gold/43475-cash-behind-arms-decision-to-overrule-chairman-motsepe-on-harmonys-r3-5bn-rights-issue/

Mediclinic. 27 October 2016. 'Patrice Motsepe's plan for cheaper private healthcare'. https://doctorsportal.mediclinic.co.za/Lists/News/DoctorsDispForm.aspx?ID=1630&ContentTypeId=0x010057A3FE46DA122B48A1BA84CA4F16E388

Mendoza, J. 21 August 2021. 'The truth about the deadly Vaal Reefs tragedy'. Grunge. https://www.grunge.com/492948/the-truth-about-the-deadly-vaal-reefs-tragedy/

Milken Institute. 7 August 2020. Conversations with Mike Milken: Precious Moloi-Motsepe, co-founder and CEO, Motsepe Foundation. https://mikemilken.com/podcast/Conversations-with-MM-Precious-Motsepe-0872020.pdf

Miningmx.com. 2022. 'Rainmakers and Potstirrers: Patrice Motsepe'. https://www.miningmx.com/rainmakers/profile/70

Mitchley, A. 24 January 2020. 'Patrice Motsepe tells Donald Trump "Africa loves America, Africa loves you" – but not everyone agrees'. News24. https://www.news24.com/news24/SouthAfrica/News/in-tweets-motsepe-tells-trump-africa-loves-america-but-not-everyone-agrees-20200124

Mjo, O. 3 December 2018. 'Horror stories of crime mar Global Citizen Festival'. Sunday Times. https://www.timeslive.co.za/news/south-africa/2018-12-03-horror-stories-of-crime-mar-global-citizen-festival/

Mlotha, S. 2 August 2020. 'Tsichlas: Why I sold Downs to Motsepe'. Kickoff. https://www.kickoff.com/news/articles/south-africa-news/categories/news/premiership/anastasia-tsichlas-why-i-sold-mamelodi-sundowns-to-patrice-motsepe/682740

Mlotha, S. 4 March 2021. 'Shakes: Patrice blocked my Chiefs move'. https://www.kickoff.com/news/articles/south-africa-news/categories/news/premiership/manqoba-shakes-ngwenya-how-i-joined-mamelodi-sundowns-over-kaizer-chiefs/695498

Mnyandu, M. 5 February 2022. 'Infantino – African Super League is different from the European version'. iDiskiTimes. https://www.idiskitimes.co.za/international/african-football/infantino-african-super-league-is-different-from-the-european-version/

Mogoatlhe, L. 29 November 2018. 'This book is helping South Africans empower themselves and change their lives'. Global Citizen. https://www.globalcitizen.org/en/content/precious-little-black-book-motsepe-foundation/

Mohale, B. 1 September 2021. 'Dear Mr President, please call us: Business is ready and waiting to be part of getting SA out of this mess'. Daily Maverick. https://www.dailymaverick.co.za/opinionista/2021-09-01-dear-mr-president-please-call-us-business-is-ready-and-waiting-to-be-part-of-getting-sa-out-of-this-mess/

Moholoha, R, Molefe, M and Bambani, C. 8 October 2012. '"Hands off Neeskens": Motsepe warns fans'. TimesLive. https://www.timeslive.co.za/news/south-africa/2012-10-08-hands-off-neeskens-motsepe-warns-fans/

Molefe, M. 27 February 2021. 'Motsepe confirms Downs successor if he wins CAF'. Soccer Laduma. https://www.soccerladuma.co.za/news/articles/local/categories/mamelodi-sundowns/motsepe-s-downs-successor-confirmed/695171

Molefe, M. 16 November 2021. 'Revealed: Downs' bonus structure'. Soccer Laduma. https://www.soccerladuma.co.za/news/articles/local/categories/mamelodi-sundowns/how-downs-reward-players-and-coaches/708645

Moloantoa, D. 6 October 2020. 'A century of Pretoria's Holy Redeemer Catholic Church'. The Heritage Portal. https://www.theheritageportal.co.za/article/century-pretorias-holy-redeemer-catholic-church

Molwedi, P. 12 November 2001. 'NAFCOC boss faces arrest over statutory rape'. IOL. https://www.iol.co.za/news/south-africa/nafcoc-boss-faces-arrest-over-statutory-rape-76726

Moon, M. 24 March 2021. 'Patrice Motsepe – The man who would save African football?' African Business. https://african.business/2021/03/trade-investment/patrice-motsepe-the-man-who-would-save-african-football/

Moonda, F. 1 October 2012. 'Sundowns coach Neeskens attacked'. Africa ESPN. https://africa.espn.com/football/news/story/_/id/1176798/mamelodi-sundowns-coach-johan-neeskens-attacked-by-fans

Moreotsene, L. 10 December 2007. 'Time running out, Igesund'. SowetanLive. https://www.sowetanlive.co.za/news/2007-12-10-time-running-out-igesund/

Motecwane, K. 17 March 2022. 'CAF responds to Pitso's VAR calls'. Soccer Laduma. https://www.soccerladuma.co.za/news/articles/international/categories/african-football/the-confederation-of-african-football-says-it-s-difficult-to-implement-var-in-all-of-africa/714701

Motsepe Foundation. n.d. 'ABC Motsepe Eisteddfod Music Competition'. https://www.motsepefoundation.org/sports-music-and-arts/abc-motsepe-sasce-eisteddfod/

Motsepe Foundation. n.d. 'Dr Precious Moloi-Motsepe'. https://www.motsepefoundation.org/dr-precious-moloi-motsepe/

Motsepe Foundation. n.d. 'Kay Motsepe Schools Cup: Football' https://www.motsepefoundation.org/sports-music-and-arts/kay-motsepe-schools-cup-football/

Motsepe, GJM. 15 August 1996. Truth and Reconciliation Commission. https://www.justice.gov.za/trc/hrvtrans/pretoria/motsepe.htm

Motshwane, G. 10 December 2019. 'The battle of the billionaires: Who will prevail?' SowetanLive. https://www.sowetanlive.co.za/sport/soccer/2019-12-10-the-battle-of-the-billionaires-who-will-prevail/

Motshwane, G. 17 September 2021. 'Jay-Z and company ready to rock Mzansi with Sundowns signing'. City Press. https://www.news24.com/citypress/sport/jay-z-and-company-ready-to-rock-mzansi-with-sundowns-signing-20210917

Moyo, A. 10 August 2021. 'Patrice Motsepe, Absa launch R6.5bn renewable energy fund'. ITWeb. https://www.itweb.co.za/content/xA9POvNZOaKvo4J8

Moyo, L. 14 July 2017. 'Another African payday for Downs'. Kickoff. https://www.kickoff.com/news/articles/world-news/categories/news/caf-champions-league/mamelodi-sundowns-again-in-the-money-as-restructured-caf-champions-league-pays-dividends/580736

Mpete, M. 11 March 2021. 'Top football legends endorse Motsepe's ascendancy'. Daily Sun. https://www.dailysun.co.za/dailysun/sport/top-football-legends-endorse-motsepes-ascendancy-20210310

Mphahlele, M. 16 May 2019. '"Sundowns creates millionaires," says coach Pitso Mosimane'. SowetanLive. https://www.sowetanlive.co.za/sport/soccer/2019-05-16-sundowns-creates-millionaires-says-coach-pitso-mosimane/

Mphahlele, M. 25 May 2020. 'Motsepe on his stake in the Bulls: "Rugby brings black and white South Africans together"'. TimesLive. https://www.timeslive.co.za/sport/rugby/2020-05-25-motsepe-on-his-stake-in-the-bulls-rugby-brings-black-and-white-south-africans-together/

Mphaki, A. 16 June 2018. 'Kaizer Chiefs captain among hundreds killed'. Abaphenyi Media Group. http://www.abaphenyi.co.za/news/2018/06/16/kaizer-chiefs-captain-among-hundreds-killed/

Mungadze, S. 14 November 2021. 'Motsepe's ARC joins consortium to seal R1.5bn fintech deal'. ITWeb. https://www.itweb.co.za/content/raYAyqodOX3vJ38N

Munro, C. 16 August 2014. 'Billionaire Buys $1 Million Picasso Sketch at Leonardo DiCaprio Gala'. Artnet News. https://news.artnet.com/art-world/billionaire-buys-1-million-picasso-sketch-at-leonardo-dicaprio-gala-79143

Munusamy, R. 20 December 2012. 'Cyril Ramaphosa: the return of Nelson Mandela's chosen one'. The Guardian. https://www.theguardian.com/world/2012/dec/20/cyril-ramaphosa-return-nelson-mandela

Mutumi, PPJ. 2021 Preservation, Conservation, and Advocacy: A Study of the Parktown Westcliff Heritage Trust (PWHT) in Heritage Management, 1965-2011. Research Report, University of the Witwatersrand. https://wiredspace.wits.ac.za/jspui/bitstream/10539/11863/1/Mutumi%20Prue%20MA%20Research%20Report%20FINAL.pdf

Mvoko, V. 16 November 2011. 'Patrice Motsepe on the threat of nationalization'. https://www.forbes.com/sites/kerryadolan/2011/11/16/patrice-motsepe-on-the-threat-of-nationalization/

MyBroadband. 21 June 2021. 'ARC co-CEOs' incredible R370 million bet'. https://mybroadband.co.za/news/business/402501-arc-co-ceos-incredible-r370-million-bet.html

Myburgh Chemaly, J. 27 March 2017. 'Dr Precious Moloi Motsepe on AFI designers and the rise of the African fashion industry'. Wanted Online. https://www.wantedonline.co.za/fashion-and-grooming/2017-03-20-the-best-or-nothing/

News24. 21 October 2001. 'Reluctant Motsepe leads NAFCOC rebels'. https://www.news24.com/news24/reluctant-motsepe-leads-nafcoc-rebels-20011021

News24. 5 December 2004. 'Sundowns coach warned'. https://www.news24.com/news24/sundowns-coach-warned-20041205

News24. 27 February 2008. 'Explosion needs answers'. The Witness. https://www.news24.com/witness/archive/Explosion-needs-answers-20150430

News24. 7 September 2011. 'Busa leaders kicked out of summit – report'. https://www.news24.com/fin24/busa-leaders-kicked-out-of-summit-report-20110907

News24. 26 June 2012. 'Jovial Zuma dines with mining bosses'. https://www.news24.com/News24/jovial-zuma-dines-with-mining-bosses-20150430

News24. 28 October 2012. 'ANC makes money in Mangaung – report' https://www.news24.com/fin24/anc-makes-money-in-mangaung-report-20121028-2

News24. 31 January 2013. 'ANC salutes Motsepe'. https://www.news24.com/news24/anc-salutes-motsepe-20150429

News24. 11 September 2015. 'SA tycoon's pricey pictures land up in Sars sales bin'. https://www.news24.com/News24/sa-tycoons-pricey-pictures-land-up-in-sars-sales-bin-20150911

News24. 25 October 2016. 'Motsepe: Players must divvy up the winnings'. https://www.news24.com/Sport/motsepe-players-must-divvy-up-the-winnings-20161025

News24. 4 September 2017. '"Brave Kusasalethu miners died like warriors in battle"'. AllAfrica. https://allafrica.com/stories/201709050112.html

News24. 4 September 2017. 'Minister tells Patrice Motsepe to pay Kusasalethu miners "decent salaries"'. https://www.news24.com/News24/minister-tells-patrice-motsepe-to-pay-kusasalethu-miners-decent-salaries-20170904

News24. 28 July 2018. 'Malema's warning to Patrice Motsepe: "We are watching you"'. https://www.news24.com/News24/malemas-warning-to-patrice-motsepe-we-are-watching-you-20180728

News24. 9 May 2019. 'Andile Mngxitama ordered to retract from bashing Patrice Motsepe'. https://www.news24.com/News24/andile-mngxitama-ordered-to-retract-from-bashing-patrice-motsepe-20190509

News24. 28 January 2020. 'Patrice Motsepe apologises for telling US President Donald Trump "Africa loves you"'. https://www.news24.com/news24/SouthAfrica/News/just-in-patrice-motsepe-apologises-for-telling-us-president-donal-trump-africa-loves-you-20200128

Ngidi, N. 10 September 2020. 'South Africa: The three pillars of Mamelodi Sundowns' success'. New Frame. https://allafrica.com/stories/202009160880.html

Ngobeni, V. 14 December 2005. 'Cappa was not pushed, says Motsepe'. Sapa. https://www.iol.co.za/capeargus/sport/cappa-was-not-pushed-says-motsepe-552435

Njilo, N. 18 November 2021. 'Cyril Ramaphosa and Patrice Motsepe donated money to ANC ahead of election'. TimesLive. https://www.timeslive.co.za/politics/2021-11-18-cyril-ramaphosa-and-patrice-motsepe-donated-money-to-anc-ahead-of-election/

Njilo, N. 30 December 2021. '"We want to save the ANC": Concerned party members want Patrice Motsepe as president'. TimesLive. https://www.timeslive.co.za/politics/2021-12-30-we-want-to-save-the-anc-concerned-party-members-want-patrice-motsepe-as-president/

Nkanjeni, U. 25 February 2022. '"Hypocrite" or 'securing the bag"?: Malema under fire after EFF received R2m from Motsepe's companies'. TimesLive. https://www.timeslive.co.za/politics/2022-02-25-hypocrite-or-securing-the-bag-malema-under-fire-after-eff-received-r2m-from-motsepes-companies/

Nkanjeni, U. 14 March 2022. 'Pitso Mosimane: "Sundowns must leave me alone. I've moved on"'. TimesLive. https://www.timeslive.co.za/sport/soccer/2022-03-14-pitso-mosimane-sundowns-must-leave-me-alone-ive-moved-on/

REFERENCES

Ntloko, M. 10 January 2017. 'I would sell Dolly for R5, says a vexed Motsepe'. BusinessLive. https://www.businesslive.co.za/bd/sport/soccer/2017-01-10-i-would-sell-dolly-for-r5-says-a-vexed-motsepe/

Ntloko. M. 1 September 2020. 'Premiership champions Mamelodi Sundowns unveil their new kit'. TimesLive. https://www.timeslive.co.za/sport/soccer/2020-09-01-premiership-champions-mamelodi-sundowns-unveil-their-new-kit/

Ntloko, M. 31 May 2021. 'Tension between Mosimane and former club Sundowns continues to escalate'. SowetanLive. https://www.sowetanlive.co.za/sport/soccer/2021-05-31-tension-between-mosimane-and-former-club-sundowns-continues-to-escalate/

Okeleji. O. 21 June 2019. 'What does FIFA's takeover of CAF mean for African football?' Al Jazeera. https://www.aljazeera.com/sports/2019/6/21/what-does-fifas-takeover-of-caf-mean-for-african-football

O'Malley. 1994. 'The Reconstruction and Development Programme (RDP)' https://omalley. nelsonmandela.org/omalley/index.php/site/q/03lv02039/04lv02103/05lv02120/06 lv02126.htm

Onyii. 7 February 2020. '#CAFPwCAuditReport: How Ahmad's inner circle binged on $24 million CAF cash'. Fifa Colonialism. https://fifacolonialism.com/cafpwcauditreport-how-ahmads-inner-circle-binged-on-24-million-caf-cash/

Panja, T. 19 June 2019. 'FIFA takes control in Africa, where the sport is in chaos'. The New York Times. https://www.nytimes.com/2019/06/19/sports/fifa-takes-control-of-soccer-in-africa-where-the-sport-is-in-chaos.html

Parliamentary Monitoring Group. 2 April 2003. 'Black Empowerment in the Mining Sector'. https://pmg.org.za/committee-meeting/2342/

Pavitt, M. 1 March 2021. 'Motsepe expected to become CAF President with rivals reportedly set to withdraw'. Inside the Games. https://www.insidethegames.biz/articles/1104840/ motsepe-football-caf-president-election

People. 6 December 1976. 'What the world needs now is love, sweet love – especially the beauty contest of the same name'. https://people.com/archive/what-the-world-needs-now-is-love-sweet-love-especially-the-beauty-contest-of-the-same-name-vol-6-no-23/

Pillay, B. 19 March 2022. 'Mamelodi Sundowns chairman Tlhopane Motsepe responds to Al Ahly's complaint, states no supporters blocked Bus'. Sports Brief. https://sportsbrief.com/ football/mamelodi-sundowns/1b501-mamelodi-sundowns-chairman-tlhopane-motsepe-responds-al-ahlys-complaint-states-no-supporters-blocked-bus/

Pinnock, D. 12 October 2017. 'West Coast phosphate mine interdicted to stop drawing fossil water'. Conservation Action Trust. https://conservationaction.co.za/media-articles/west-coast-phosphate-mine-interdicted-stop-drawing-fossil-water/

Plaatjes, E. 7 February 2015. 'Action leadership: Learn from the world's top business leaders'. Ventures Africa. https://venturesafrica.com/action-leadership-learn-from-the-worlds-top-business-leaders/

Polity. 21 September 2002. Address by the president of South Africa, Thabo Mbeki, at the NAFCOC Conference, Sun City. https://www.polity.org.za/article/mbeki-nafcoc-conference-21092002-2002-09-21

Qobo, M. 19 January 2016. 'Why the rich should do more to save the world'. The Conversation. https://theconversation.com/why-the-rich-should-do-more-to-save-the-world-52944

Ramalepe, P. 7 March 2022. 'Ramaphosa scores R2.1 million for Ankole cow in cattle auction thanks to Motsepe'. Business Insider SA. https://www.businessinsider.co.za/ramaphosa-sells-ankole-cow-for-r21-million-2022-3

Ramphekwa, H. 24 March 2009. 'Familiar face returns to coach Sundowns'. Cape Argus. https://www.iol.co.za/capeargus/sport/familiar-face-returns-to-coach-sundowns-600061

Rankhumise, SP. 2017. 'The Bakgatla ba ga Motsha under the Native policy of the Transvaal, 1852-1910'. Thesis. North-West University. http://dspace.nwu.ac.za/bitstream/handle/10394/35164/RANKHUMISE_SP.pdf

Richardson, J. 19 March 2021. 'Who is Tlhopane Motsepe?'. The South African. https://www.thesouthafrican.com/sport/soccer/psl-south-africa/tlhopane-motsepe-gets-seal-of-approval-from-sundowns-coach/

Robinson, S. 17 April 2005. 'South Africa: The New Rand Lords'. Time. http://content.time.com/time/subscriber/article/0,33009,1050314,00.html

Robinson, S. 6 June 2005. 'Welcome to the Club'. Time. http://content.time.com/time/world/article/0,8599,2050149,00.html

Ross, S. 21 January 2022. 'What are the best measurements of economic growth?'. investopedia.com. https://www.investopedia.com/ask/answers/032515/what-are-best-measurements-economic-growth.asp

Ryan, B. 17 March 2015. 'Motsepe issues Zambia royalty warning'. MiningMX. https://www.miningmx.com/news/base-metals/12556-motsepe-issues-zambia-royalty-warning/

Ryan, B. 16 March 2017. 'Motsepe will shut mines rather than bow to misled communities'. Miningmx. https://www.miningmx.com/news/markets/29279-motsepe-will-shut-mines-rather-bow-politicised-communities/

SABC News. 16 March 2021. 'SAFA President Dr Danny Jordaan on Motsepe's CAF presidency'. YouTube https://www.youtube.com/watch?v=GLnjFi3BGac

Sang, K. 16 July 2021. 'CAF Champions League: Al Ahly will beat Kaizer Chiefs if "lucky charm" Motsepe attends final – Mosimane'. Goal. https://www.goal.com/en/news/caf-champions-league-mosimane-al-ahly-will-beat-kaizer/fspefgs5pvrs1bd286sasjsl0

Sapa. 20 July 2011. 'BMF leaves BUSA'. SowetanLive. https://www.sowetanlive.co.za/business/2011-07-04-bmf-leaves-busa/

Sapa. 27 May 2012. 'City Press editor: "I don't respond to threats"'. Mail&Guardian. https://mg.co.za/article/2012-05-27-city-press-editor-i-dont-respond-to-threats/

SA Rugby Mag. 9 December 2021. 'Roc Nation boss: SA rugby players have no voice'. https://www.sarugbymag.co.za/yormark-sa-rugby/

Schenk, S and De Swardt, C. 5 December 2011. 'Safe Hands: Building Integrity and Transparency at FIFA'. Transparency International. https://www.transparency.org/files/content/pressrelease/20111205_TI-S_FIFA_SafeHands_EN.pdf

Selisho, K. 8 April 2019. 'Bridgette Radebe accused of interfering in Botswana politics'. The Citizen. https://www.citizen.co.za/news/news-world/news-africa/2114014/bridgette-radebe-accused-of-interfering-in-botswana-politics/

Sentinel News Service. 11 November 2015. 'Keep a Child Alive raises $3.8 for children and families impacted by HIV and AIDS'. Los Angeles Sentinel. https://lasentinel.net/keep-a-child-alive-raises-3-8-for-children-and-families-impacted-by-hiv-and-aids.html

Serrao, C. 30 November 2015. 'Tech billionaires team up to take on climate change. Wired. https://www.wired.com/2015/11/zuckerberg-gates-climate-change-breakthrough-energy-coalition/

Sguazzin, A. 27 January 2022. 'Sun Exchange sees bright future in Africa'. BusinessLive. https://www.businesslive.co.za/bloomberg/news/2022-01-27-sun-exchange-sees-bright-future-in-africa/

Shabolyo, N. 23 November 2016. 'Africa's first black billionaire, Patrice Motsepe, thanks Zambians'. High Commission of the Republic of Zambia, Pretoria. http://www.zambiapretoria.net/africas-first-black-billionaire-patrice-motsepe-thanks-zambians/

Shah, N. 13 November 2018. 'These dignitaries are attending the Global Citizen festival: Mandela 100'. Global Citizen. https://www.globalcitizen.org/en/content/mandela-100-dignitary-announcement/

Shah, N and Gralki, P. 28 September 2019. Global Citizen. 'Almost $1B in commitments made at 2019 Global Citizen festival'. https://www.globalcitizen.org/en/content/impact-report-2019/

Shevel, A. 4 September 2011. 'The Rich List – Patrice Motsepe tops it'. Sunday Times. https://www.timeslive.co.za/sunday-times/lifestyle/2011-09-04-the-rich-list-patrice-motsepe-tops-it/

Sibembe, Y. 7 March 2021. 'Patrice Motsepe's historic bid for president of CAF moves closer to reality'. Daily Maverick. https://www.dailymaverick.co.za/article/2021-03-07-patrice-motsepes-historic-bid-for-president-of-caf-moves-closer-to-reality/

Sibembe, Y. 17 May 2021. 'New CAF president Patrice Motsepe says his team will score for African football'. Daily Maverick. https://www.dailymaverick.co.za/article/2021-03-17-new-caf-president-patrice-motsepe-says-his-team-will-score-for-african-football/

Sifile, L. 4 September 2017. '#KusasalethuMemorial: "Pay mineworkers decent salaries"'. IOL. https://www.iol.co.za/news/south-africa/gauteng/kusasalethumemorial-pay-mineworkers-decent-salaries-11074023

Sikwane, O. 14 March 2016. 'Leaders battle over community's R26 billion wealth'. GroundUp. https://www.groundup.org.za/article/fight-soul-bakgatla-ba-kgafela/

SL International. 19 November 2021. 'Ghana FA sends message to Motsepe after SAFA complaint'. Soccer Laduma. https://www.soccerladuma.co.za/news/articles/international/categories/african-football/ghana-fa-president-we-don-t-expect-patrice-motsepe-to-take-sides/708809

Smith, A. 14 July 2019. 'Trump says congresswomen of color should "go back" and fix the places they "originally came from"'. NBC News. https://www.nbcnews.com/politics/donald-trump/trump-says-progressive-congresswomen-should-go-back-where-they-came-n1029676

Soccer Laduma. 8 May 2014. 'Igesund lauds Motsepe and Mosimane. https://www.soccerladuma.co.za/news/articles/local/categories/german-bundesliga/gordon-igesund-has-heaped-praise-on-pitso-and-motsepe/161737

Soccer Laduma. 27 February 2019. 'Throwback – How Teko Modise won Sundowns the title in 2014'. https://www.soccerladuma.co.za/news/articles/local/categories/south-africa/throwback-how-teko-modise-won-sundowns-the-title-in-2014/650926

Solomons, S. 4 April 2018. 'Joint partners condemn senseless attacks on Modikwa mineworkers'. Mining Review Africa. https://www.miningreview.com/southern-africa/joint-partners-condemn-senseless-attacks-modikwa-mineworkers/

Sports Club. 21 May 2021. 'Pitso's agency MT Sports responds to Sundowns lawsuit'. https://www.sportsclub.co.za/pitsos-agency-mt-sports-responds-to-sundowns-lawsuit-1/

Stockenstroom, S. 8 October 2018. 'Joburg Fashion Week a hit with Asian fusion'. Sunday World Lifestyle. https://www.sowetanlive.co.za/sundayworld/lifestyle/2018-10-08-joburg-fashion-week-a-hit-with-asian-fusion/

Stoddard, E. 6 September 2021. 'Annual results: Patrice Motsepe's African Rainbow Minerals reports 136% spike in earnings, flags Transnet woes'. Daily Maverick. https://www.dailymaverick.co.za/article/2021-09-06-annual-results-patrice-motsepes-african-rainbow-minerals-reports-136-spike-in-earnings-flags-transnet-woes/

Strohschein, J. 3 December 2021. 'Patrice Motsepe: CAF President by the grace of Infantino'. DW. https://www.dw.com/en/patrice-motsepe-caf-president-by-the-grace-of-infantino/a-56852726

Strydom, M. 13 January 2017. 'It was Motsepe who insisted on R25-million buyout clause: Keagan Dolly's dad'. SowetanLive. https://www.sowetanlive.co.za/sport/soccer/2017-01-13-it-was-motsepe-who-insisted-on-r25-million-buyout-clause-keagan-dollys-dad/

Strydom, M. 26 February 2021. 'CAF presidential candidate Patrice Motsepe confirms who will run Mamelodi Sundowns'. SowetanLive. https://www.sowetanlive.co.za/sport/soccer/2021-02-26-caf-presidential-candidate-patrice-motsepe-confirms-who-will-run-mamelodi-sundowns/

Strydom, M. 17 March 2021. 'Why Patrice Motsepe has high hopes for his new secretary-general Veron Mosengo-Omba'. DispatchLIVE. https://www.dispatchlive.co.za/sport/2021-03-17-why-patrice-motsepe-has-high-hopes-for-his-new-secretary-general-veron-mosengo-omba/

Strydom, M. 9 September 2021. 'Tlhopie Motsepe: Sundowns' coaching trinity ensured transition in life after Pitso'. SowetanLive. https://www.sowetanlive.co.za/sport/soccer/2021-09-09-tlhopie-motsepe-sundowns-coaching-trinity-ensured-transition-in-life-after-pitso/ Accessed 19 April 2022.

Strydom, M. 21 September 2021. 'Tlhopie Motsepe targets fellow millennials to expand Sundowns' fan base'. SowetanLive. https://www.sowetanlive.co.za/sport/soccer/2021-09-21-tlhopie-motsepe-targets-fellow-millennials-to-expand-sundowns-fan-base/

Strydom, M. 21 December 2021. 'CAF appoints Infront France to manage TV broadcast services of major tournaments'. HeraldLIVE. https://www.heraldlive.co.za/sport/soccer/2021-12-21-caf-appoints-infront-france-to-manage-tv-broadcast-services-of-major-tournaments/

SuperSport. 10 November 2020. 'Safa explains Motsepe nomination for CAF president'. https://supersport.com/general/xtra/news/201110_Safa_explains_Motsepe_nomination_for_Caf_President

Tau, P. 20 July 2011. '"We helped keep Mandela safe"'. The Star. https://www.iol.co.za/the-star/we-helped-keep-mandela-safe-1102738

Teye, PN. 21 October 2021. 'CAF president Motsepe touts Ghana's World Cup-winning credentials'. Goal. https://www.goal.com/en-gh/news/caf-president-motsepe-touts-ghana-world-cup-winning/z72o8j209lja1o62lw6bbnezh

The Giving Pledge. n.d. https://givingpledge.org/pledger?pledgerId=253

Theunissen, G. 8 October 2020. 'Patrice Motsepe's investment firm is under fire – it's now promising new deals and dividends'. ARC. https://africanrainbowcapital.co.za/patrice-motsepes-investment-firm-is-under-fire-its-now-promising-new-deals-and-dividends/

TikTok. 6 January 2022. 'TikTok unites African football fans through partnership with Confederation of African Football'. https://newsroom.tiktok.com/en-africa/tiktok-sponsors-caf

TimesLive. 18 February 2019. 'I come from old money, my hands are clean, says Patrice Motsepe'. https://www.timeslive.co.za/politics/2019-02-18-i-come-from-old-money-my-hands-are-clean-says-patrice-motsepe/

Timm, S. 3 February 2020. 'Former law student turned tech founder sells art platform to Precious Moloi-Motsepe'. VentureBurn. https://ventureburn.com/2020/02/sa-art-platform-wezart-acquired-by-afi/

Tlhoaele, D. 17 October 2013. 'Motsepe donates millions to develop his home town'. Pretoria Rekord. https://rekord.co.za/307646/motsepe-donates-millions-to-develop-his-home-town/

Tshwaku, K. 13 March 2022. 'Mosimane fires broadside at 'Downs after bus blocked en route to stadium: What do you want from me?'. News24. https://www.news24.com/sport/soccer/mosimane-fires-broadside-at-downs-after-bus-blocked-en-route-to-stadium-what-do-you-want-from-me-20220313

Tyler, E. 16 November 2021. 'Climate finance for transition away from coal: a chance to change history in SA'. Eyewitness News. https://ewn.co.za/2021/11/16/climate-finance-for-transition-away-from-coal-a-chance-to-change-history-in-sa

University of Johannesburg. 21 January 2016. 'UJ's Dr Mzukisi Qobo on philanthrocapitalists'. https://www.uj.ac.za/news/ujs-dr-mzukisi-qobo-on-philanthrocapitalists/

Van Diemen, E. 29 September 2021. 'How South Africa can power ahead with green energy ambitions through R750bn financing plan'. Daily Maverick. https://www.dailymaverick.co.za/article/2021-09-29-how-south-africa-can-power-ahead-with-green-energy-ambitions-through-r750bn-financing-plan/

Vanek, M. 22 May 2017. 'Black Business Council, Business Unity South Africa terminate co-operation at Nedlac'. CNBCAfrica. https://www.cnbcafrica.com/2017/black-business-council-vs-business-unity-south-africa/

Van Zyl, J. 20 March 2014. 'Sanlam and Ubuntu-Botho BEE partnership delivers R15-billion in value'. Sanlam. https://www.sanlam.co.za/mediacentre/media-category/media-releases/Sanlam%20and%20Ubuntu-Botho%20BEE%20Partnership%20delivers%20R15-Billion%20in%20Value

Vardien, T. 10 March 2021. '7 standout quotes from soon-to-be new CAF president Patrice Motsepe'. News24. https://www.news24.com/sport/Soccer/BafanaBafana/7-standout-quotes-from-soon-to-be-new-caf-president-patrice-motsepe-20210310

Veblen, A. 26 May 2013. 'Cap crusaders'. Vogue. https://en.vogue.me/archive/international/cap-crusaders-amfar-red-carpet-cannes-love-gold/

Ventures Africa. 17 July 2012. 'Lord of the Mines: Billionaire Patrice Motsepe'. https://venturesafrica.com/lord-of-the-mines-patrice-motsepe/

Wa ka Ngobeni, E. 19 October 2001. 'NAFCOC relocates despite "ousting" of its leader'. Mail&Guardian. https://mg.co.za/article/2001-10-19-nafcoc-relocates-despite-ousting-of-its-leader/

Watts, H. 2 September 2011. 'South Africa's billionaire Patrice Motsepe in talks with Ratan Tata for JV in financial, minerals business'. India Times. https://economictimes.indiatimes.com/industry/indl-goods/svs/metals-mining/south-africas-billionaire-patrice-motsepe-in-talks-with-ratan-tata-for-jv-in-financial-minerals-business/articleshow/9829914.cms

Weinberg, T. May 2015. 'The contested status of 'communal land tenure' in South Africa'. Rural status report 3. University of the Western Cape. https://media.africaportal.org/documents/PLAAS_Rural_Report_Book_3_-_Tara_-_Web.pdf

Why Africa. 20 September 2021. 'Kropz cleared to start production at Elandsfontein in SA'. https://www.whyafrica.co.za/kropz-cleared-to-start-production-at-elandsfontein-in-sa/

Wirfengla, I. 27 January 2022. 'Inside the stampede at Olembé Stadium'. New Frame. https://www.newframe.com/inside-the-stampede-at-olembe-stadium/

World Economic Forum. 15 November 2019. 'World Economic Forum appoints two new members to its board of trustees'. https://www.weforum.org/press/2019/11/world-economic-forum-appoints-two-new-members-to-its-board-of-trustees/

Young, J. 11 January 2021. 'How Pitso Mosimane built a dynasty with Mamelodi Sundowns'. BTL. https://breakingthelines.com/manager-analysis/how-pitso-mosimane-built-a-dynasty-with-mamelodi-sundowns/

Zarabi, S. 22 May 2022. 'Change in the air as the well-heeled WEF veterans make it to spring-time Davos'. BusinessToday.In. https://www.businesstoday.in/opinion/columns/story/change-in-the-air-as-the-well-heeled-wef-veterans-make-it-to-spring-time-davos-334588-2022-05-22

Zuma, J. 12 November 2015. 'South Africa's position on climate change ahead of UNFCCC COP 21 Summit'. The Presidency. https://www.thepresidency.gov.za/content/south-africa%E2%80%99s-position-climate-change-ahead-unfccc-cop-21-summit

Acknowledgements

My sincere thanks to editor Tracey Hawthorne, who pulled the manuscript apart like a detective, and patiently and cleverly dealt with every detail of it. Thanks to publisher Gill Moodie with her strong backbone, an excellent barometer of the public appetite. Thanks also to the many brilliant colleagues, writers, historians and journalists whose absorbing work, insights and inputs allowed me to put a book together. Without each other, we cannot produce.

Loving thanks to my friends, who never fail to check in and check up, and keep believing that it's possible to live the life of an author; and especially to my sister Deborah, my beloved children, Angela, Nathanael, Isabella and Heath, and lovely Kayla, as they seem happy to have endless conversations about why, and how, and if – those conversations being essential to the work of any writer, especially of non-fiction. Thanks also to Priscilla Nkosi, my assistant and helper, and to JH for 35 years of a very strange but compelling bond.

My gratitude goes to everyone who buys and enjoys and supports South African books, and books about Africa. Rage against the machine!

Notes

Prologue

1   Trump's reply was reportedly, 'You're doing a great job, thank you very much.' Mitchley, A. 24 January 2020. 'Patrice Motsepe tells Donald Trump "Africa loves America, Africa loves you" – but not everyone agrees'. News24. https://www.news24.com/news24/SouthAfrica/News/in-tweets-motsepe-tells-trump-africa-loves-america-but-not-everyone-agrees-20200124 Accessed 11 May 2022.

2   The Pew Research Center found that 'while most countries in the world had low confidence in Mr Trump to do the right thing in world affairs, he garnered 65% support in Kenya and 58% in Nigeria'. BBC News. 24 January 2020. 'Patrice Motsepe's "Africa loves Trump" comment divides opinion'. https://www.bbc.com/news/world-africa-51235485 Accessed 11 May 2022.

3   Harris, JF, Eder F and Heath, R. 22 January 2020. 'Trump roars, and Davos shrugs'. Politico.com. https://www.politico.com/news/magazine/2020/01/22/donald-trump-davos-102147 Accessed 28 May 2022.

4   Smith, A. 14 July 2019. 'Trump says congresswomen of color should "go back" and fix the places they "originally came from"'. NBC News. https://www.nbcnews.com/politics/donald-trump/trump-says-progressive-congresswomen-should-go-back-where-they-came-n1029676 Accessed 11 May 2022. The congresswomen were Alexandria Ocasio-Cortez of New York, Ayanna Pressley of Massachusetts, Rashida Tlaib of Michigan and Ilhan Omar of Minnesota.

5   News24. 28 January 2020. 'Patrice Motsepe apologises for telling US President Donald Trump "Africa loves you"'. https://www.news24.com/news24/SouthAfrica/News/just-in-patrice-motsepe-apologises-for-telling-us-president-donal-trump-africa-loves-you-20200128 Accessed 11 May 2022.

6   Harmony Gold had issued over 60 million shares, raising about R3.47 billion, in order to pay the upfront cash element of the purchase of two companies – Mponeng and Mine Waste Solutions – from AngloGold Ashanti. ARM, a 13.77-percent shareholder in Harmony Gold, had not followed its rights to subscribe to the shares.

7   McKay, D. 31 August 2020. 'Cash behind ARM's decision to overrule chairman Motsepe on Harmony's R3.5bn rights issue'. Miningmx. https://www.miningmx.com/news/gold/43475-cash-behind-arms-decision-to-overrule-chairman-motsepe-on-harmonys-r3-5bn-rights-issue/ Accessed 14 April 2022.

8   Plaatjes, E. 7 February 2015. 'Action leadership: Learn from the world's top business leaders'. Ventures Africa. https://venturesafrica.com/action-leadership-learn-from-the-worlds-top-business-leaders/ Accessed 13 May 2022.

9   Fin24. 10 October 2002. 'Motsepe is Entrepreneur 2002'. News24. https://www.news24.com/fin24/motsepe-is-entrepeneur-2002-20021010 Accessed 13 May 2022.

10 BusinessTech. 1 September 2020. 'Patrice Motsepe on encouraging investment – and why he won't leave South Africa'. https://businesstech.co.za/news/business/430494/patrice-motsepe-on-encouraging-investment-and-why-he-wont-leave-south-africa/ Accessed 13 May 2022.

11 Shabolyo, N. 23 November 2016. 'Africa's first black billionaire, Patrice Motsepe, thanks Zambians'. High Commission of the Republic of Zambia, Pretoria. http://www.

zambiapretoria.net/africas-first-black-billionaire-patrice-motsepe-thanks-zambians/ Accessed 11 May 2022. He was addressing a gathering of more than 80 kings and chiefs from South Africa, Zambia, Lesotho, eSwatini, Zimbabwe, Namibia and Botswana at a meeting hosted by the Motsepe Foundation and the African Rainbow Minerals Broad-Based Economic Empowerment (ARM BBEE) Trust. The ARM BBEE Trust was established in 2006 'to ensure that as many of our people as possible benefit from the mining industry'. Beneficiaries were five ARM Provincial Rural Upliftment Trusts, the National Women's Upliftment Trust, the ZCC Church Trust, the South African Democratic Teachers Union, and the National Education, Health and Allied Workers Union, which together represented about 400 000 workers, entrepreneurs, community leaders and women- and youth-owned small businesses.

12 Creamer, M. 7 September 2018. 'ARM mulling 'very exciting" growth opportunities – Motsepe'. Engineering News. https://www.polity.org.za/print-version/arm-mulling-very-exciting-growth-opportunities-motsepe-2018-09-07 Accessed 13 May 2022.

1. A night in Rabat: The arrival of the contender

1   *Copa Mundial* is Spanish for 'World Cup'.

2   Panja, T. 19 June 2019. 'FIFA takes control in Africa, where the sport is in chaos'. The New York Times. https://www.nytimes.com/2019/06/19/sports/fifa-takes-control-of-soccer-in-africa-where-the-sport-is-in-chaos.html Accessed 10 May 2022.

3   UEFA (Europe), CAF (Africa), CONCACAF (North and Central America), CONMEBOL (South America), OFC (New Zealand and South Pacific island nations) and AFC (Asia). FIFA stands at the head of these confederations, which in turn organise and regulate the game in their areas, based on the overall statutes and policies of FIFA.

4   FIFA had itself been through a massive crisis in 2015 which had 'threatened its very existence and involved crimes uncovered by the Federal Bureau of Investigation and Internal Revenue Service' in the USA as these had 'largely occurred at the confederation level in the Americas'. Panja, T. 19 June 2019. 'FIFA takes control in Africa, where the sport is in chaos'. The New York Times. https://www.nytimes.com/2019/06/19/sports/fifa-takes-control-of-soccer-in-africa-where-the-sport-is-in-chaos.html Accessed 10 May 2022.

5   Okeleji. O. 21 June 2019. 'What does FIFA's takeover of CAF mean for African football?' Al Jazeera. https://www.aljazeera.com/sports/2019/6/21/what-does-fifas-takeover-of-caf-mean-for-african-football Accessed 13 April 2022.

6   Onyii. 7 February 2020. '#CAFPwCAuditReport: How Ahmad's inner circle binged on $24 million CAF cash'. Fifa Colonialism. https://fifacolonialism.com/cafpwcauditreport-how-ahmads-inner-circle-binged-on-24-million-caf-cash/ Accessed 13 April 2022.

7   Kunti, S. 25 February 2021. '"African football must become the best in the world": Billionaire Patrice Motsepe lays out his plan to become continent's soccer boss'. Forbes. https://www.forbes.com/sites/samindrakunti/2021/02/25/mining-billionaire-patrice-motsepe-launches-manifesto-to-run-african-soccer/ Accessed 10 May 2022.

8   Angola, Botswana, Comoros, Lesotho, Madagascar, Malawi, Mauritius, Mozambique, Namibia, Seychelles, South Africa, eSwatini, Zambia, Zimbabwe and Reunion.

9   Gibbs, H. 23 February 2021. 'Cosafa backs Patrice Motsepe's "business acumen" to help CAF in tough period'. IOL. https://www.iol.co.za/sport/soccer/africa/cosafa-backs-patrice-motsepes-business-acumen-to-help-caf-in-tough-period-1eb105c2-5780-4964-8db6-2770671c2bf8 Accessed 10 May 2022.

10 Kickoff. 10 April 2015. '"Mazembe can't afford SA players"'. https://www.kickoff.com/news/articles/world-news/categories/news/caf-champions-league/mazembe-boss-moise-katumbi-discusses-sa-players/558126 Accessed 10 May 2022.

11 Sibembe, Y. 7 March 2021. 'Patrice Motsepe's historic bid for president of CAF moves closer to reality'. Daily Maverick. https://www.dailymaverick.co.za/article/2021-03-07-patrice-motsepes-historic-bid-for-president-of-caf-moves-closer-to-reality/ Accessed 10 May 2022.

12 Forbes. 2 May 2018. 'Forbes releases 2018 list of the world's most powerful people'. https://www.forbes.com/profile/gianni-infantino/ Accessed 29 May 2022.

13 Those companies included African Rainbow Capital, African Rainbow Minerals and Sanlam.

14 SABC News. 16 March 2021. 'SAFA President Dr Danny Jordaan on Motsepe's CAF presidency'. YouTube https://www.youtube.com/watch?v=GLnjFi3BGac Accessed 11 April 2022.

15 Kunti, S. 25 February 2021. '"African football must become the best in the world": Billionaire Patrice Motsepe lays out his plan to become continent's soccer boss'. Forbes. https://www.forbes.com/sites/samindrakunti/2021/02/25/mining-billionaire-patrice-motsepe-launches-manifesto-to-run-african-soccer/ Accessed 10 May 2022.

16 SABC News. 16 March 2021. 'SAFA President Dr Danny Jordaan on Motsepe's CAF presidency'. YouTube https://www.youtube.com/watch?v=GLnjFi3BGac Accessed 11 April 2022.

17 The World Economic Forum, founded in 1971, is based in Switzerland. It's mostly funded by its 1 000 member companies. It views its mission as 'improving the state of the world by engaging business, political, academic, and other leaders of society to shape global, regional, and industry agendas'.

2. The dazzle and the dark side: Taking the reins at CAF

1 Pavitt, M. 1 March 2021. 'Motsepe expected to become CAF President with rivals reportedly set to withdraw'. Inside the Games. https://www.insidethegames.biz/articles/1104840/motsepe-football-caf-president-election Accessed 10 May 2022.

2 Al Mouahidi, K. 4 March 2021. 'Election to the CAF: The clarification of Jacques Anouma from Côte d'Ivoire'. MedAfricaTimes. https://medafricatimes.com/22667-election-to-the-caf-the-clarification-of-jacques-anouma-from-cote-divoire.html Accessed 10 May 2022.

3 Francsjeux.com. 8 March 2021. 'With Patrice Motsepe, Gianni Infantino secures the voices of Africa'. https://www.francsjeux.com/2021/03/08/with-patrice-motsepe-gianni-infantino-secures-the-voices-of-africa/ Accessed 10 May 2022.

4 Chukwu, S. 13 March 2021 'Motsepe cannot shake off Fifa influence, but he can succeed with CAF governance reform'. Goal. https://www.goal.com/en-za/news/motsepe-cannot-shake-off-fifa-influence-but-he-can-succeed/1q1rtp85mp5rk1uol62jq1lxjz Accessed 10 May 2022. The other vice-presidents were Souleiman Hassan Waberi of Djibouti, Seidou Mbombo Njoya of Cameroon and Kanizat Ibrahim of Comoros.

5 Onyii. 7 February 2020. '#CAFPwCAuditReport: How Ahmad's inner circle binged on $24 million CAF cash'. Fifa Colonialism. https://fifacolonialism.com/cafpwcauditreport-how-ahmads-inner-circle-binged-on-24-million-caf-cash/ Accessed 23 May 2022. Initiated in 2016 under Infantino, FIFA Forward expends capital on promoting football, with the FIFA congress granting each of its member associations financial support to help eliminate economic inequalities in football. FIFA Forward's deposits are in a separate escrow account and can only be accessed if a project has been identified and its finances agreed to by a relevant committee.

6 Conn, D. 16 March 2017. 'Issa Hayatou deposed after 29 years as CAF president by Ahmad Ahmad'. The Guardian. https://www.theguardian.com/football/2017/mar/16/issa-hayatou-caf-president-ahmad-ahmad-madagascar-fa-fifa Accessed 10 May 2022.

7 FIFA chief Gianni Infantino had close links to UEFA, having previously been its secretary-general before he became FIFA president in 2016. This followed a complicated series of events, starting when Infantino acted in the post of the world governing body's leader in 2015 when then president Sepp Blatter was suspended over an irregular payment to UEFA president Michel Platini. Blatter and Platini were then both banned by FIFA. Infantino ran officially for FIFA president in 2016, beating rival Issa Hayatou, who had previously been CAF president for 29 years.

8   Chukwu, S. 13 March 2021 'Motsepe cannot shake off Fifa influence, but he can succeed with CAF governance reform'. Goal. https://www.goal.com/en-za/news/motsepe-cannot-shake-off-fifa-influence-but-he-can-succeed/1q1rtp85mp5rk1uol62jq1lxjz Accessed 10 May 2022.

9   CNBCAfrica. 16 May 2021. 'Rwandan President praises new mindset for African football'. https://www.cnbcafrica.com/2021/rwandan-president-praises-new-mindset-for-african-football/ Accessed 11 April 2022.

10 FIFA found that Bwalya had accepted bribes and banned him for two years from taking part in any football activity. In 2019, FIFA reduced Bwalya's ban to time served, but this did not absolve him as he remained guilty of corruption.

11 Baloyi, C, Khoza, N and Ndebele, S. 12 March 2021. 'Motsepe told: Prioritise African unity, TV rights deal'. SowetanLive. https://www.sowetanlive.co.za/sport/soccer/2021-03-12-motsepe-told-prioritise-african-unity-tv-rights-deal/ Accessed 11 April 2022.

12 Mpete, M. 11 March 2021. 'Top football legends endorse Motsepe's ascendancy'. Daily Sun. https://www.dailysun.co.za/dailysun/sport/top-football-legends-endorse-motsepes-ascendancy-20210310 Accessed 12 April 2022.

13 Baleka, M. 12 March 2021. 'There is so much to admire about Patrice Motsepe, says Norman Arendse'. IOL. https://www.iol.co.za/sport/soccer/africa/there-is-so-much-to-admire-about-patrice-motsepe-says-norman-arendse-bbcd073e-715a-4c4b-9623-337e3ba5ffef Accessed 10 May 2022.

14 Strohschein, J. 3 December 2021. 'Patrice Motsepe: CAF President by the grace of Infantino'. DW. https://www.dw.com/en/patrice-motsepe-caf-president-by-the-grace-of-infantino/a-56852726 Accessed 13 April 2022.

15 Koubakin, R. 2 March 2021. 'CAF election: African football is at a crossroads'. DW. https://www.dw.com/en/caf-election-african-football-is-at-a-crossroads/a-56720175 Accessed 13 April 2022.

16 Edwards, P. 8 March 2021. 'Motsepe to become CAF president as Ahmad appeal fails'. BBC Sport Africa. https://www.bbc.com/sport/africa/56323524 Accessed 23 May 2022.

17 CAF Online. 23 April 2021. 'President Motsepe takes his office at CAF headquarters'. https://www.cafonline.com/news-center/news/caf-president-dr-patrice-motsepe-holds-key-meetings-in-cairo Accessed 23 May 2022.

18 Ibid.

19 Strydom, M. 17 March 2021. 'Why Patrice Motsepe has high hopes for his new secretary-general Veron Mosengo-Omba'. DispatchLIVE. https://www.dispatchlive.co.za/sport/2021-03-17-why-patrice-motsepe-has-high-hopes-for-his-new-secretary-general-veron-mosengo-omba/ Accessed 17 May 2022.

20 Sibembe, Y. 17 May 2021. 'New CAF president Patrice Motsepe says his team will score for African football'. Daily Maverick. https://www.dailymaverick.co.za/article/2021-03-17-new-caf-president-patrice-motsepe-says-his-team-will-score-for-african-football/ Accessed 30 March 2022.

21 Kunti, S. 16 March 2021. 'Motsepe backs Veron to hit the ground running at CAF and tells TV it is time to pay Africans'. Inside World Football. https://www.insideworldfootball.com/2021/03/16/motsepe-backs-veron-hit-ground-running-caf-tells-tv-time-pay-africans/ Accessed 17 May 2022.

22 CAFonline. 23 April 2021. 'President Motsepe takes his office at CAF headquarters'. https://www.cafonline.com/news-center/news/caf-president-dr-patrice-motsepe-holds-key-meetings-in-cairo Accessed 13 April 2022.

23 Kickoff Lifestyle. 6 May 2021. 'Motsepe confirms R145m donation'. https://www.kickoff.com/lifestyle/categories/community/patrice-motsepe-foundation-donates-r145m-to-fifa-caf-pan-african-school-championship/698759 Accessed 13 April 2022.

24 Motsepe Foundation. n.d. 'Kay Motsepe Schools Cup: Football' https://www.motsepefoundation.org/sports-music-and-arts/kay-motsepe-schools-cup-football/ Accessed 10 May 2022.

25 Billebault, A. 13 July 2021. 'Football: Heads have been rolling ever since South Africa's Patrice Motsepe arrived at the CAF'. The Africa Report. https://www.theafricareport.com/107602/football-heads-have-been-rolling-ever-since-south-africas-patrice-motsepe-arrived-at-the-caf/ Accessed 13 April 2022.

26 Ibid.

27 Teye, PN. 21 October 2021. 'CAF president Motsepe touts Ghana's World Cup-winning credentials'. Goal. https://www.goal.com/en-gh/news/caf-president-motsepe-touts-ghana-world-cup-winning/z72o8j209lja1o62lw6bbnezh Accessed 13 April 2022.

28 Mark, J. 22 November 2021. 'Safa say referee complaint is valid, confident ahead of Fifa response'. The Citizen. https://www.citizen.co.za/sport/soccer/local-soccer/2913441/safa-referee-complaint-valid-confident-fifa-response/ Accessed 29 May 2022.

29 SL International. 19 November 2021. 'Ghana FA sends message to Motsepe after SAFA complaint'. Soccer Laduma. https://www.soccerladuma.co.za/news/articles/international/categories/african-football/ghana-fa-president-we-don-t-expect-patrice-motsepe-to-take-sides/708809 Accessed 13 April 2022.

30 Kickoff. 29 November 2021. 'Motsepe wades in on standard of African refs'. Chronicle. https://www.chronicle.co.zw/motsepe-wades-in-on-standard-of-african-refs/ Accessed 13 April 2022.

3. The birth of the Brazilians: How Sundowns was made

1 Masilela, J. 1 November 2018. 'Retired Bela-Bela educator Cisco Maphokga also played in the Soweto Derby'. The Post. https://diepos.co.za/52435/retired-bela-bela-educator-cisco-maphokga-also-played-soweto-derby/ Accessed 12 April 2022.

2 Moon, M. 24 March 2021. 'Patrice Motsepe – The man who would save African football?' African Business. https://african.business/2021/03/trade-investment/patrice-motsepe-the-man-who-would-save-african-football/ Accessed 10 May 2022.

3 Sixty years later, of course, a black South African would be the president of the association.

4 Mphaki, A. 16 June 2018. 'Kaizer Chiefs captain among hundreds killed'. Abaphenyi Media Group. http://www.abaphenyi.co.za/news/2018/06/16/kaizer-chiefs-captain-among-hundreds-killed/ Accessed 12 April 2022.

5 Jacobs, S. 21 January 2014. 'Mr Big Bucks and the Mamelodi Sundowns'. The Far Post. https://roadsandkingdoms.com/2014/mr-big-bucks-and-the-mamelodi-sundowns/ Accessed 12 April 2022.

6 Gleeson, M. 22 December 2013. 'Obituary: Zola Mahobe – Soccer boss who lived large on loot'. Sunday Times Lifestyle. https://www.timeslive.co.za/sunday-times/lifestyle/2013-12-22-obituary-zola-mahobe-soccer-boss-who-lived-large-on-loot/ Accessed 12 April 2022.

7 This means that the team that scores more goals in total advances. If the aggregate score is tied, then the winner is the club that scored more goals on its opponent's field (usually referred to as 'the away goals rule').

8 Mlotha, S. 2 August 2020. 'Tsichlas: Why I sold Downs to Motsepe'. Kickoff. https://www.kickoff.com/news/articles/south-africa-news/categories/news/premiership/anastasia-tsichlas-why-i-sold-mamelodi-sundowns-to-patrice-motsepe/682740 Accessed 12 April 2022.

9 Mlotha, S. 4 March 2021. 'Shakes: Patrice blocked my Chiefs move'. https://www.kickoff.com/news/articles/south-africa-news/categories/news/premiership/manqoba-shakes-ngwenya-how-i-joined-mamelodi-sundowns-over-kaizer-chiefs/695498 Accessed 12 April 2022.

4. A crisis of coaches: Sundowns' battle for control

1 News24. 5 December 2004. 'Sundowns coach warned'. https://www.news24.com/news24/sundowns-coach-warned-20041205 Accessed 12 April 2022.

2   Ngobeni, V. 14 December 2005. 'Cappa was not pushed, says Motsepe'. Sapa. https://www.iol.co.za/capeargus/sport/cappa-was-not-pushed-says-motsepe-552435 Accessed 10 May 2022.

3   Ibid.

4   Ibid.

5   Moreotsene, L. 10 December 2007. 'Time running out, Igesund'. SowetanLive. https://www.sowetanlive.co.za/news/2007-12-10-time-running-out-igesund/ Accessed 10 May 2022.

6   Matshe, N. 21 December 2007. 'Motsepe, Igesund in tense crisis meeting'. IOL. https://www.iol.co.za/capeargus/sport/motsepe-igesund-in-tense-crisis-meeting-582877 Accessed 10 May 2022.

7   Soccer Laduma. 8 May 2014. 'Igesund lauds Motsepe and Mosimane. https://www.soccerladuma.co.za/news/articles/local/categories/german-bundesliga/gordon-igesund-has-heaped-praise-on-pitso-and-motsepe/161737 Accessed 10 May 2022.

8   Cape Argus. 22 December 2008. 'Motsepe slates coach Michel for no-show'. https://www.iol.co.za/capeargus/sport/motsepe-slates-coach-michel-for-no-show-596739 Accessed 17 May 2022.

9   Ramphekwa, H. 24 March 2009. 'Familiar face returns to coach Sundowns'. Cape Argus. https://www.iol.co.za/capeargus/sport/familiar-face-returns-to-coach-sundowns-600061 Accessed 17 May 2022.

10 On 21 March 1960, after a day of demonstrations against the hated pass laws, a crowd of about 7 000 protesters went to the police station in Sharpeville. The police opened fire on them, killing 69 people and injuring 180 others. Many were shot in the back as they fled.

11 Lerman, S. 5 February 2011. 'Downs coach steps down after death threats'. Sapa. https://www.timeslive.co.za/sport/soccer/2011-02-05-downs-coach-steps-down-after-death-threats/ Accessed 10 May 2022.

12 Ibid.

13 Moonda, F. 1 October 2012. 'Sundowns coach Neeskens attacked'. Africa ESPN. https://africa.espn.com/football/news/story/_/id/1176798/mamelodi-sundowns-coach-johan-neeskens-attacked-by-fans Accessed 10 May 2022.

14 Moholoha, R, Molefe, M and Bambani, C. 8 October 2012. '"Hands off Neeskens": Motsepe warns fans'. TimesLive. https://www.timeslive.co.za/news/south-africa/2012-10-08-hands-off-neeskens-motsepe-warns-fans/ Accessed 10 May 2022.

15 Mvoko, V. 16 November 2011. 'Patrice Motsepe on the threat of nationalization'. https://www.forbes.com/sites/kerryadolan/2011/11/16/patrice-motsepe-on-the-threat-of-nationalization/ Accessed 12 April 2022.

5. The big time: The Pitso Mosimane years

1   Kickoff. 20 August 2013. 'Analysing Motsepe's decade in charge'. https://www.kickoff.com/news/articles/south-africa-news/categories/news/premiership/patrice-motsepes-lack-of-success-at-mamelodi-sundowns/545365 Accessed 12 April 2022.

2   Billiat would score 22 goals for Sundowns in the PSL and a penalty in the 2014-15 Nedbank Cup. He performed well, too, at the FIFA Club World Cup Japan in 2016 on a legendary outing with Sundowns.

3   There was anger at FIFA, as the federation did not back the Zimbabwe Football Association's decision to sanction the players and managers because the association had acted without its involvement during the disciplinary process. In the end, the bannings were lifted in 2018, although the personal harm and that to the Zimbabwe Football Association remained for some time.

4   Young, J. 11 January 2021. 'How Pitso Mosimane built a dynasty with Mamelodi Sundowns'. BTL. https://breakingthelines.com/manager-analysis/how-pitso-mosimane-built-a-dynasty-with-mamelodi-sundowns/ Accessed 10 May 2022.

5   Soccer Laduma. 27 February 2019. 'Throwback – How Teko Modise won Sundowns the title in 2014'. https://www.soccerladuma.co.za/news/articles/local/categories/south-africa/throwback-how-teko-modise-won-sundowns-the-title-in-2014/650926 Accessed 10 May 2022.
6   Gleeson, M. 7 December 2016. 'Second-chance Sundowns hit Club World Cup ahead of schedule'. Reuters. https://www.reuters.com/article/ozasp-uk-soccer-club-mamelodi-idAFKBN13W0L0 Accessed 13 April 2022.
7   Ngidi, N. 10 September 2020. 'South Africa: The three pillars of Mamelodi Sundowns' success'. New Frame. https://allafrica.com/stories/202009160880.html Accessed 10 May 2022.
8   Kickoff. 24 October 2016. 'Mosimane ends Motsepe's wait'. https://www.kickoff.com/news/articles/world-news/categories/news/caf-champions-league/mamelodi-sundowns-patrice-motsepe-credits-pitso-mosimane-after-champions-league-triumph/573647 Accessed 12 April 2022.
9   Ibid.
10 Vardien, T. 10 March 2021. '7 standout quotes from soon-to-be new CAF president Patrice Motsepe'. News24. https://www.news24.com/sport/Soccer/BafanaBafana/7-standout-quotes-from-soon-to-be-new-caf-president-patrice-motsepe-20210310 Accessed 13 April 2022.
11 CAF Online. 10 December 2016. 'Billiat out to make the Sundowns shine'. https://www.cafonline.com/news-center/news/billiat-out-to-make-the-sundowns-shine Accessed 13 April 2022.
12 Amounts for these high-level trades within football are conventionally given in euros or pounds, as those are the currencies in which the buyouts would be done, not in rands.
13 Strydom, M. 13 January 2017. 'It was Motsepe who insisted on R25-million buyout clause: Keagan Dolly's dad'. SowetanLive. https://www.sowetanlive.co.za/sport/soccer/2017-01-13-it-was-motsepe-who-insisted-on-r25-million-buyout-clause-keagan-dollys-dad/ Accessed 10 May 2022.
14 Ntloko, M. 10 January 2017. 'I would sell Dolly for R5, says a vexed Motsepe'. BusinessLive. https://www.businesslive.co.za/bd/sport/soccer/2017-01-10-i-would-sell-dolly-for-r5-says-a-vexed-motsepe/ Accessed 17 May 2022.
15 Kickoff. 13 January 2017. '"Motsepe was misinformed on Dolly"'. https://www.kickoff.com/news/articles/south-africa-news/categories/news/psl-transfer-news/patrice-motsepe-was-misinformed-on-keagan-dolly-sundowns-made-9-changes-to-contract-in-disputed-buyout-clause/575781 Accessed 13 April 2022.
16 Kickoff. 17 January 2017. 'Downs set for internal investigation'. https://www.kickoff.com/news/articles/south-africa-news/categories/news/premiership/mamelodi-sundowns-set-for-internal-investigation-into-keagan-dolly-contract-mistake/575868 Accessed 17 May 2022.
17 Kickoff. 13 January 2017. 'How Sundowns won Dolly DRC case'. https://www.kickoff.com/news/articles/south-africa-news/categories/news/psl-transfer-news/how-mamelodi-sundowns-won-psl-drc-keagan-dolly-contract-dispute-case-patrice-motsepe/575670 Accessed 13 April 2022.
18 Bongani Zungu, Nyasha Mushekwi, Percy Tau, Bennett Mnguni, Siaka Tiene, Siboniso Gaxa and Siyanda Xulu were among other players who would also be able to pursue careers in Europe having been honed at Sundowns.
19 Collins, N. 7 January 2017. 'Goodbye Dolly! Why South Africa's shining talent must go to Europe, before it's too late'. Neal and Pray. http://neal-collins.blogspot.com/2017/01/goodbye-dolly-why-south-africas-shining.html Accessed 10 May 2022.
20 Ngidi, N. 10 September 2020. 'South Africa: The three pillars of Mamelodi Sundowns' success'. New Frame. https://allafrica.com/stories/202009160880.html Accessed 10 May 2022.

21 Kaizer Chiefs. 7 January 2017. https://www.kaizerchiefs.com/news/congratulations-sundowns-motaung/ Accessed 13 April 2022.

22 Kickoff. 11 May 2018. 'Sundowns boss hails importance of Barca visit'. https://www.kickoff.com/news/articles/south-africa-news/categories/news/mamelodi-sundowns/mamelodi-sundowns-president-patrice-mots/589324 Accessed 19 April 2022.

23 Ibid.

6. The broadsides and the bucks: A new era begins

1 Moyo, L. 14 July 2017. 'Another African payday for Downs'. Kickoff. https://www.kickoff.com/news/articles/world-news/categories/news/caf-champions-league/mamelodi-sundowns-again-in-the-money-as-restructured-caf-champions-league-pays-dividends/580736 Accessed 10 May 2022.

2 Molefe, M. 16 November 2021. 'Revealed: Downs' bonus structure'. Soccer Laduma. https://www.soccerladuma.co.za/news/articles/local/categories/mamelodi-sundowns/how-downs-reward-players-and-coaches/708645 Accessed 10 May 2022.

3 Ibid.

4 News24. 25 October 2016. 'Motsepe: Players must divvy up the winnings'. https://www.news24.com/Sport/motsepe-players-must-divvy-up-the-winnings-20161025 Accessed 13 April 2022.

5 Mphahlele, M. 16 May 2019. '"Sundowns creates millionaires," says coach Pitso Mosimane'. SowetanLive. https://www.sowetanlive.co.za/sport/soccer/2019-05-16-sundowns-creates-millionaires-says-coach-pitso-mosimane/ Accessed 10 May 2022.

6 The competition was held every year until 2021, when its dates were complicated by delays caused by covid-19. It had been hosted by Brazil, Japan, the United Arab Emirates, Morocco and Qatar, and South Africa had put in a bid to host it in 2022.

7 Ditlhobolo, A. 1 October 2020. 'Pitso Mosimane's top 10 moments as Mamelodi Sundowns coach'. Goal. https://www.goal.com/en/lists/pitso-mosimanes-top-10-moments-as-mamelodi-sundowns-coach/12hwn1mxp1prp1ngshougaey23 Accessed 10 May 2022.

8 Mphahlele, M. 16 May 2019. '"Sundowns creates millionaires," says coach Pitso Mosimane'. SowetanLive. https://www.sowetanlive.co.za/sport/soccer/2019-05-16-sundowns-creates-millionaires-says-coach-pitso-mosimane/ Accessed 10 May 2022.

9 Ibid.

10 Fakude, E. 4 December 2019. 'Five reasons Pitso will stay with Downs'. Kickoff. https://www.kickoff.com/news/articles/south-africa-news/categories/news/premiership/five-reasons-pitso-mosimane-wants-to-renew-his-mamelodi-sundowns-contract/668795 Accessed 13 April 2022.

11 Ibid.

12 Ibid.

13 Sports Club. 21 May 2021. 'Pitso's agency MT Sports responds to Sundowns lawsuit'. https://www.sportsclub.co.za/pitsos-agency-mt-sports-responds-to-sundowns-lawsuit-1/ Accessed 13 April 2022.

14 Ibid.

15 Ntloko, M. 31 May 2021. 'Tension between Mosimane and former club Sundowns continues to escalate'. SowetanLive. https://www.sowetanlive.co.za/sport/soccer/2021-05-31-tension-between-mosimane-and-former-club-sundowns-continues-to-escalate/ Accessed 13 April 2022.

16 Sang, K. 16 July 2021. 'CAF Champions League: Al Ahly will beat Kaizer Chiefs if "lucky charm" Motsepe attends final – Mosimane'. Goal. https://www.goal.com/en/news/caf-champions-league-mosimane-al-ahly-will-beat-kaizer/fspefgs5pvrs1bd286sasjsl0 Accessed 10 May 2022.

17 Nkanjeni, U. 14 March 2022. 'Pitso Mosimane: "Sundowns must leave me alone. I've moved on"'. TimesLive. https://www.timeslive.co.za/sport/soccer/2022-03-14-pitso-mosimane-sundowns-must-leave-me-alone-ive-moved-on/ Accessed 13 April 2022.

18 Tshwaku, K. 13 March 2022. 'Mosimane fires broadside at 'Downs after bus blocked en route to stadium: What do you want from me?'. News24. https://www.news24.com/sport/soccer/mosimane-fires-broadside-at-downs-after-bus-blocked-en-route-to-stadium-what-do-you-want-from-me-20220313 Accessed 13 April 2022.

19 Gumede. N. 17 March 2022. 'Mosimane slams Motsepe, likens his CAF leadership to that of Hayatou'. Phakaaathi. https://www.citizen.co.za/sport/soccer/local-soccer/3052262/mosimane-slams-motsepe-likens-his-caf-leadership-to-that-of-hayatou/ Accessed 13 April 2022.

20 South Africa's apartheid regime eventually started a process towards democracy in the early 1990s. Sudan gained independence towards Britain in 1955. Egypt was recognised as a sovereign state by Britain in 1922. Ethiopia was never colonised.

21 Edwards, P. 14 January 2021. 'How CAF went from stopping Hayatou's pension to honouring him'. BBC. https://www.bbc.com/sport/africa/55654829 Accessed 13 April 2022.

22 Gumede. N. 17 March 2022. 'Mosimane slams Motsepe, likens his CAF leadership to that of Hayatou'. Phakaaathi. https://www.citizen.co.za/sport/soccer/local-soccer/3052262/mosimane-slams-motsepe-likens-his-caf-leadership-to-that-of-hayatou/ Accessed 13 April 2022.

23 Enhanced video reviews may determine if a call made on the field was correct or not. Depending on the circumstances, the tech allows a referee to correct a mistake as a result of a clear and obvious error.

24 Gumede. N. 17 March 2022. 'Mosimane slams Motsepe, likens his CAF leadership to that of Hayatou'. Phakaaathi. https://www.citizen.co.za/sport/soccer/local-soccer/3052262/mosimane-slams-motsepe-likens-his-caf-leadership-to-that-of-hayatou/ Accessed 13 April 2022.

25 Motecwane, K. 17 March 2022. 'CAF responds to Pitso's VAR calls'. Soccer Laduma. https://www.soccerladuma.co.za/news/articles/international/categories/african-football/the-confederation-of-african-football-says-it-s-difficult-to-implement-var-in-all-of-africa/714701 Accessed 13 April 2022.

7. A millennial in the chair: Tlhopie Motsepe

1   Molefe, M. 27 February 2021. 'Motsepe confirms Downs successor if he wins CAF'. Soccer Laduma. https://www.soccerladuma.co.za/news/articles/local/categories/mamelodi-sundowns/motsepe-s-downs-successor-confirmed/695171 Accessed 10 May 2022.

2   Richardson, J. 19 March 2021. 'Who is Tlhopane Motsepe?'. The South African. https://www.thesouthafrican.com/sport/soccer/psl-south-africa/tlhopane-motsepe-gets-seal-of-approval-from-sundowns-coach/ Accessed 18 May 2022.

3   Ibid.

4   Strydom, M. 26 February 2021. 'CAF presidential candidate Patrice Motsepe confirms who will run Mamelodi Sundowns'. SowetanLive. https://www.sowetanlive.co.za/sport/soccer/2021-02-26-caf-presidential-candidate-patrice-motsepe-confirms-who-will-run-mamelodi-sundowns/ Accessed 19 April 2022.

5   Ibid.

6   Ntloko, M. 1 September 2020. 'Premiership champions Mamelodi Sundowns unveil their new kit'. TimesLive. https://www.timeslive.co.za/sport/soccer/2020-09-01-premiership-champions-mamelodi-sundowns-unveil-their-new-kit/ Accessed 13 April 2022.

7   Fakude, E. 14 December 2020. 'Diouf: Downs among biggest in the world'. Kickoff. https://www.kickoff.com/news/articles/south-africa-news/categories/news/premiership/el-hadji-diouf-explains-attendance-at-mamelodi-sundowns-50th-anniversary-event/691113 Accessed 13 April 2022.

8   Strydom, M. 21 September 2021. 'Tlhopie Motsepe targets fellow millennials to

expand Sundowns' fan base'. SowetanLive. https://www.sowetanlive.co.za/sport/soccer/2021-09-21-tlhopie-motsepe-targets-fellow-millennials-to-expand-sundowns-fan-base/ Accessed 19 April 2022.

9 Strydom, M. 9 September 2021. 'Tlhopie Motsepe: Sundowns' coaching trinity ensured transition in life after Pitso'. SowetanLive. https://www.sowetanlive.co.za/sport/soccer/2021-09-09-tlhopie-motsepe-sundowns-coaching-trinity-ensured-transition-in-life-after-pitso/ Accessed 19 April 2022.

10 Faver, D. 29 April 2022. 'Rulani's challenge To Chiefs, Pirates: We need stronger rivals'. Soccer Laduma. https://www.soccerladuma.co.za/news/articles/local/categories/mamelodi-sundowns/rulani-mokwena-s-challenge-to-chiefs-and-pirates/ Accessed 10 May 2022.

11 Gower, P. 8 March 2021. 'TuksSport and Mamelodi Sundowns form a partnership to scientifically enhance the game of football'. University of Pretoria. https://www.up.ac.za/football/news/post_2957159-tukssport-tukssport-and-mamelodi-sundowns-form-a-partnership-to-scientifically-enhance-the-game-of-football Accessed 19 April 2022.

12 Hendricks, A. 29 July 2019. 'The new football champions of Stellenbosch'. New Frame. https://www.newframe.com/the-new-football-champions-of-stellenbosch/ Accessed 19 April 2022.

13 Motshwane, G. 10 December 2019. 'The battle of the billionaires: Who will prevail?' SowetanLive. https://www.sowetanlive.co.za/sport/soccer/2019-12-10-the-battle-of-the-billionaires-who-will-prevail/ Accessed 10 May 2022.

14 Pillay, B. 19 March 2022. 'Mamelodi Sundowns chairman Tlhopane Motsepe responds to Al Ahly's complaint, states no supporters blocked bus'. Sports Brief. https://sportsbrief.com/football/mamelodi-sundowns/13501-mamelodi-sundowns-chairman-tlhopane-motsepe-responds-al-ahlys-complaint-states-no-supporters-blocked-bus/ Accessed 13 April 2022.

15 Roc Nation was founded in 2008 and has since become one of the world's biggest entertainment companies. Its agency, Roc Nation Sports, was launched in 2013, and became Roc Nation Unified in 2022. Roc Nation Unified supplies marketing, branding and sponsorship strategies, as well as philanthropic and communication strategies, to artists, athletes, events, venues, leagues, teams and brands.

16 Motshwane, G. 17 September 2021. 'Jay-Z and company ready to rock Mzansi with Sundowns signing'. City Press. https://www.news24.com/citypress/sport/jay-z-and-company-ready-to-rock-mzansi-with-sundowns-signing-20210917 Accessed 14 May 2022.

17 Impey, S. 8 June 2020. '"We didn't sign Siya the rugby star": How Roc Nation is building the Kolisi brand'. SportsPro. https://www.sportspromedia.com/analysis/siya-kolisi-roc-nation-springboks-rugby-world-cup-south-africa-coronavirus/ Accessed 14 May 2022.

18 SA Rugby Mag. 9 December 2021. 'Roc Nation boss: SA rugby players have no voice'. https://www.sarugbymag.co.za/yormark-sa-rugby/ Accessed 14 May 2022.

19 Mphahlele, M. 25 May 2020. 'Motsepe on his stake in the Bulls: "Rugby brings black and white South Africans together"'. TimesLive. https://www.timeslive.co.za/sport/rugby/2020-05-25-motsepe-on-his-stake-in-the-bulls-rugby-brings-black-and-white-south-africans-together/ Accessed 19 April 2022.

8. Not a moment's silence: The first year at CAF

1 Football Ghana. 21 October 2021. 'CAF president Patrice Motsepe defends why World Cup every two years will help Africa'. https://footballghana.com/caf-president-patrice-motsepe-defends-why-world-cup-every-two-years-will-help-africa Accessed 11 May 2022.

2 AP News. 13 October 2021. 'French football league opposes plans for biennial World Cup'. https://apnews.com/article/soccer-sports-europe-france-fifa-3c9fe2f628fddde1c2381533f0b2e93d Accessed 13 April 2022.

3 Gibbs, H. 7 December 2021. 'FIFA's love affair with CAF is fuel for world football bust-up'. IOL. https://www.iol.co.za/sport/soccer/africa/fifas-love-affair-with-caf-is-fuel-for-world-football-bust-up-b7e8ef94-4685-43bf-8c05-c19ee6adb3a2 Accessed 13 April 2022.

4 The Fédération Internationale des Associations de Footballeurs Professionnels is the worldwide representative organisation for 65 000 professional footballers in 67 national players' associations.

5 Associated Press. 19 May 2021. 'Saudi Arabia formally proposes World Cups every two years'. ESPN. https://africa.espn.com/football/fifa-world-cup/story/4389476/saudi-arabia-formally-proposes-world-cups-every-two-years Accessed 11 May 2022.

6 Gibbs, H. 7 December 2021. 'FIFA's love affair with CAF is fuel for world football bust-up'. IOL. https://www.iol.co.za/sport/soccer/africa/fifas-love-affair-with-caf-is-fuel-for-world-football-bust-up-b7e8ef94-4685-43bf-8c05-c19ee6adb3a2 Accessed 13 April 2022.

7 BBC Sport. 31 March 2022. 'FIFA did not propose biennial World Cup'. https://www.bbc.com/sport/football/60937907 Accessed 18 May 2022.

8 Ibid.

9 Chikamhi, E. 7 February 2022. 'Zimbabwe: Proposed African Super League excites Dynamos'. AllAfrica. https://allafrica.com/stories/202202070169.html Accessed 13 April 2022.

10 Ibid.

11 Lambley, G. 22 October 2021. 'Patrice Motsepe backs idea for Soccer World Cup every 2 years for "benefit of African football"'. The South African. https://www.thesouthafrican.com/sport/soccer/patrice-motsepe-backs-idea-for-soccer-world-cup-every-2-years-for-benefit-of-african-football/ Accessed 13 April 2022.

12 Kunti, S. 7 February 2022. 'More African Super League talk as Motsepe says it will be FIFA run and privately funded'. Inside World Football. https://www.insideworldfootball.com/2022/02/07/african-super-league-talk-motsepe-says-will-fifa-run-privately-funded/ Accessed 13 April 2022.

13 Mnyandu, M. 5 February 2022. 'Infantino – African Super League is different from the European version'. iDiskiTimes. https://www.idiskitimes.co.za/international/african-football/infantino-african-super-league-is-different-from-the-european-version/ Accessed 13 April 2022.

14 Strydom, M. 21 December 2021. 'CAF appoints Infront France to manage TV broadcast services of major tournaments'. HeraldLIVE. https://www.heraldlive.co.za/sport/soccer/2021-12-21-caf-appoints-infront-france-to-manage-tv-broadcast-services-of-major-tournaments/ Accessed 13 April 2022.

15 Ibid.

16 Cotterill, J, Massoudi, A and Blitz, R. 10 February 2015. 'Dalian Wanda buys Sepp Blatter nephew's sports rights agency'. Financial Times. https://www.ft.com/content/92157ce8-b070-11e4-a2cc-00144feab7de Accessed 30 May 2022.

17 TikTok. 6 January 2022. 'TikTok unites African football fans through partnership with Confederation of African Football'. https://newsroom.tiktok.com/en-africa/tiktok-sponsors-caf Accessed 14 May 2022.

18 Wirfengla, I. 27 January 2022. 'Inside the stampede at Olembé Stadium'. New Frame. https://www.newframe.com/inside-the-stampede-at-olembe-stadium/ Accessed 11 May 2022.

19 Eyewitness News. 26 January 2022. 'African football boss blames closed gate for Cup of Nations tragedy'. https://ewn.co.za/2022/01/26/african-football-boss-blames-closed-gate-for-cup-of-nations-tragedy Accessed 19 April 2022.

20 Mvoko, V. 16 November 2011. 'Patrice Motsepe on the threat of nationalization'. https://www.forbes.com/sites/kerryadolan/2011/11/16/patrice-motsepe-on-the-threat-of-nationalization/ Accessed 19 April 2022.

21 BBC Africa. 6 April 2022. 'Afcon 2023: Ivory Coast progress "reassures" CAF president Patrice Motsepe'. https://www.modernghana.com/sports/1150136/afcon-2023-ivory-coast-progress-reassures-caf.html Accessed 11 May 2022.

9. Crushing the devil: How a family was made

1   The nickname for *Forbes*'s list of those claiming to have more than a billion dollars in the bank, named for the American convention of separating thousands with commas ($1,000,000,000).
2   Amanze, J. n.d. 'Motsepe, Cuthbert Alban Ramasodi'. Dictionary of African Christian Biography. https://dacb.org/stories/botswana/motsepe-cuthbert/ Accessed 11 May 2022.
3   Mandela and Magano had got to know each other through the operations of Umkhonto we Sizwe, the militant underground established by Mandela in 1961. Later, Mandela and Magano would spend 17 years together in prison on Robben Island. Mandela would be there for a decade longer than his friend.
4   Tau, P. 20 July 2011. '"We helped keep Mandela safe"'. The Star. https://www.iol.co.za/the-star/we-helped-keep-mandela-safe-1102738 Accessed 11 May 2022.
5   Amanze, J. n.d. 'Motsepe, Cuthbert Alban Ramasodi'. Dictionary of African Christian Biography. https://dacb.org/stories/botswana/motsepe-cuthbert/ Accessed 11 May 2022.
6   Motsepe, GJM. 15 August 1996. Truth and Reconciliation Commission. https://www.justice.gov.za/trc/hrvtrans/pretoria/motsepe.htm Accessed 11 May 2022.
7   Gordon, D. 28 July 2009. 'Daughter of exile traces the pulse of Y-Generation'. Business Day. https://www.hci.co.za/2009/07/28/daughter-of-exile-traces-the-pulse-of-y-generation/ Accessed 11 May 2022.
8   Kubheka, T. 14 December 2015. 'Patrice Motsepe brings early Christmas to Soweto children'. Eyewitness News. https://ewn.co.za/2015/12/14/Patrice-Motsepe-brings-early-Christmas-to-Soweto-children Accessed 11 May 2022.
9   Laurence, P. 30 September 2010. 'Bridgette Radebe, the ANCYL and nationalisation'. Politicsweb. https://www.politicsweb.co.za/news-and-analysis/bridgette-radebe-the-ancyl-and-nationalisation Accessed 15 April 2022.
10 Ibid.
11 Radebe, who joined the ANC in 1976, was jailed on Robben Island after being convicted of terrorism. He was minister of public works under Nelson Mandela, minister of public enterprises and then transport under Thabo Mbeki, minister of constitutional and justice development and then minister in the presidency under Jacob Zuma, and minister of energy and mineral resources under Cyril Ramaphosa. Radebe is considered a possible choice for deputy president if Ramaphosa wins at the ANC's elective conference in December 2022.
12 People. 6 December 1976. 'What the world needs now is love, sweet love – especially the beauty contest of the same name'. https://people.com/archive/what-the-world-needs-now-is-love-sweet-love-especially-the-beauty-contest-of-the-same-name-vol-6-no-23/ Accessed 11 May 2022.
13 Masilela, J. 13 December 2015. 'Memories of village boy called Tlhopane'. Sunday Independent. https://www.iol.co.za/sundayindependent/memories-of-village-boy-called-tlhopane-1959581 Accessed 11 May 2022.
14 Bishop, C. 2017. *Africa's Billionaires: Inspirational stories from the continent's wealthiest people*. Penguin Books.
15 Ventures Africa. 17 July 2012. 'Lord of the Mines: Billionaire Patrice Motsepe'. https://venturesafrica.com/lord-of-the-mines-patrice-motsepe/ Accessed 11 April 2022.
16 Barnard, M. 2015. 'The Motsepe Ethic: An exploration of the role of the BEE power elite'. Research Report, University of the Witwatersrand. https://wiredspace.wits.ac.za/jspui/bitstream/10539/18389/2/the%20motsepe%20ethic%20final%20sub.pdf Accessed 11 April 2022.

17 Ibid.
18 Bophuthatswana was one of ten 'bantustans' (or 'homelands') set aside for black inhabitants of South Africa as part of the policy of apartheid. The others were Lebowa, Transkei, Ciskei, Venda, Gazankulu, KaNgwane, KwaNdebele, KwaZulu and QwaQwa.
19 TimesLive. 18 February 2019. 'I come from old money, my hands are clean, says Patrice Motsepe'. https://www.timeslive.co.za/politics/2019-02-18-i-come-from-old-money-my-hands-are-clean-says-patrice-motsepe/ Accessed 11 April 2022.
20 Cobley, AG. 1986. '"On the shoulders of giants": The black petty bourgeoisie in politics and society in South Africa, 1924 to 1950'. Thesis. University of London. https://eprints.soas.ac.uk/33865/1/11010655.pdf Accessed 11 May 2022.
21 Brummer, S. 28 January 2000. 'Granite mining scars Bakgatla village'. Mail&Guardian. https://mg.co.za/article/2000-01-28-granite-mining-scars-bakgatla-village/ Accessed 11 April 2022.
22 Cantwell, L. 2015. 'Chiefly Power in a Frontline State: Kgosi Linchwe II, the Bakgatla and Botswana in the South African Liberation Struggle, 1948–1994'. *Journal of Southern African Studies*, 41(2), 255-272.
23 Mangope was born in 1923 into a ruling family of chiefs, and became leader of the Mathlathowa region in what is now North West when he was 21. He was made first chief minister of Bophuthatswana in 1972, and then his Bophuthatswana Democratic Party took power in 1977 when the bantustan was declared 'independent' from apartheid South Africa.

10. The careful curation: Precious Moloi-Motsepe

1   Milken Institute. 7 August 2020. 'Conversations with Mike Milken: Precious Moloi-Motsepe, co-founder and CEO, Motsepe Foundation'. https://mikemilken.com/podcast/Conversations-with-MM-Precious-Motsepe-0872020.pdf Accessed 11 April 2022.
2   Koka, M. 13 August 2020. 'I wasn't willing to sacrifice family for career: Dr Precious Moloi-Motsepe'. SowetanLive. https://www.sowetanlive.co.za/news/south-africa/2020-08-13-i-wasnt-willing-to-sacrifice-family-for-career-dr-precious-moloi-motsepe/ Accessed 11 May 2022.
3   Hughes, A. 28 September 2018. 'Founder of African Fashion International partners with Global Citizens Festival'. WWD. https://www.yahoo.com/lifestyle/founder-african-fashion-international-partners-132238855.html Accessed 14 April 2022.
4   Channel24. 26 March 2017. 'Dr Precious Moloi-Motsepe celebrates a decade of fashion with AFI'. Yahoo!News. https://uk.news.yahoo.com/dr-precious-moloi-motsepe-celebrates-decade-fashion-afi-074809389.html Accessed 11 May 2022.
5   Mail&Guardian. 8 August 2013. 'A rendezvous for great design'. https://mg.co.za/article/2013-08-08-00-a-rendezvous-for-great-design/ Accessed 14 April 2022.
6   Fashion4Development. n.d. 'Agents of change: Dr Precious Moloi-Motsepe' http://www.fashion4development.com/dr-precious Accessed 25 May 2022.
7   Myburgh Chemaly, J. 27 March 2017. 'Dr Precious Moloi Motsepe on AFI designers and the rise of the African fashion industry'. Wanted Online. https://www.wantedonline.co.za/fashion-and-grooming/2017-03-20-the-best-or-nothing/ Accessed 14 April 2022.
8   Hughes, A. 28 September 2018. 'Founder of African Fashion International partners with Global Citizens Festival'. WWD. https://www.yahoo.com/lifestyle/founder-african-fashion-international-partners-132238855.html Accessed 14 April 2022.
9   Myburgh Chemaly, J. 27 March 2017. 'Dr Precious Moloi Motsepe on AFI designers and the rise of the African fashion industry'. Wanted Online. https://www.wantedonline.co.za/fashion-and-grooming/2017-03-20-the-best-or-nothing/ Accessed 14 April 2022.
10 Franca Sozzani was *Vogue Italia* editor-in-chief.
11 Hughes, A. 28 September 2018. 'Founder of African Fashion International partners with Global Citizens Festival'. WWD. https://www.yahoo.com/lifestyle/founder-african-fashion-international-partners-132238855.html Accessed 11 May 2022.

12 Ibid.
13 Stockenstroom, S. 8 October 2018. 'Joburg Fashion Week a hit with Asian fusion'. Sunday World Lifestyle. https://www.sowetanlive.co.za/sundayworld/lifestyle/2018-10-08-joburg-fashion-week-a-hit-with-asian-fusion/ Accessed 11 May 2022.
14 Hughes, A. 28 September 2018. 'Founder of African Fashion International partners with Global Citizens Festival'. WWD. https://www.yahoo.com/lifestyle/founder-african-fashion-international-partners-132238855.html Accessed 14 April 2022.
15 Ibid.
16 Milken Institute. 7 August 2020. 'Conversations with Mike Milken: Precious Moloi-Motsepe, co-founder and CEO, Motsepe Foundation'. https://mikemilken.com/podcast/Conversations-with-MM-Precious-Motsepe-0872020.pdf Accessed 11 April 2022.
17 Ibid.
18 Ibid.
19 Ibid.
20 Ehlers, A. 2015. 'The Helpmekaar: Rescuing the "volk" through reading, writing and arithmetic, c.1916-c.1965'. *Historia*, 60(2), 87-108.
21 Mogoatlhe, L. 29 November 2018. 'This book is helping South Africans empower themselves and change their lives'. Global Citizen. https://www.globalcitizen.org/en/content/precious-little-black-book-motsepe-foundation/ Accessed 11 May 2022.
22 Motsepe Foundation. n.d. 'ABC Motsepe Eisteddfod Music Competition'. https://www.motsepefoundation.org/sports-music-and-arts/abc-motsepe-sasce-eisteddfod/ Accessed 11 May 2022.
23 Channel24. 26 March 2017. 'Dr Precious Moloi-Motsepe celebrates a decade of fashion with AFI'. Yahoo!News. https://uk.news.yahoo.com/dr-precious-moloi-motsepe-celebrates-decade-fashion-afi-074809389.html Accessed 11 May 2022.
24 Jacobs, C. 14 April 2019. 'Condé Nast International Luxury Conference where the fashionably late and truly fabulous gather'. Sunday Times. https://www.timeslive.co.za/sunday-times/lifestyle/fashion-and-beauty/2019-04-14-cond-nast-international-luxury-conference-where-the-fashionably-late-and-truly-fabulous-gather/ Accessed 11 May 2022.

11. Bottomless flutes: How the billions get bought

1 Robinson, S. 17 April 2005. 'South Africa: The New Rand Lords'. Time. http://content.time.com/time/subscriber/article/0,33009,1050314,00.html Accessed 12 May 2022.
2 Ibid.
3 Ibid.
4 Robinson, S. 6 June 2005. 'Welcome to the Club'. Time. http://content.time.com/time/world/article/0,8599,2050149,00.html Accessed 12 May 2022.
5 Mahlangu, JK. 25 February 2019. @kennydior. https://twitter.com/kennydior/status/1099994119668158464?lang=en Accessed 11 May 2022.
6 Mvoko, V. 16 November 2011. 'Patrice Motsepe on the threat of nationalization'. https://www.forbes.com/sites/kerryadolan/2011/11/16/patrice-motsepe-on-the-threat-of-nationalization/ Accessed 11 May 2022.
7 Bishop, C. 2017. *Africa's Billionaires: Inspirational stories from the continent's wealthiest people.* Penguin Books.
8 Gundan, F. 30 December 2014. 'South African billionaire Patrice Motsepe spends 68-million rands on Cape Town luxury retreat'. Forbes. https://www.forbes.com/sites/faraigundan/2014/12/30/south-african-billionaire-patrice-motsepe-spends-68-million-rands-on-cape-town-luxury-retreat/ Accessed 19 April 2022.
9 Ibid.
10 Shevel, A. 4 September 2011. 'The Rich List – Patrice Motsepe tops it'. Sunday Times. https://www.timeslive.co.za/sunday-times/lifestyle/2011-09-04-the-rich-list-patrice-motsepe-tops-it/ Accessed 12 May 2022.

11 Ibid.

12 Ibid.

13 The way the newspaper saw it, Oppenheimer's estimate had to exclude his family's 40 percent interest in De Beers. Had that not been the case, he would have outweighed Motsepe.

14 Dolan, KA. 16 November 2011. 'Africa's 40 Richest: 2011'. Forbes. https://www.forbes.com/sites/kerryadolan/2011/11/16/africas-40-richest/ Accessed 8 April 2022.

15 Drum Digital. 22 February 2013. 'Minister of police Nathi Mthethwa weds'. News24. https://www.news24.com/drum/News/minister-of-police-nathi-mthethwa-weds-20170728 Accessed 11 May 2022.

16 Veblen, A. 26 May 2013. 'Cap crusaders'. Vogue Arabia. https://en.vogue.me/archive/international/cap-crusaders-amfar-red-carpet-cannes-love-gold/ Accessed 11 May 2022.

17 Francis, J. 27 May 2013. 'Cannes amfAR Gala: We rub shoulders with Leonardo DiCaprio, Jessica Chastain and more at the star-studded charity night'. Fashion. https://fashionmagazine.com/flare/celebrity/amfar-gala-2013-cannes/ Accessed 11 April 2022.

18 Veblen, A. 26 May 2013. 'Cap crusaders'. Vogue Arabia. https://en.vogue.me/archive/international/cap-crusaders-amfar-red-carpet-cannes-love-gold/ Accessed 11 May 2022.

19 Munro, C. 16 August 2014. 'Billionaire Buys $1 Million Picasso Sketch at Leonardo DiCaprio Gala'. Artnet News. https://news.artnet.com/art-world/billionaire-buys-1-million-picasso-sketch-at-leonardo-dicaprio-gala-79143 Accessed 14 April 2022.

20 Ibid.

21 News24. 11 September 2015. 'SA tycoon's pricey pictures land up in Sars sales bin'. https://www.news24.com/News24/sa-tycoons-pricey-pictures-land-up-in-sars-sales-bin-20150911 Accessed 11 May 2022.

22 Ibid.

23 Timm, S. 3 February 2020. 'Former law student turned tech founder sells art platform to Precious Moloi-Motsepe'. VentureBurn. https://ventureburn.com/2020/02/sa-art-platform-wezart-acquired-by-afi/ Accessed 11 May 2022.

24 Motsepe Foundation. n.d. 'Dr Precious Moloi-Motsepe'. https://www.motsepefoundation.org/dr-precious-moloi-motsepe/ Accessed 11 May 2022.

25 Timm, S. 3 February 2020. 'Former law student turned tech founder sells art platform to Precious Moloi-Motsepe'. VentureBurn. https://ventureburn.com/2020/02/sa-art-platform-wezart-acquired-by-afi/ Accessed 11 May 2022.

26 Daniel, L. 3 May 2021. 'President Ramaphosa's Ankole cattle just sold for R2.7 million – with bull "Mufasa" voted best'. Business Insider SA. https://zambezinews24.com/president-ramaphosas-ankole-cattle-just-sold-for-r2-7-million-with-bull-mufasa-voted-best/ Accessed 11 May 2022.

27 Ramalepe, P. 7 March 2022. 'Ramaphosa scores R2.1 million for Ankole cow in cattle auction thanks to Motsepe'. Business Insider SA. https://www.businessinsider.co.za/ramaphosa-sells-ankole-cow-for-r21-million-2022-3 Accessed 11 May 2022.

28 Ibid.

12. The patriotic bourgeoisie: Inside the club

1 Motsepe Foundation. n.d. 'Dr Precious Moloi-Motsepe'. https://www.motsepefoundation.org/dr-precious-moloi-motsepe/ Accessed 23 May 2022.

2 Mahlaka, R. 18 April 2021. 'Forbes 2021 billionaires list: During the pandemic, the very rich got very much richer – even in South Africa'. Daily Maverick. https://www.dailymaverick.co.za/article/2021-04-18-forbes-2021-billionaires-list-during-the-pandemic-the-very-rich-got-very-much-richer-even-in-south-africa/ Accessed 19 May 2022.

3 Sentinel News Service. 11 November 2015. 'Keep a Child Alive raises $3.8 for children and families impacted by HIV and AIDS'. Los Angeles Sentinel. https://lasentinel.net/

keep-a-child-alive-raises-3-8-for-children-and-families-impacted-by-hiv-and-aids. html Accessed 11 May 2022.

4   Ibid.
5   Shah, N. 13 November 2018. 'These dignitaries are attending the Global Citizen festival: Mandela 100'. Global Citizen. https://www.globalcitizen.org/en/content/ mandela-100-dignitary-announcement/ Accessed 19 May 2022.
6   The concert was a triumph, but the night didn't end well. South Africans took to Twitter 'to detail their crime horror stories … with some explaining how they were mugged at gunpoint [or threatened with a knife] outside the stadium, with no police in sight'. The Motsepes weren't blamed. Mjo, O. 3 December 2018. 'Horror stories of crime mar Global Citizen Festival'. Sunday Times. https://www.timeslive.co.za/news/ south-africa/2018-12-03-horror-stories-of-crime-mar-global-citizen-festival/ Accessed 11 May 2022.
7   Shah, N and Gralki, P. 28 September 2019. Global Citizen. 'Almost $1B in commitments made at 2019 Global Citizen festival'. https://www.globalcitizen.org/en/content/ impact-report-2019/ Accessed 19 May 2022.
8   Cobbett, E and Friesen, E. 2014. 'Motsepe's Gift: or how Philanthropy serves Capitalism in South Africa'. *Selected Themes in African Political Studies: Political Conflict and Stability.* Springer.
9   University of Johannesburg. 21 January 2016. 'UJ's Dr Mzukisi Qobo on philanthro-capitalists'. https://www.uj.ac.za/news/ujs-dr-mzukisi-qobo-on-philanthrocapitalists/ Accessed 19 April 2022.
10   Ibid.
11   I-Net Bridge. 20 January 2013. 'Patrice Motsepe donates half his wealth'. BusinessTech. https://businesstech.co.za/news/trending/30852/patrice-motsepe-donates-half-his-wealth/ Accessed 12 April 2022.
12   In February 2020, then American president Donald Trump granted Milken a full pardon.
13   The Giving Pledge. n.d. https://givingpledge.org/pledger?pledgerId=253 Accessed 12 April 2022.
14   News24. 31 January 2013. 'ANC salutes Motsepe'. https://www.news24.com/news24/ anc-salutes-motsepe-20150429 Accessed 12 April 2022.
15   SuperSport. 10 November 2020. 'Safa explains Motsepe nomination for CAF president'. https://supersport.com/general/xtra/news/201110_Safa_explains_Motsepe_nomination_ for_Caf_President Accessed 12 April 2022.

13. A royal family: The Bakgatla ba Mmakau

1   Motsepe and Kgafela are related through Kgafela's mother, the queen mother, Kathleen Nono Motsepe, known as Mofumagadi Kathy or Mma Seingwaeng (mother of Seingwaeng, her only daughter), who was born in Pretoria in 1943, a princess within the Bakgatla ba Mmakau royal family.
2   Harden, B. 11 April 1988. 'Chief Linchwe gets his way'. The Washington Post. https:// www.washingtonpost.com/archive/politics/1988/04/11/chief-linchwe-ii-gets-his-way/03f14b57-7a5f-407d-bfd0-b25ece0a42cb/ Accessed 12 April 2022.
3   Cantwell, L. 2015. 'Chiefly Power in a Frontline State: Kgosi Linchwe II, the Bakgatla and Botswana in the South African Liberation Struggle, 1948–1994'. *Journal of Southern African Studies*, 41(2), 255-272.
4   Ibid.
5   Sikwane, O. 14 March 2016. 'Leaders battle over community's R26 billion wealth'. GroundUp.   https://www.groundup.org.za/article/fight-soul-bakgatla-ba-kgafela/ Accessed 12 April 2022.
6   The crisis in Moruleng reached such a low point in 2015 that Kgafela – a practising attorney in Botswana – threw his hands up and said he no longer wished to be

recognised as a paramount chief in South Africa, where he'd been living for years. North West premier Supra Mahumapelo set up a commission of inquiry in 2018 to probe succession disputes there once and for all, and the commission endorsed Kgafela.

7 'House' here relates to the wives of the king, and means that Manonwana Seamego and Moemise Motsepe were both born of the king's third wife.

8 Moloantoa, D. 6 October 2020. 'A century of Pretoria's Holy Redeemer Catholic Church'. The Heritage Portal. https://www.theheritageportal.co.za/article/century-pretorias-holy-redeemer-catholic-church Accessed 12 May 2022.

9 Historian Tara Weinberg describes this as a 'strongly debated term, employed by the colonial and apartheid governments in a crude or simplistic way, to describe African customary land tenure systems as "group-based", that is, opposite to individual property ownership in Europe'. Weinberg, T. May 2015. 'The contested status of 'communal land tenure' in South Africa'. Rural status report 3. University of the Western Cape. https://media.africaportal.org/documents/PLAAS_Rural_Report_Book_3_-_Tara_-_Web.pdf Accessed 11 May 2022.

10 Rankhumise, SP. 2017. 'The Bakgatla ba ga Motsha under the Native policy of the Transvaal, 1852-1910'. Thesis. North-West University. http://dspace.nwu.ac.za/bitstream/handle/10394/35164/RANKHUMISE_SP.pdf Accessed 23 May 2022.

11 Liebenberg, J. 2006. 'Critical evaluation of the late-restitution process (from the landowner's perspective): The case of Krelingspost, North West province, 2005. *Urban Changes in Different Scales: Systems and Structures*. International Geographical Union.

12 Tlhoaele, D. 17 October 2013. 'Motsepe donates millions to develop his home town'. Pretoria Rekord. https://rekord.co.za/307646/motsepe-donates-millions-to-develop-his-home-town/ Accessed 12 April 2022.

13 IOL. 13 September 2017. 'Protesters claim Motsepes use cash to get control of tribe'. https://www.iol.co.za/pretoria-news/protesters-claim-motsepes-use-cash-to-get-control-of-tribe-11194748 Accessed 14 May 2022.

14. Trying his luck: The birth of African Rainbow Minerals

1 Miningmx.com. 2022. 'Rainmakers and Potstirrers: Patrice Motsepe'. https://www.miningmx.com/rainmakers/profile/70 Accessed 19 May 2022.

2 Stoddard, E. 6 September 2021. 'Annual results: Patrice Motsepe's African Rainbow Minerals reports 136% spike in earnings, flags Transnet woes'. Daily Maverick. https://www.dailymaverick.co.za/article/2021-09-06-annual-results-patrice-motsepes-african-rainbow-minerals-reports-136-spike-in-earnings-flags-transnet-woes/ Accessed 19 May 2022.

3 Gencor was the result of a 1980 merger between the General Mining and Finance Corporation and the Union Corporation, two of the first South African mining companies set up after the discovery of gold in the 1890s. In 1994, it acquired the mining division of Billiton, which demerged in 1997, taking Gencor's non-precious business. Gencor merged its gold assets with Gold Fields to become Gold Fields Limited in 1998.

4 Ventures Africa. 17 July 2012. 'Lord of the Mines: Billionaire Patrice Motsepe'. https://venturesafrica.com/lord-of-the-mines-patrice-motsepe/ Accessed 11 April 2022.

5 Adams, S. 6 March 2008. 'The Prince of Mines'. Forbes. https://www.forbes.com/forbes/2008/0324/088.html?sh=12ea68ad3afe Accessed 11 April 2022.

6 Bishop, C. 2017. *Africa's Billionaires: Inspirational stories from the continent's wealthiest people*. Penguin Books.

7 Ibid.

8 News24. 21 October 2001. 'Reluctant Motsepe leads NAFCOC rebels'. https://www.news24.com/news24/reluctant-motsepe-leads-nafcoc-rebels-20011021 Accessed 11 April 2022.

9 Adams, S. 6 March 2008. 'The Prince of Mines'. Forbes. https://www.forbes.com/forbes/2008/0324/088.html Accessed 11 April 2022.

10 Ibid.
11 Ventures Africa. 17 July 2012. 'Lord of the Mines: Billionaire Patrice Motsepe'. https://venturesafrica.com/lord-of-the-mines-patrice-motsepe/ Accessed 11 April 2022.
12 Mvoko, V. 16 November 2011. 'Patrice Motsepe on the threat of nationalization'. Forbes. https://www.forbes.com/sites/kerryadolan/2011/11/16/patrice-motsepe-on-the-threat-of-nationalization/ Accessed 12 May 2022.
13 Adams, S. 6 March 2008. 'The Prince of Mines'. Forbes. https://www.forbes.com/forbes/2008/0324/088.html Accessed 11 April 2022.
14 Mendoza, J. 21 August 2021. 'The truth about the deadly Vaal Reefs tragedy'. Grunge. https://www.grunge.com/492948/the-truth-about-the-deadly-vaal-reefs-tragedy/ Accessed 12 May 2022.
15 Ibid.
16 Ventures Africa. 17 July 2012. 'Lord of the Mines: Billionaire Patrice Motsepe'. https://venturesafrica.com/lord-of-the-mines-patrice-motsepe/ Accessed 11 April 2022.
17 Adams, S. 6 March 2008. 'The Prince of Mines'. Forbes. https://www.forbes.com/forbes/2008/0324/088.html Accessed 11 April 2022.
18 Ibid.
19 Bishop, C. 2017. *Africa's Billionaires: Inspirational stories from the continent's wealthiest people*. Penguin Books.
20 IOL. 17 May 2002. 'Empowerment hits gold'. https://www.iol.co.za/business-report/economy/empowerment-hits-gold-778604 Accessed 17 May 2022.
21 The deal with ARMgold valued the new company at around $2.8 billion (about R17 billion at the time). Harmony issued 63.67 million new shares to ARMgold shareholders, giving a merger ratio of two Harmony shares for every three ordinary shares held in ARMgold. ARMgold paid a special dividend of R5 a share before the merger. Motsepe retained a preference for paying out dividends.
22 Fin24. 20 June 2004. 'Exciting future awaits Motsepe'. https://www.news24.com/fin24/exciting-future-awaits-motsepe-20040620 Accessed 12 April 2022.
23 Ibid.

15. 'Here are the deals': The fight for business

1   Polity. 21 September 2002. Address by the president of South Africa, Thabo Mbeki, at the NAFCOC Conference, Sun City. https://www.polity.org.za/article/mbeki-nafcoc-conference-21092002-2002-09-21 Accessed 12 April 2022.
2   IOL. 27 November 2000. 'NAFCOC drafts plan for SACOB unity pact'. https://www.iol.co.za/business-report/economy/nafcoc-drafts-plan-for-sacob-unity-pact-784852 Accessed 26 February 2022.
3   News24. 21 October 2001. 'Reluctant Motsepe leads NAFCOC rebels'. https://www.news24.com/news24/reluctant-motsepe-leads-nafcoc-rebels-20011021 Accessed 12 April 2022.
4   Ibid.
5   Ibid.
6   Ibid.
7   Wa ka Ngobeni, E. 19 October 2001. 'NAFCOC relocates despite "ousting" of its leader'. Mail&Guardian. https://mg.co.za/article/2001-10-19-nafcoc-relocates-despite-ousting-of-its-leader/ Accessed 20 May 2022.
8   Mail&Guardian. 1 October 2002. 'Black business has a bold new face'. https://mg.co.za/article/2002-10-01-black-business-has-a-bold-new-face/ Accessed 12 April 2022.
9   Polity. 21 September 2002. Address by the president of South Africa, Thabo Mbeki, at the NAFCOC Conference, Sun City. https://www.polity.org.za/article/mbeki-nafcoc-conference-21092002-2002-09-21 Accessed 12 April 2022.
10 Ibid.
11 IOL. 13 October 2003. 'NAFCOC members' R2bn windfall'. https://www.iol.co.za/

business-report/economy/nafcoc-members-r2bn-windfall-773885 Accessed 12 May 2022.

12 Mail&Guardian. 1 October 2002. 'Black business has a bold new face'. https://mg.co.za/article/2002-10-01-black-business-has-a-bold-new-face/ Accessed 12 April 2022.

13 Ibid.

14 Ibid.

15 IOL. 3 October 2002. 'SA Chamber of Business gets new CEO'. https://www.iol.co.za/news/south-africa/sa-chamber-of-business-gets-new-ceo-95505 Accessed 22 May 2022.

16 Parliamentary Monitoring Group. 2003. 'CHAMSA (Chambers of Commerce & Industry of South Africa) Medium Term Budget Policy Statement – Commentary to the Joint Budget Committee'. https://static.pmg.org.za/docs/2003/appendices/031118chamsa.htm Accessed 24 May 2022.

17 Bonang Mohale would go on to serve as the chief executive of Business Unity South Africa.

18 Mohale, B. 1 September 2021. 'Dear Mr President, please call us: Business is ready and waiting to be part of getting SA out of this mess'. Daily Maverick. https://www.dailymaverick.co.za/opinionista/2021-09-01-dear-mr-president-please-call-us-business-is-ready-and-waiting-to-be-part-of-getting-sa-out-of-this-mess/ Accessed 12 May 2022.

19 Ibid.

20 Sapa. 20 July 2011. 'BMF leaves BUSA'. SowetanLive. https://www.sowetanlive.co.za/business/2011-07-04-bmf-leaves-busa/ Accessed 14 April 2022.

21 News24. 7 September 2011. 'Busa leaders kicked out of summit – report'. https://www.news24.com/fin24/busa-leaders-kicked-out-of-summit-report-20110907 Accessed 14 April 2022.

22 IOL. 21 September 2011. 'Unity of black, white business crucial: Motsepe'. https://www.iol.co.za/business-report/economy/unity-of-black-white-business-crucial-motsepe-1142092 Accessed 22 May 2022.

23 Fin24. 8 September 2011. 'Motsepe to chair black business body'. https://www.news24.com/Fin24/Motsepe-to-chair-black-business-body-20110908 Accessed 14 April 2022.

24 Chauke, A. 22 September 2011. '"Racial discord bad for business": Motsepe'. TimesLive. https://www.timeslive.co.za/news/south-africa/2011-09-22-racial-discord-bad-for-business-motsepe-/ Accessed 14 April 2022

25 Ibid.

26 Ibid.

27 Ibid.

28 Survé, executive chairman of Independent Media and founder of the Sekunjalo Group, has since seen Sekunjalo featured in a damning official inquiry into its relationship with its main funder, the R2.3-trillion state asset manager the Public Investment Corporation. By 2022, banking groups would not do business with Survé's companies. In addition, his newspapers suffered major reputational damage over a story about a decuplet birth in South Africa. Other media outlets identified the story as a hoax.

29 Engineering News. 14 April 2011. 'Seize Brics opportunities – Zuma implores SA business'. https://www.engineeringnews.co.za/print-version/seize-brics-opportunities-zuma-implores-sa-business-2011-04-14 Accessed 14 April 2022.

30 Vanek, M. 22 May 2017. 'Black Business Council, Business Unity South Africa terminate co-operation at Nedlac'. CNBCAfrica. https://www.cnbcafrica.com/2017/black-business-council-vs-business-unity-south-africa/ Accessed 12 May 2022.

31 IOL. 20 April 2019. 'BBC, BUSA will work together to help the economy'. https://www.iol.co.za/business-report/economy/bbc-busa-will-work-together-to-help-the-economy-20907940 Accessed 12 May 2022.

16. From pillar to post: Empowerment and loss

1   Bailey, S. 31 July 2002. 'Godsell, Motsepe call for empowerment calm'. AllAfrica. https://allafrica.com/stories/200208010502.html Accessed 12 April 2022.
2   Itano, N. 14 November 2003. 'South African mines in a 3-way deal'. The New York Times. https://www.nytimes.com/2003/11/14/business/south-african-mines-in-a-3-way-deal.html Accessed 12 May 2022.
3   Josselsohn, D. 8 August 2003. 'Agreement to merge between African Rainbow Minerals and Exploration (Pty) Ltd and African Rainbow Minerals Gold Ltd and Harmony Gold Mining Company Limited'. Notarial certificate. https://www.sec.gov/Archives/edgar/data/1023514/000120561303000189/exhibit4_14.htm Accessed 12 May 2022.
4   Guest, R. 23 December 2004. 'The World's Most Extreme Affirmative Action Program'. WSJ. https://www.wsj.com/articles/SB110376334634607918 Accessed 13 May 2022.
5   Hlongwane, S. 31 January 2013. 'South Africa's only black billionaire donates half his fortune to charity'. The Guardian. https://www.theguardian.com/world/2013/jan/31/south-african-billionaire Accessed 13 May 2022.
6   Itano, N. 14 November 2003. 'South African mines in a 3-way deal'. The New York Times. https://www.nytimes.com/2003/11/14/business/south-african-mines-in-a-3-way-deal.html. Accessed 22 May 2022.
7   City Press. 25 April 2010. 'Miners fail to meet BEE targets'. Fin24. https://www.news24.com/fin24/miners-fail-to-meet-bee-targets-20100425 Accessed 13 May 2022.
8   Sipho Nkosi was CEO of heavy-minerals producer Exxaro Resources after the merger of Eyesizwe, a coal company he formed with other entrepreneurs, and Kumba Resources, a JSE-listed company. He completed an MBA at the University of Massachusetts in 1986. Nkosi – who retired in 2015 – was appointed to the presidency in South Africa in 2022 to lead an initiative to cut government red tape to promote the ease of doing business. Impala Platinum, the world's second-largest platinum company, was formed as a subsidiary of Union Corporation in 1966 before entering a prospecting accord with the Royal Bafokeng Nation in 1968.
9   City Press. 25 April 2010. 'Miners fail to meet BEE targets'. Fin24. https://www.news24.com/fin24/miners-fail-to-meet-bee-targets-20100425 Accessed 12 April 2022.
10 Ibid.
11 IOL. 11 October 2004. 'Motsepe says he lost R500m on Modikwa platinum mine'. https://www.iol.co.za/business-report/companies/motsepe-says-he-lost-r500m-on-modikwa-platinum-mine-759355 Accessed 22 May 2022.
12 Environmental Justice Atlas. n.d. 'Anglo American Platinum Modikwa Mine in Maandagshoek, Limpopo, South Africa'. https://ejatlas.org/conflict/modiwa-platinum-mine-in-maandagshoek-limpopo-south-africa Accessed 13 May 2022.
13 Ibid.
14 Claassens, A. 2019. 'Mining magnates and traditional leaders: the role of law in elevating elite interests and deepening exclusion 2002-2018'. Mistra. https://mistra.org.za/wp-content/uploads/2019/10/Aninka-Claassens_-Working-Paper_Final.pdf Accessed 24 May 2022.
15 The Environmental Justice Atlas (EJ Atlas) emanated out of the Institute of Environmental Science and Technology at the Universitat Autònoma de Barcelona and collated data from different sources about communities around the world struggling for human rights. Its researchers covered Maandagshoek's issues for years. Environmental Justice Atlas. n.d. 'Anglo American Platinum Modikwa Mine in Maandagshoek, Limpopo, South Africa'. https://ejatlas.org/conflict/modiwa-platinum-mine-in-maandagshoek-limpopo-south-africa Accessed 13 May 2022.
16 Duda, T. 5 April 2017. 'Op-Ed: Communal land belongs to the people, not to the chiefs'. Daily Maverick. https://www.dailymaverick.co.za/article/2017-04-05-op-ed-communal-land-belongs-to-the-people-not-to-the-chiefs/ Accessed 13 May 2022.

17 Environmental Justice Atlas. n.d. 'Anglo American Platinum Modikwa Mine in Maandagshoek, Limpopo, South Africa'. https://ejatlas.org/conflict/modiwa-platinum-mine-in-maandagshoek-limpopo-south-africa Accessed 13 May 2022.

18 Ibid.

19 Mvoko, V. 16 November 2011. 'Patrice Motsepe on the threat of nationalization'. Forbes. https://www.forbes.com/sites/kerryadolan/2011/11/16/patrice-motsepe-on-the-threat-of-nationalization/ Accessed 13 April 2022.

20 Dube, M. 5 December 2021. 'Motsepe's mine in reparation row'. Mail&Guardian. https://mg.co.za/news/2021-12-05-motsepes-mine-in-reparation-row/ Accessed 13 April 2022.

21 Ryan, B. 16 March 2017. 'Motsepe will shut mines rather than bow to misled communities'. Miningmx. https://www.miningmx.com/news/markets/29279-motsepe-will-shut-mines-rather-bow-politicised-communities/ Accessed 13 May 2022.

22 Ibid.

23 Ibid.

24 Bishop, C. 2017. *Africa's Billionaires: Inspirational stories from the continent's wealthiest people*. Penguin Books.

25 Ryan, B. 16 March 2017. 'Motsepe will shut mines rather than bow to misled communities'. Miningmx. https://www.miningmx.com/news/markets/29279-motsepe-will-shut-mines-rather-bow-politicised-communities/ Accessed 13 April 2022.

26 Ibid.

27 Solomons, S. 4 April 2018. 'Joint partners condemn senseless attacks on Modikwa mineworkers'. Mining Review Africa. https://www.miningreview.com/southern-africa/joint-partners-condemn-senseless-attacks-modikwa-mineworkers/ Accessed 13 May 2022.

28 The Human Rights Commission is the national institution established in 1995 to support constitutional democracy. It is committed to promote respect for, observance of and protection of human rights for everyone without fear or favour.

29 Dube, M. 5 December 2021. 'Motsepe's mine in reparation row'. Mail&Guardian. https://mg.co.za/news/2021-12-05-motsepes-mine-in-reparation-row/ Accessed 13 April 2022.

30 Ibid.

31 Ibid.

32 Ibid.

33 Sifile, L. 4 September 2017. '#KusasalethuMemorial: "Pay mineworkers decent salaries"'.IOL.https://www.iol.co.za/news/south-africa/gauteng/kusasalethumemorial-pay-mineworkers-decent-salaries-11074023 Accessed 15 April 2022.

34 News24. 4 September 2017. '"Brave Kusasalethu miners died like warriors in battle"'. AllAfrica. https://allafrica.com/stories/201709050112.html Accessed 15 April 2022.

35 News24. 4 September 2017. 'Minister tells Patrice Motsepe to pay Kusasalethu miners "decent salaries"'. https://www.news24.com/News24/minister-tells-patrice-motsepe-to-pay-kusasalethu-miners-decent-salaries-20170904 Accessed 15 April 2022.

36 African Rainbow Minerals. 2008. Annual Report. https://www.arm.co.za/archive/files/annual/2008/default.htm Accessed 24 May 2022.

37 Ibid.

38 News24. 27 February 2008. 'Explosion needs answers'. The Witness. https://www.news24.com/witness/archive/Explosion-needs-answers-20150430 Accessed 23 May 2022.

39 Engineering News. 8 April 2020. 'Amendments to the Mineral and Petroleum Resources Development Regulations'. https://www.engineeringnews.co.za/article/amendments-to-the-mineral-and-petroleum-resources-development-regulations-2020-04-08 Accessed 12 May 2022.

40 ARM owned 83 percent of its ARM Mining Consortium (ARM MC) through a 100-percent-held subsidiary, ARM Platinum. A separate percentage of ARM MC was held on behalf of the Maandagshoek farm communities.

41 Parliamentary Monitoring Group. 2 April 2003. 'Black Empowerment in the Mining Sector'. https://pmg.org.za/committee-meeting/2342/ Accessed 12 May 2022.

17. The changing order: Capital diversified

1   Adams, S. 6 March 2008. 'The Prince of Mines'. Forbes. https://www.forbes.com/forbes/2008/0324/088.html?sh=12ea68ad3afe Accessed 13 May 2022.
2   Ibid.
3   IOL. 9 September 2016. 'Motsepe slams policy uncertainty'. https://www.iol.co.za/business-report/companies/motsepe-slams-policy-uncertainty-2066115 Accessed 15 April 2022.
4   De Ionno, P. 18 June 2000. 'R500m proposal for the fostering of junior mining sector'. IOL. https://www.iol.co.za/business-report/companies/r500m-proposal-for-the-fostering-of-junior-mining-sector-794324 Accessed 12 April 2022.
5   Creamer, M. 7 September 2018. 'ARM mulling "very exciting" growth opportunities – Motsepe'. Engineering News. https://www.engineeringnews.co.za/article/arm-mulling-very-exciting-growth-opportunities-motsepe-2018-09-07/rep_id:4136 Accessed 12 May 2022.
6   Ibid.
7   Offering Motsepe diversification into the financial services industry, that deal would go on to deliver R15 billion in value after the first decade (up to 2013).
8   Van Zyl, J. 20 March 2014. 'Sanlam and Ubuntu-Botho BEE partnership delivers R15-billion in value'. Sanlam. https://www.sanlam.co.za/mediacentre/media-category/media-releases/Sanlam%20and%20Ubuntu-Botho%20BEE%20Partnership%20delivers%20R15-Billion%20in%20Value Accessed 12 May 2022.
9   Ibid.
10 From 2003 to 2015, its market value went from about R14 billion to about R150 billion.
11 Fin24. 19 December 2016. 'Motsepe turns down Sanlam chair position for Van Zyl'. https://www.news24.com/Fin24/motsepe-turns-down-sanlam-chair-position-for-van-zyl-20161219 Accessed 14 April 2022.
12 eNCA. 18 April 2018. 'DA welcomes Johan van Zyl's resignation from Steinhoff board'. https://www.enca.com/money/da-welcomes-johan-van-zyls-resignation-from-steinhoff-board Accessed 14 April 2022.
13 UBI's shareholding, comprising Sizanani-Thusanang-Helpmekaar Investments (55%), is owned by Motsepe and his family, the Sanlam Ubuntu-Botho Community Development Trust (20%) and BBBEE groups (25%).
14 MyBroadband. 21 June 2021. 'ARC co-CEOs' incredible R370 million bet'. https://mybroadband.co.za/news/business/402501-arc-co-ceos-incredible-r370-million-bet.html Accessed 12 July 2022.
15 Theunissen, G. 8 October 2020. 'Patrice Motsepe's investment firm is under fire – it's now promising new deals and dividends'. ARC. https://africanrainbowcapital.co.za/patrice-motsepes-investment-firm-is-under-fire-its-now-promising-new-deals-and-dividends/ Accessed 14 April 2022.
16 Theunissen explained that 'UBI General Partner, the BEE management company owned by UBI which is in turn Sanlam's BEE partner, would have been required to pay 95% of the fee to the unlisted ARC via its parent, UBI, as an investment services fee. The money would then have been returned to the ARC Fund to follow its rights under the new share issuance.' Ibid.
17 Buthelezi, L. 2 November 2020. 'Battle of the stock exchanges: A2X's plans to take JSE's market share. Fin24. https://www.news24.com/fin24/markets/battle-of-the-stock-exchanges-a2xs-plans-to-take-jses-market-share-20201102 Accessed 12 May 2022.
18 Mediclinic. 27 October 2016. 'Patrice Motsepe's plan for cheaper private healthcare'. https://doctorsportal.mediclinic.co.za/Lists/News/DoctorsDispForm.aspx?ID=1630 Accessed 12 May 2022.

19 Mungadze, S. 14 November 2021. 'Motsepe's ARC joins consortium to seal R1.5bn fintech deal'. ITWeb. https://www.itweb.co.za/content/raYAyqodOX3vJ38N Accessed 12 May 2022.
20 Ibid.
21 World Economic Forum. 15 November 2019. 'World Economic Forum appoints two new members to its board of trustees'. https://www.weforum.org/press/2019/11/world-economic-forum-appoints-two-new-members-to-its-board-of-trustees/ Accessed 24 May 2022.
22 Theunissen, G. 8 October 2020. 'Patrice Motsepe's investment firm is under fire – it's now promising new deals and dividends'. Business Insider. https://www.businessinsider.co.za/motesepes-arc-investments-faces-trouble-2020-10 Accessed 14 April 2022.
23 Bloomberg News. 26 February 2013. 'Motsepe: Mining assets are a good buy'. IOL. https://www.iol.co.za/business-report/companies/motsepe-mining-assets-are-a-good-buy-1477329 Accessed 14 April 2022.

18. Mobilising energy: All colours green

1 Ryan, B. 17 March 2015. 'Motsepe issues Zambia royalty warning'. MiningMX. https://www.miningmx.com/news/base-metals/12556-motsepe-issues-zambia-royalty-warning/ Accessed 12 May 2022.
2 Watts, H. 2 September 2011. 'South Africa's billionaire Patrice Motsepe in talks with Ratan Tata for JV in financial, minerals business'. India Times. https://economictimes.indiatimes.com/industry/indl-goods/svs/metals-mining/south-africas-billionaire-patrice-motsepe-in-talks-with-ratan-tata-for-jv-in-financial-minerals-business/articleshow/9829914.cms Accessed 14 April 2022.
3 Ibid.
4 Breakthrough Energy Ventures was initially known as the Breakthrough Energy Coalition, when, in 2015, a group of 28 international investors (billionaires, really) from ten countries met at the United Nations Climate Change Conference and decided to complement Gates's Mission Innovation through risk capital. That's when it changed its name from 'Coalition' to 'Ventures' to indicate the influx of money.
5 Serrao, C. 30 November 2015. 'Tech billionaires team up to take on climate change. Wired. https://www.wired.com/2015/11/zuckerberg-gates-climate-change-breakthrough-energy-coalition/ Accessed 18 April 2022.
6 Qobo, M. 19 January 2016. 'Why the rich should do more to save the world'. The Conversation. https://theconversation.com/why-the-rich-should-do-more-to-save-the-world-52944 Accessed 12 May 2022.
7 Zuma, J. 12 November 2015. 'South Africa's position on climate change ahead of UNFCCC COP 21 Summit'. The Presidency. https://www.thepresidency.gov.za/content/south-africa%E2%80%99s-position-climate-change-ahead-unfccc-cop-21-summit Accessed 18 April 2022.
8 Tyler, E. 16 November 2021. 'Climate finance for transition away from coal: a chance to change history in SA'. Eyewitness News. https://ewn.co.za/2021/11/16/climate-finance-for-transition-away-from-coal-a-chance-to-change-history-in-sa Accessed 12 May 2022.
9 Van Diemen, E. 29 September 2021. 'How South Africa can power ahead with green energy ambitions through R750bn financing plan'. Daily Maverick. https://www.dailymaverick.co.za/article/2021-09-29-how-south-africa-can-power-ahead-with-green-energy-ambitions-through-r750bn-financing-plan/ Accessed 18 April 2022.
10 Absa. 6 August 2021. 'African Rainbow Energy and Absa launch investment platform'. https://www.absa.co.za/media-centre/press-statements/2021/african-rainbow-and-absa-launch-a-renewable-energy-investment-platform/ Accessed 24 May 2022.
11 Burger, S. 3 November 2021. 'Ikamva consortium to build 1.27 GW of new wind, solar in South Africa'. Engineering News. https://www.engineeringnews.co.za/article/

ikamva-consortium-to-build-127-gw-of-new-wind-solar-in-south-africa-2021-11-03 Accessed 18 April 2022.
12 Absa. 6 August 2021. 'African Rainbow Energy and Absa launch investment platform'. https://www.absa.co.za/media-centre/press-statements/2021/african-rainbow-and-absa-launch-a-renewable-energy-investment-platform/ Accessed 24 May 2022.
13 Moyo, A. 10 August 2021. 'Patrice Motsepe, Absa launch R6.5bn renewable energy fund'. ITWeb. https://www.itweb.co.za/content/xA9POvNZOaKvo4J8 Accessed 19 April 2022.
14 IOL. 26 February 2013. 'Motsepe: Mining assets are a good buy'. https://www.iol.co.za/business-report/companies/motsepe-mining-assets-are-a-good-buy-1477329 Accessed 19 April 2022.
15 CSIR. 5 August 2021. 'CSIR releases power sector statistics for first-half of 2021'. https://www.csir.co.za/csir-releases-power-sector-statistics-first-half-2021 Accessed 31 May 2022.
16 Buthelezi, L. 14 September 2021. 'Motsepe's African Rainbow Capital to exit Metrofibre and coal mining as it "prunes" portfolio. News24. https://www.news24.com/fin24/companies/motsepes-african-rainbow-capital-to-exit-metrofibre-and-coal-mining-as-it-prunes-portfolio-20210914 Accessed 18 April 2022.
17 Ibid.
18 Why Africa. 20 September 2021. 'Kropz cleared to start production at Elandsfontein in SA'. https://www.whyafrica.co.za/kropz-cleared-to-start-production-at-elandsfontein-in-sa/ Accessed 19 April 2022.
19 Pinnock, D. 12 October 2017. 'West Coast phosphate mine interdicted to stop drawing fossil water'. Conservation Action Trust. https://conservationaction.co.za/media-articles/west-coast-phosphate-mine-interdicted-stop-drawing-fossil-water/ Accessed 18 April 2022.
20 Gosling, M. 18 October 2017. 'Mine hits back over West Coast aquifer'. GroundUp. https://www.groundup.org.za/article/west-coast-mine-says-stopping-it-pumping-out-aquifer-will-only-cause-more-harm/ Accessed 19 April 2022.
21 Why Africa. 20 September 2021. 'Kropz cleared to start production at Elandsfontein in SA'. https://www.whyafrica.co.za/kropz-cleared-to-start-production-at-elandsfontein-in-sa/ Accessed 19 April 2022.
22 Sguazzin, A. 27 January 2022. 'Sun Exchange sees bright future in Africa'. BusinessLive. https://www.businesslive.co.za/bloomberg/news/2022-01-27-sun-exchange-sees-bright-future-in-africa/ Accessed 18 April 2022.
23 Ibid.
24 Bloomberg. 27 January 2022. 'Bitcoin-paying South African solar company plans expansion'. BusinessTech. https://businesstech.co.za/news/energy/553494/bitcoin-paying-south-african-solar-company-plans-expansion/ Accessed 12 May 2022.

19. The post-liberation gospel: Keeping the ANC afloat

1 702. 29 March 2022. 'ANC is tax compliant, the R102-million Sars debt is an old story – Mashatile'. https://www.702.co.za/articles/441880/anc-is-tax-compliant-the-r102-million-sars-debt-is-an-old-story-mashatile Accessed 13 May 2022.
2 Njilo, N. 18 November 2021. 'Cyril Ramaphosa and Patrice Motsepe donated money to ANC ahead of election'. TimesLive. https://www.timeslive.co.za/politics/2021-11-18-cyril-ramaphosa-and-patrice-motsepe-donated-money-to-anc-ahead-of-election/ Accessed 11 April 2022.
3 Before the Political Party Funding Act took effect in 2021, parties didn't have to declare their funders, so previously it wasn't known how much money Motsepe gave to the ANC or any other entity.
4 Cele, S. 29 July 2018. 'SA does not belong to the Motsepe family – Malema'. City Press. https://www.news24.com/citypress/news/sa-does-not-belong-to-the-motsepe-family-malema-20180729 Accessed 18 April 2022.

5   The notorious Gupta brothers, Ajay, Atul and Rajesh, were implicated in state capture in South Africa during the 2010s.

6   News24. 28 July 2018. 'Malema's warning to Patrice Motsepe: "We are watching you"'. https://www.news24.com/News24/malemas-warning-to-patrice-motsepe-we-are-watching-you-20180728 Accessed 18 April 2022.

7   Nkanjeni, U. 25 February 2022. '"Hypocrite' or 'securing the bag"?: Malema under fire after EFF received R2m from Motsepe's companies'. TimesLive. https://www.timeslive.co.za/politics/2022-02-25-hypocrite-or-securing-the-bag-malema-under-fire-after-eff-received-r2m-from-motsepes-companies/ Accessed 18 April 2022.

8   O'Malley. 1994. 'The Reconstruction and Development Programme (RDP)' https://omalley.nelsonmandela.org/omalley/index.php/site/q/03lv02039/04lv02103/05lv021 20/06lv02126.htm Accessed 23 May 2022.

9   Ross, S. 21 January 2022. 'What are the best measurements of economic growth?'. investopedia.com. https://www.investopedia.com/ask/answers/032515/what-are-best-measurements-economic-growth.asp 23 May 2022.

10   O'Malley. 1994. 'The Reconstruction and Development Programme (RDP)' https://omalley.nelsonmandela.org/omalley/index.php/site/q/03lv02039/04lv02103/05lv021 20/06lv02126.htm Accessed 24 May 2022.

11   Creamer, M. 9 December 2009. 'Mine nationalisation okay if good for South Africa – Patrice Motsepe'. Mining Weekly. https://www.miningweekly.com/article/mine-nationalisation-okay-if-good-for-south-africa-patrice-motsepe-2009-12-09   Accessed 13 May 2022.

12   Ibid.

13   Chauke, A. 22 September 2011. '"Racial discord bad for business": Motsepe'. TimesLive. https://www.timeslive.co.za/news/south-africa/2011-09-22-racial-discord-bad-forbusiness-motsepe-/ Accessed 14 April 2022

14   Mvoko, V. 16 November 2011. 'Patrice Motsepe on the threat of nationalization'. Forbes. https://www.forbes.com/sites/kerryadolan/2011/11/16/patrice-motsepe-on-the-threat-of-nationalization/ Accessed 19 April 2022.

15   Ibid.

16   Jordan, ZP. 16 December 1997. 'The National Question in post-'94 South Africa (abridged)'. African National Congress. https://www.anc1912.org.za/50th-national-conference-the-national-question-in-post-94-south-africa-a-discussion-paper-in-preparation-for-the-50th-national-conference-abridged/ Accessed 11 May 2022.

17   Cobbett, E and Friesen, E. 2014. 'Motsepe's Gift: or how Philanthropy serves Capitalism in South Africa'. *Selected Themes in African Political Studies: Political Conflict and Stability.* Springer.

20. Guests of the president: The patronage years

1   Haffajee, F. 28 May 2012. 'The Spear is down – out of care and fear'. City Press. https://www.news24.com/news24/columnists/ferial-haffajee/The-Spear-is-down-out-of-care-and-fear-20120528-2 Accessed 13 May 2022.

2   Sapa. 27 May 2012. 'City Press editor: "I don't respond to threats"'. Mail&Guardian. https://mg.co.za/article/2012-05-27-city-press-editor-i-dont-respond-to-threats/ Accessed 13 May 2022.

3   Haffajee, F. 28 May 2012. @ferialhaffajee. https://twitter.com/ferialhaffajee/status/207042839174062080 Accessed 13 May 2022.

4   Basson, A. 5 March 2010. 'Crony capitalists on JZ's coat-tails'. *Mail&Guardian.* https://mg.co.za/article/2010-03-05-crony-capitalists-on-jzs-coattails/ Accessed 15 April 2022.

5   News24. 28 October 2012. 'ANC makes money in Mangaung – report' https://www.news24.com/fin24/anc-makes-money-in-mangaung-report-20121028-2 Accessed 15 April 2022.

6   News24. 26 June 2012. 'Jovial Zuma dines with mining bosses'. https://www.news24.

com/News24/jovial-zuma-dines-with-mining-bosses-20150430 Accessed 13 May 2022.
7   Du Plessis, C. 26 June 2012. 'Zuma in jovial mood at glamorous ANC fund-raising event'. The Witness. https://www.news24.com/amp/witness/archive/Zuma-in-jovial-mood-at-glamorous-ANC-fund-raising-event-20150430 Accessed 15 April 2022.
8   Battersby, J. 24 December 2015. 'Brilliant: John Battersby unpacks Nenegate, Jacob Zuma's greatest blunder'. Fin24. https://www.news24.com/Fin24/brilliant-john-battersby-unpacks-nenegate-jacob-zumas-greatest-blunder-20151224 Accessed 15 April 2022.
9   Ibid.
10 The title of a 1990s megahit by South African pop superstar Brenda Fassie about being the girlfriend 'on the side'.
11 IOL. 9 September 2016. 'Motsepe slams policy uncertainty'. https://www.iol.co.za/business-report/companies/motsepe-slams-policy-uncertainty-2066115 Accessed 13 May 2022.
12 Njilo, N. 30 December 2021. '"We want to save the ANC": Concerned party members want Patrice Motsepe as president'. TimesLive. https://www.timeslive.co.za/politics/2021-12-30-we-want-to-save-the-anc-concerned-party-members-want-patrice-motsepe-as-president/ Accessed 13 May 2022.
13 An Emmanuel Makgoga was an activist and leader of the Maandagshoek Development Committee that protested in 2006 (see chapter 16). It could not be confirmed that this was the same Emmanuel Makgoga.
14 Njilo, N. 30 December 2021. '"We want to save the ANC": Concerned party members want Patrice Motsepe as president'. TimesLive. https://www.timeslive.co.za/politics/2021-12-30-we-want-to-save-the-anc-concerned-party-members-want-patrice-motsepe-as-president/ Accessed 13 May 2022.
15 Blignaut, M. 10 July 2018. 'Move over Cyril! Patrice Motsepe dubbed SA's new president after booking Beyoncé'. Briefly. https://briefly.co.za/14098-move-cyril-patrice-motsepe-dubbed-sas-president-booking-beyonce.html Accessed 13 May 2022.

21. Perilous optics: Looking into the future

1   BusinessTech. 18 January 2018. 'Here's the full list of South Africans going to Davos in 2018'. https://businesstech.co.za/news/business/219819/heres-the-full-list-of-south-africans-going-to-davos-in-2018/ Accessed 15 April 2022.
2   Ramaphosa had been married twice before and had two children, Tulisa and Andile, with his ex-wives Nomazizi Mtshotshisane and Hope. Motsepe's nephew and two nieces – Tumelo, Kiki and Mashudu – are from the marriage of Ramaphosa and Tshepo Motsepe.
3   Hartley, R. 12 November 2017. 'How Ramaphosa nearly became Nelson Mandela's deputy'. Sunday Times. https://www.timeslive.co.za/sunday-times/news/2017-11-11-how-ramaphosa-nearly-became-nelson-mandelas-deputy/ Accessed 13 May 2022.
4   Munusamy, R. 20 December 2012. 'Cyril Ramaphosa: the return of Nelson Mandela's chosen one'. The Guardian. https://www.theguardian.com/world/2012/dec/20/cyril-ramaphosa-return-nelson-mandela Accessed 13 May 2022.
5   New Africa Investments Limited was South Africa's black economic empowerment forerunner, designed to plough money into the hands of black South Africans through attracting institutional investors – most significantly insurance company Metropolitan Life, a successful Sanlam subsidiary.
6   'Cadre deployment' was an ANC policy to place its most loyal members in jobs in government to keep its hands on power. 'Redeployment' took place when cadres could not be 'deployed', and were instead placed in pivotal roles in the private sector.
7   Creamer, M. 16 March 2015. 'ARM's Motsepe urges serious govt intervention on Eskom let down'. Polity. https://www.polity.org.za/article/arms-motsepe-urges-serious-govt-intervention-on-eskom-let-down-2015-03-16 Accessed 13 April 2022.

8   Ibid.
9   Davis, R. 22 February 2019. 'It is perfectly legitimate to scrutinise Ramaphosa's business buddies during his presidency – here's why'. Daily Maverick. https://www.dailymaverick. co.za/article/2019-02-22-it-is-perfectly-legitimate-to-scrutinise-ramaphosas-business-buddies-during-his-presidency-heres-why/ Accessed 18 April 2022.
10 Ibid.
11 Ibid.
12 Selisho, K. 8 April 2019. 'Bridgette Radebe accused of interfering in Botswana politics'. The Citizen. https://www.citizen.co.za/news/news-world/news-africa/2114014/bridgette-radebe-accused-of-interfering-in-botswana-politics/ Accessed 14 May 2022.
13 Du Plessis, C. 29 November 2019. 'Court stops Botswana paper from publishing negative stories about Patrice Motsepe'. Daily Maverick. https://www.dailymaverick. co.za/article/2019-11-29-court-stops-botswana-paper-from-publishing-negative-stories-about-patrice-motsepe/ Accessed 14 May 2022.
14 Madisa, K. 14 June 2019. '"He's a family friend" – Motsepe defends meeting with Botswana's Ian Khama'. SowetanLive. https://www.sowetanlive.co.za/news/south-africa/2019-06-14-hes-a-family-friend-motsepe-defends-meeting-with-botswanas-ian-khama/ Accessed 14 May 2022.
15 Cilliers, C. 9 June 2019. 'Malema promises to speak about "powerful SA family" in Botswana "plot" against government. The Citizen. https://www.citizen.co.za/news/south-africa/politics/2141020/malema-promises-to-speak-about-powerful-sa-family-in-botswana-plot-against-government/ Accessed 14 May 2022.
16 News24. 9 May 2019. 'Andile Mngxitama ordered to retract from bashing Patrice Motsepe'. https://www.news24.com/News24/andile-mngxitama-ordered-to-retract-from-bashing-patrice-motsepe-20190509 Accessed 14 May 2022.
17 Cilliers, C. 9 June 2019. 'Malema promises to speak about "powerful SA family" in Botswana "plot" against government. The Citizen. https://www.citizen.co.za/news/south-africa/politics/2141020/malema-promises-to-speak-about-powerful-sa-family-in-botswana-plot-against-government/ Accessed 14 May 2022.
18 Mahlakoana, T. 'Motsepe's lawyers head to Botswana to address political meddling claims'. Eyewitness News. https://ewn.co.za/2019/06/13/motsepe-s-lawyers-travelled-to-botswana-to-address-political-meddling-claims Accessed 14 May 2022.
19 Alaka, J. 26 April 2022. 'CAF President urges African businesses, governments to invest in football'. Premium Times. https://www.premiumtimesng.com/sports/football/526063-caf-president-urges-african-businesses-governments-to-invest-in-football.html Accessed 14 May 2022.

22. Stakeholder theory: Disruption as a process

1   Zarabi, S. 22 May 2022. 'Change in the air as the well-heeled WEF veterans make it to spring-time Davos'. BusinessToday.In. https://www.businesstoday.in/opinion/columns/story/change-in-the-air-as-the-well-heeled-wef-veterans-make-it-to-spring-time-davos-334588-2022-05-22 Accessed 23 May 2022.
2   Kagan, J. 24 October 2021. 'World Economic Forum: WEF'. investopedia.com. https://www.investopedia.com/terms/w/world-economic-forum.asp Accessed 23 May 2022.
3   Economist Intelligence (EIU). 13 May 2022. 'Democracy Index 2021'. https://www.eiu.com/n/campaigns/democracy-index-2021/ Accessed 23 May 2022.
4   Ibid.
5   Dillon, K. 4 February 2020. 'Disruption 2020: An interview with Clayton M. Christensen'. MITSloan Management Review. https://sloanreview.mit.edu/article/an-interview-with-clayton-m-christensen/ 23 May 2022.

Patrice Motsepe's shareholdings

1   MyBroadband. 27 July 2021. 'All the companies Patrice Motsepe owns'. https://
    mybroadband.co.za/news/business/407384-all-the-companies-patrice-motsepe-owns.
    html Accessed 1 June 2022.

Index

CPSIA information can be obtained
at www.ICGtesting.com
Printed in the USA
LVHW030606300822
727116LV00012B/352